W9-AOD-937

spirituality 101

{ **the indispensable guide to keeping—or finding— your spiritual life on campus** }

Harriet L. Schwartz
with contributions by college students from 30 campuses across the United States

Walking Together, Finding the Way
SKYLIGHT PATHS Publishing
Woodstock, Vermont

Spirituality 101:
The Indispensable Guide to Keeping—or Finding—Your Spiritual Life on Campus
First Printing 2004
© 2004 by Harriet L. Schwartz

Library of Congress Cataloging-in-Publication Data
Schwartz, Harriet L.
Spirituality 101 : the indispensable guide to keeping or finding your spiritual life on campus / Harriet L. Schwartz.
p. cm.
Includes bibliographical references.
ISBN 1-59473-000-8 (pbk.)
1. College students—Religious life. I. Title: Spirituality one hundred and one. II. Title: Spirituality one hundred one. III. Title.
BL625.9.C64 S39 2004
204'.4'088378198—dc22
                                                                                    2003023930

Manufactured in the United States of America

SkyLight Paths Publishing is creating a place where people of different spiritual traditions come together for challenge and inspiration, a place where we can help each other understand the mystery that lies at the heart of our existence.

SkyLight Paths sees both believers and seekers as a community that increasingly transcends traditional boundaries of religion and denomination—people wanting to learn from each other, walking together, finding the way.

SkyLight Paths, "Walking Together, Finding the Way" and colophon are trademarks of LongHill Partners, Inc., registered in the U.S. Patent and Trademark Office.

Walking Together, Finding the Way
Published by SkyLight Paths Publishing
A Division of LongHill Partners, Inc.
Sunset Farm Offices, Route 4, P.O. Box 237
Woodstock, VT 05091
Tel (802) 457-4000 Fax (802) 457-4004
www.skylightpaths.com

For my grandmothers, with love.

This book is for people of all traditions. More than forty students and campus professionals, each firmly positioned within his or her own spiritual faith tradition, have written thoughtful and valuable contributions. Representing various Christian, Jewish, Muslim, Buddhist, Hindu, and other traditions—as can be seen in the Contributors section at the end of this book—*Spirituality 101* is meant to provide an opening for discussion among people of any and all faiths and to be a helpful guide for students and educators on college campuses everywhere.

CONTENTS

INTRODUCTION

Who do you want to be?

Are you spiritual? Religious? Still figuring it out?

Does your faith jump-start your day or get you through long nights?

Does your faith rein you in, or set you free?

How is college impacting your spirituality?

Do you feel called by your faith, or does it drive you?

Has faith been a point of connection with others, or a reminder that you are different?

In this time and place, has your faith tradition been a positive or a negative—for you, your family, and your people (whomever you consider "your people" to be)?

Are you proud of what your spiritual tradition stands for and how it is perceived? If so, how will you continue to support that? If not, will you reinvent it on a personal level and perhaps even become an activist?

Who do you want to be?

You may be looking for answers, but this book is about the questions.

Sure, there is plenty of advice between the front and back covers. And you will have many opportunities to learn from other students who have explored their own spirituality and found their own answers along the way. But first and foremost, this book is about helping you frame and explore the questions that you face as you explore your spirituality.

This book is a conversation. I began this conversation by seeking students from all over the country, from as many traditions as possible, who, by writing and contributing their own experiences, would lead us by example—show us their questions, their searching, their answers. To solicit student and staff contributions, I contacted campus faith leaders, faculty members of related disciplines, student organization leaders, and staff at relevant national organizations.

As students began to respond to my call for submissions, the process became more and more exciting. I imagined these dynamic storytellers with a vast range of experiences, all eagerly sharing their lives with us readers, all these diverse points of view, all under "one tent." **Imagine sitting with a group of students, one who solidified his Christianity while studying in Australia, another who can take you inside a Buddhist retreat, and another who shares with you the tale of her interview for rabbinical school**. These students, and more than twenty-five others who wrote, did so independently and not in dialogue with each other. Taken as a whole, however, the contributions in this book became a new conversation. Although the essays were divided into categories, the themes overlap as stories affirm and sometimes challenge each other. We as readers make the discussion three-dimensional.

The students who have contributed their writings to this book are thoughtful, committed to their own growth and that of others, at times funny, and at times very serious. Their stories have energized me and motivated me to continue exploring my own spiritual growth and commitments. You will find these stories to be a fascinating and inspiring collection of ideas and emotions. At times you may feel validated when a writer articulates something you have been feeling but hadn't yet put into words. At other times, you will be challenged as you are faced with ideas that differ from your own perspective.

One of the most fascinating points that emerges again and again in the student contributions is the importance of engaging in discussions and in communities with people who come from differing points of view. Although many of us often seek the comfort of communities of "people like us," the stories in this book point strongly to the power of bumping up against ideas different from our own. Many people fear that coming to understand a new perspective will dilute their own commitments. In fact, the opposite proves to be true. Time and again, the student writers who learned the most about themselves did so while learning to understand and living alongside students who brought a different experience to the table. This kind of exploring requires curiosity balanced with conviction and confidence balanced with an open mind.

So, take your time with this book. Savor the questions. Seek to become comfortable living in a space of not always knowing. Find good companions. And enjoy the journey. Wisdom often arrives when we have the opportunity to think and wonder aloud.

FINDING YOUR PLACE: WHO DO YOU WANT TO BE?

You have unpacked your bags and boxes. You have bought your books and figured out where to get the cheapest pizza. And now you wonder.

You wonder whether you will like your classes. You wonder whether it will be hard to meet people. You wonder where on campus you will get involved. Finally, you have a vague wondering about how you will do spiritually in this new place. At this time, you can't really articulate what that means, but if you were to reflect on it four years from now, you would realize this is a question that has both subtle and visible answers. Who will you be in relation to others—classmates, professors, and friends? Who will you be in relation to the religion you were (or were not) raised with? Will you make time for spiritual practice? Who are you now in relation to the person you want to be?

If you grew up involved in a particular faith tradition, college is the time when you continue to solidify your commitment, redefine that commitment for yourself, or, in some cases, reject that tradition and find a new sense of spirituality that suits you better. If you grew up without involvement in a faith community, college may very well be the time when you begin to sort out your own sense of spirituality.

1

You have chosen your college—maybe for serious and specific reasons, such as believing it will give you the perfect spiritual environment in which to study, or maybe for less specific but nonetheless compelling reasons, feeling the campus just seemed "right" when you visited, for example. Or maybe it's the school that offered you the most financial aid (a persuasive reason indeed!). Regardless, the school that you have committed to will provide you with a host of spiritual challenges.

You may be someone who was seeking relative spiritual safety when picking your school, deciding to go to a religiously affiliated college with "people like you." Indeed, you will find yourself surrounded by students, faculty, and staff who share your same tradition, on a campus with plenty of opportunities for worship, service, study, and other manifestations of your faith. You will also find yourself on a campus with plenty of people who share your tradition but who are, in other ways, very different from you. Perhaps their urban spiritual sense differs from your rural perspective on faith, or their family's financial situation gave them a very different childhood from yours.

Maybe you consciously chose to attend a religiously affiliated school even though you don't belong to the faith which the school's history is rooted in. Perhaps religious affiliation didn't seem like such a big influence growing up, and so you didn't think it would be a big factor in campus life. If you made this choice, chances are that being surrounded by students devoted to their tradition (even if it is different from yours) will motivate you to explore the role of spirituality in your own life. What will you learn from these students, faculty, and staff? Will you see them as spiritual role models, whose faith inspires your own searching? Will you seek to learn more about their traditions?

You may have decided to go to a secular college or university. Whether you attend a small private liberal arts college or a large state university, you will still encounter challenges to your spirituality. Those challenges may come in the form of class discussions, friends, teammates, fraternity brothers or sorority sisters, professors—the list goes on. One of the most important relationships you will deal with, particularly early in your college career, is the relationship with your roommate. Even if you and your roommate don't turn out to be close friends, this relationship is important because it will significantly impact your quality of life. If you and your roommate get along, then the room can be a place to call home.

Some of us like to have our world rocked, our assumptions shaken—we like the questions as much as the answers. Others want stability, safety, a faith we can count on. Regardless of your preferred mode, life on campus will challenge you and change you.

WELCOME TO THE JUNGLE
ALICE CHEN

My freshman year at college, my dorm was classic. We had the nerds, the athletes, the naked bed-hopping, the blokes everyone avoided, the puke in the toilets, the drunken fights, the religious fanatic who weirded everyone out, the strange no-show who lent his room out for sexual activities, and the late-night chats about anything from romance to the ethics of snipers. We had fun, and not all of it would've been sanctioned by a church, synagogue, mosque, or temple. A lot of times, students from religious backgrounds (especially the strict ones) feel as though they're entering some sort of battle zone. Assuredly, they've probably been heavily warned by parents and others about the hellhole they are about to descend into while trying to get an education.

The deal with college and education is that you learn in class and out of class. You learn some things are right, some are wrong, some are gray territory, and others need broader views. If you're living in a dorm situation, you're most likely thrown in with people from all over the world (or country or state) with all sorts of pasts. Some love to drink and party and others have a book stapled to their heads. You become friends with some, and then you begin to

Trust yourself. Create the kind of self that you will be happy to live with all your life.

—GOLDA MEIR

question whether drinking or flirting or believing in something other than your faith is really that bad.

Although it's risky and possibly the hugest fear of your religious (or nonreligious) parents, you should question what you believe, whether you're religious or not. You shouldn't just stop at the questioning stage, which is unfortunately what too many people do. Don't settle for easy answers, but do get answers. Find people you trust from within your own faith tradition and also from outside of your own faith tradition. What they tell you will help you sort through your questions, especially if they have been thinking about the same issues. It also helps to read up on an issue or to take a class. Suppose you have an issue with abortion and your faith. You could take a class on public policy, women's history, the health care system, or ethics. At the same time, you could be dialoguing with friends, advisors, and colleagues about the topic. You might find that abortion addresses topics of compassion and then investigate what compassion looks like in your faith. You could find your life's passion and purpose simply by asking the question: What is it I believe and why?

The key is to be open to change and self-examination. One friend of mine changed her view on East Asian people after having previously believed they were a rather self-serving, cold lot. Her view wasn't going to change until she had seen some East Asians who weren't self-serving and cold and whose existence challenged her belief. Once my friend had a living contradiction in front of her, she set about discovering why she held that belief. She could have still come to the conclusion that East Asians were bad, but at least she would have had a tried-and-tested opinion. You need to explore faith in the same way because you need to know why you believe what you believe.

You need to know the "why," especially when it comes to issues and religious codes of behavior. You're making a lot of your own decisions in college, and you're more independent (or should be). When your new friends want to go drinking and you don't, you have to know why they do and why you don't. Most people aren't hostile to different points of view, but they do want an explanation. They want to know why you go kosher (better for your health? religious reverence? cultural habits?). Even if they don't agree with your reasoning, they will respect you more if you can give them a reasoning to disagree with. Likewise, you'll feel more confident if you know why you wear a head covering, and your confidence and thinking will show others that your faith isn't blind. What's more, being thoughtful about your faith also helps show others that, unlike portrayals on TV, all religious people haven't just emptied their brains of reason.

When you know your whys, your faith will also be stronger and more personal. The more personal your faith is, the better you'll be able to make decisions with more wisdom. It's like knowing a person. There are days when I'll walk by a shop or read a book and think, "Hey, my sister would really like this." Sometimes I can give the reasoning behind that thought, but other times it's intuition. The better I know someone, the more these intuitive thoughts occur. The more you know your faith, the more you will be able to use your intuition to make decisions that satisfy your faith. Your faith becomes a part of you and it can change, just as a person changes, but you still know what it looks like.

Some people will still laugh at you or think you're weird. Others might avoid you. Still others may not understand even when you explain your views. Let it roll off you. If faith is important to you, hold on and don't let go. Your understanding of faith may change and mature over time, and so will your application of faith. You may find that alcohol is of the devil one year and the next year it's not so bad after all when used responsibly. The keys are to keep learning about your faith, to know your faith, and to identify how it affects you. If your faith tradition says to keep your wits about you at all times, don't go snorting cocaine. If your faith tradition emphasizes moderation in all things, don't go bingeing at the buffet.

If you're feeling lonely with your faith, find other people like you so you can have some support. Find a faith group on campus or start one. These people may still challenge your understanding of your faith, but at least they will supportively challenge you and guide your path toward answers. Don't write off those who laugh at you either. They are probably also trying to figure out what life is about and how to deal with the freedom of college. They might just be using their freedom badly (like Mr. Dorm-sex-renter in my freshman house).

Your freedom and independence in college allows you the opportunity to learn from everyone you meet, even if the lesson is "I don't want to be like him." You don't have to test everything out personally to know whether something's good for you or not. Being a good observer of your fellow students' actions and the consequences can help you figure out a lot about what you want to do. Fortunately, with few exceptions, your school's probably not the moral and religious cesspool you or your parents might fear. Even if it is, you can use other people's opposition to your faith to challenge, change, reaffirm, and strengthen your faith. It's like that saying about making lemonade out of lemons—get something good out of something bad, and then you'll know what it is to be educated.

SPIRITUALITY AS STRESS MANAGEMENT

A little bit of stress can be a good thing—just the motivation to get you to finish that paper for class or work on your solo one more time for the upcoming musical. Too much stress can have the opposite effect, diminishing your focus and energy and leaving you more susceptible to loss of sleep and illness.

The following students reflect on spirituality as stress management. A common theme throughout is the need to commit to your spiritual practice over time. If you sit to meditate or pray for the first time when things get rough, chances are you may not get much strength or relief from the practice. However, if you meditate or pray regularly, the practice will become a means by which you can get centered, clear your head, prioritize, and calm your nerves—and that all combines for healthy stress management.

Oh, did I mention calculus? STRESS. Many days, escaping to a club for a few shots and a dance sounded great to me, but Jesus always sounded much better. A quick prayer, and a lot of faith and reassurance from fellow believers, jump-started my life again.

—Natalie Hunte, Central Connecticut State University

People often look to Buddhist meditation as a way to chill out, but when they actually practice it they see how hard it can be! Despite the initial surprise at the difficulty of the practice, I always see people open up if they sit meditation regularly. I know that for me, sitting with my mind for a half hour a day will open tremendous space. Afterward, everything seems workable.

—Lodrö Rinzler, Wesleyan University

I have always been amazed at how quickly music can change one's state of mind. I just love that part of Shabbat services when everyone starts singing and you look up at the people around you and watch the smiles grow and frowns fade on each and every face.

—Ben Hochman, University of California, Davis

College does come with a lot of stress. The classes, social life, and responsibilities can all add up to be quite overwhelming. On top of that, the hard work doesn't always pay off and equal good grades. I guess that's when I appreciate Hinduism's teaching that God does everything for a reason. So, after a quick convo with God (Hindus believe that parents are a form of God), I'm back on my feet and ready to get back to my life.

—Tejal Patel, College of the Holy Cross

Being the overinvolved overachiever that I am, stress is a common entity that appears in my life on a regular basis. And while some of my many activities are stress relieving in and of themselves (fencing saber is a great way to get rid of any feelings of anger and frustration), sometimes sanity demands that I take time from my myriad activities to focus inward and connect with the universe. Every night before I sleep, I like to sit quietly for a few minutes and meditate, clearing my mind and just focusing on breathing and on releasing all the tensions of the day. I visualize myself connected to the Earth, and I let the Earth support me and give me strength. I suspend my waking mind and allow myself to just be, unhindered by thoughts and worries. When I finish, I feel relaxed and calm, and I can sleep peacefully until the morning, when I will awaken refreshed and renewed and ready for the next busy day.

—Laura Carroll, Smith College

THE ADMISSIONS INTERVIEW
LYNNE GEARTY

As a senior in high school, I had narrowed down my choice of the colleges I would apply to by the end of September. For my entire thirteen years of school—including kindergarten—I attended Catholic schools. When I presented my list of prospective schools to my parents, they weren't surprised to find that all the colleges were indeed affiliated with the Roman Catholic religion. Looking back, I suppose I never really gave much thought to *not* attending another Catholic school. I grew up in religious schools; I felt comfortable and at home in that type of environment. As my mother read the list she inquired about my choice to apply to all Catholic schools.

"Well, I've always been educated in these particular schools, why shouldn't I continue to?" I responded.

"That doesn't seem like a good enough reason," she replied. "Why don't you make another list of reasons why you'd like to further your education at another Catholic school?"

So I did just that. My new list consisted of about three reasons: I felt I could learn best in a Catholic school because I was accustomed to small class sizes and had encountered many driven teachers throughout my academic experience thus far. I also enjoyed being with people of my own faith whom I could relate to through a common religion and similar views. Lastly, I believed the integration of my faith and school benefited my peers and me by knitting us together on a spiritual level.

"Those are all excellent reasons," said my mother, "but have you ever considered going to a school affiliated with another faith or none at all?"

I understood what she was getting at. In a way, I'd been sheltered attending a private Catholic school for all of those years. I had never really been around or associated much with peers who were not of the same faith. Over the next few weeks I contemplated my mother's point and decided to apply to a non–Roman Catholic college. I arranged for an interview in November.

A senior planning to graduate the following spring interviewed me. She was born in and emigrated from India. Once I discovered that she practiced a faith called Jainism, I became very interested in it, as I had never heard of the religion in Catholic schools. I asked her all about Jainism. She informed me of her strictly vegetarian diet—she had never once eaten meat or poultry! I found this astonishing and intriguing. I made a mental comparison to Catholics giving up meat during Lent. My senior interviewer told me how most members of the Jain religion do not work in fields that severely harm the environment. *Wonderful,* I reflected.

This woman opened my eyes to a whole other faith in just thirty minutes. *What were other religions like?* **I wondered.** *How many others are out there that I don't know about?* I understood my mother more completely now. Although she thought Catholic schools were best for me, she recognized that I had not had enough exposure to other faiths. I wasn't well rounded concerning other religions besides my own. In my opinion, the Catholic schools I attended had done me a disservice by not incorporating other faiths into the classroom.

Although my final decision was to enroll at a Roman Catholic college, my choice was not based upon religious reasons. I'm thankful that my mother encouraged me to discover the different facets of faith on my own. Perhaps most important, she did not push me to do this; I did it in my own way and on my own terms. In college, instead of taking classes on Catholicism, I'm nurturing my religious curiosity with classes such as the religious art of Islam. For me, and like every other person, applying to college was a hectic time in my life. Unlike others, however, I believe I came away from it with a more valuable lesson rather than simply refining my ability to meet deadlines. Through this experience I've realized that no religion is necessarily "right." I have come to understand that certain faiths are only "right" for certain people.

SOME OF MY BEST FRIENDS ARE . . .
BETH KANDER

Religion has often seemed like a wedge to me. I'm Jewish and take great pride in Judaism—but I haven't always acknowledged that pride to the fullest extent. I tried to avoid conversations about religious or spiritual identity. I was reluctant to discuss openly my own heritage. Why the hesitation? I didn't want to hurt anyone's feelings, especially not the feelings of my own family members.

My mom converted to Judaism. She had been drawn to Judaism for many years, though raised Lutheran. When she met my father, a nice Jewish man, she intensified her studies and wound up converting to Judaism before they were married. My mother is comfortable sharing her story: She refers to my father as a catalyst but not a cause, and she is solid in her Jewish identity. I know it hasn't been easy for her. Her family is still all Christian, mostly Baptist and Lutheran.

I remember growing up and always going to my grandmother's house for Christmas Eve. My parents would explain to my siblings and me: "We go to celebrate Christmas with the family, because they're our family, and we love them. They share their holiday with us because they love us. But it's not our holiday."

I love my grandmother. I love everyone in my mom's family and loved spending Christmas and Easter with them. As a child, I enjoyed celebrating all the holidays but occasionally wondered why we didn't have the same ones. As I grew older, I felt that I had to be sensitive to people's feelings on all sides, hiding a little something from everyone. I didn't mention to my Jewish friends that I would be opening presents from under a tree on December 25. I didn't mention to my Christian relatives how much I loved services, youth group, and learning Hebrew.

Thank goodness for Thanksgiving. A good old nonsectarian American holiday was the best of all worlds. Both sides of my family celebrated together, and I looked forward to it each year. Hey, minus the whole religious aspect, sharing holidays with family was *great* (though many of my fellow vegetarians never did understand my great love for Turkey Day)!

By the time I left for college, I had accumulated a pretty hefty set of religion-related baggage. I wanted to avoid the religion wedge, in both family relationships and friendships. Interestingly enough, I chose Brandeis University, partially because of its sizable Jewish community. But when discussing my decision, I talked more about choosing the university for its history of social justice and its commitment to liberal arts and undergraduate academics.

I may have been pulled to Brandeis by its Jewish community, but my freshman year I was minimally involved with any sort of Jewish activity. Shying away from organized religion and avoiding taking ownership of my spirituality were responses to my feeling that all too often, religion leads more to conflict than to community. I didn't want to be too closely associated with a religion or a religious group because, to me, people were always more important than observance. I avoided Hillel events but proudly attended diversity workshops, community events, and gay/straight alliance meetings. I just avoided personal religious stuff.

I didn't even know it at the time, but in some strange way, I was actually following a commandment found in *Pirkei Avot* ("The Ethics of Our Ancestors," a central Jewish text): "You shall not separate yourself from your community." That was my central concern: I didn't want to separate myself from my community. If going to services every Friday night alienated me from my hallmates, I would choose to go into the North End of Boston with my friends rather than light Shabbat candles. If keeping kosher meant not being able to eat with a large percentage of my friends and family, I wouldn't keep kosher. Or at least I wouldn't mention it, and cite only my vegetarianism as my reason for avoiding ham-and-Swiss. The way I saw it, I was choosing community over conflict. The problem with my practices was that I *was* separating myself from an important part of my community—my Jewish community.

It was hard making the decision to get involved. I didn't want the image of "actively Jewish," and I certainly didn't want that to be my central image or one that got back to my family. I really didn't want to be lumped in as another Brandeis Jew. As it happened, my freshman-year boyfriend was Jewish, but I knew him and started dating him before college, and I assured myself that I would have dated him even if he hadn't been Jewish. I had convinced myself that I was comfortable being quietly, peripherally Jewish.

I was proud of my diverse background, my diverse friendships. Attaching to one religious group, identifying strongly with my Judaism, was something I steered fairly clear of—but after freshman year, I realized I needed something more. Personally, spiritually, I wanted to explore my Judaism. I became involved in the Reform Hillel group at my campus, BaRuCH—the Brandeis Reform Chavurah. That was when I realized the importance of religious community and personal spirituality.

Religion for me was mostly about community. Coming together once a week to rest, reflect, and share a Shabbat experience helped me feel so connected to my Shabbat crew. I started to feel a little more fulfilled. Sharing in prayer and community gathering made me feel connected not only to the people around me but also to that missing "something." It was so ironic: I had always avoided religion in order to foster community. Now I was learning that being religiously active actually helped me *create* more community.

As I became more involved religiously, I felt a heightened spiritual awareness. I found myself taking advantage of small moments to really look around me, to appreciate the blessings filling my life, to try to experience and question God and my beliefs in an active, personal way. I was becoming comfortable with my own spirituality.

Becoming comfortable *speaking* about spirituality was a more gradual process. A breakthrough moment came during my junior year. I was talking with a friend of mine. We were sitting on a hill, near a statue of Justice Louis Brandeis, the university's namesake. Our initial conversation revolved around boys, our resident advisor positions, and our families. Somehow we slid into the subject of spirituality. My friend was Indian, her family followers of Hinduism. She told me of their customs, their family celebrations of holidays, her own quest to find spirituality and discover the ways in which she could make the world a better place.

I identified so much with what she was saying. Without even thinking about it, I found myself talking about how much my Shabbat experiences each week meant to me, how my family's celebration of holidays were some of my most meaningful and important moments, but also so challenging. We talked about how trying to find a balance between secular and religious life was such a struggle for both of us. We marveled at the similarities between our values and personal thoughts about religion and spirituality.

Realizing that my friend sharing her beliefs neither alienated nor threatened me, and vice versa, led me to the further realization that such dialogue and such acceptance was possible. In the following year, I had many conversations about religion and spirituality with friends and family. The conversations always left both parties feeling privileged to have been able to discuss such a personal subject so openly.

By my senior year, I wasn't shy about my love for my Judaism. I still felt strongly that it was wrong to impose your values on someone else, but I realized that respectful dialogue without

From my perspective, good spiritual practice involves humility and compassion and ultimate forgiveness. And hopefully a degree of light-heartedness.

—MOBY

13

imposition is both possible and valuable. All of my friends, Jewish and gentile, knew of my love for Shabbat and holidays. From the moment the Shabbat candles were lit Friday night until the flickering *Havdalah* candle was extinguished each Saturday night to signify the end of Shabbat, I cherished each BaRuCH Shabbat. I learned to make time each week to take a deep breath and enjoy the moments that had come to mean so much to me. I continued my involvement with diversity programming and my secular involvements, and found that being rooted in a religious community and my own personal spirituality helped me understand and empathize with other people even more.

For my graduation, my dad, mom, brother Adam, sister Claire, and grandmother B.C.—my mom's mom—traveled from Michigan to Waltham, Massachusetts, to celebrate my commencement. They arrived Friday night and joined me for BaRuCH services. My family shared in my Shabbat experience with me, met my friends and their families, sang along with our songs. At the conclusion of the weekend, my family raved about the BaRuCH services. My grandmother, the one who always shared her Christmas with me, hugged me and said, "I am so happy that you found such a wonderful community here. I know it's going to be hard for you to leave them. This was wonderful, honey. I'm so glad I could be here."

My eyes filled with tears. My experience those four years was brought full circle by my grandmother's words. My conversation on the hill, my BaRuCH community, and my own family had all taught me the important lesson that sometimes religion isn't a wedge. Sometimes, it's not being different that's the problem—just the fear of being different.

My grandmother was right. Leaving my Shabbat crew was one of the most difficult aspects of graduating. I was so lucky to have a campus environment and a group of friends so nurturing and supportive of my questioning and growth over the course of four years. I am also lucky enough to have a diverse and loving family, supportive of my passions and pursuits. I pray that I will be lucky enough throughout my life to have a large and varied community of friends and a supportive, open-minded Jewish community as well. I hope I will always recognize the blessing that is my family. I will work to ensure that I will always be able to recognize the importance of community, religious community, and personal belief and reflection. I'm not going to let religion be a wedge in my life. I've learned the lessons of my ancestors and adapted the adages into my own life.

I will not separate myself from my communities.

FIRST *PUJA* AND THEN ON TO MASS
TEJAL PATEL

Growing up as a member of a very religious Hindu family in the United States was never easy. The practices, myths, and rituals were all completely unlike anything my friends ever did for their religions. At the end of the day, though, I went home and found that my family was there to support everything I believed and did as a Hindu. So, how was my Hinduism impacted when I immersed myself in a Catholic community?

As a result of the decision I made a year ago, I am one of the 2,700 people who make up the student body at the College of the Holy Cross and one of maybe ten Hindu students on campus. I can't say that being a religious minority at a school that's religiously affiliated is easy, but the experiences that I've had and all the things that I've learned because I am a religious minority have totally outweighed the struggle.

Specifically, one class that I took this year has opened my eyes to many different religions. The College of the Holy Cross has a program called the First Year Program (FYP), designed to inspire students to work together and identify with a common theme. The theme during my freshman year was "Since many worlds must share one world, how then shall we live?" The class I took as a member of FYP was on religious worlds. In that class, I engaged in discussions about many world religions, from Christianity to the

God's grace is like a strong wind that's always blowing. But we have to raise our own sails.

—SRI RAMAKRISHNA

religion of the Dani tribe in Africa. Each religion I learned about gave me a new opportunity to find meaning in Hinduism. I was able to compare and contrast religions; I was not only allowed but also encouraged to question the religions. Finally, I was excited to find experiences of these religions outside of the classroom setting and really sense how different religions impacted different people.

The majority of the first semester was spent trying to discover the meaning and purpose of religion. We looked at different opinions and biblical passages. Second semester began with an examination of Islam. At the end of the unit, I felt like I understood more about Islam. I wrote my paper on Islam, and the class moved on to learn about Hinduism. My excitement about learning about Hinduism was unbelievable. I was beside myself with eagerness to share my faith with the class. I brought into class anything even remotely Hindu that I could find. We completed our learning of Hinduism by actually going to a Hindu temple and participating in the activities, from joining the *puja* (Hindu religious service) to eating the Indian food that was served. After Hinduism, we studied Buddhism. Finally, we got to Christianity, the religion that I was most interested in studying. Here I was at a Jesuit institution, and I knew next to nothing about Christianity. I read, observed, listened, and engaged in the Christianity that saturated the student body at Holy Cross. I went to a Mass at the on-campus church, I read the Bible, and I talked to my Christian friends about their faith. I wrote papers on Christianity, forcing me to broaden my horizons and learn about something I knew nothing about. Finally, to expand what knowledge I gained from class, I visited an off-campus chapel. Even after many hours of studying Christianity, I knew that I had just barely skimmed the surface.

I wanted to feel overwhelmed by how much there was to learn even after studying a religion. I craved information about all of them. After watching several videos, reading many books, and attending a few lectures, I felt that I knew the basic, academic information about the religions we studied. However, I was lacking the personal experience of religion. I wanted to talk to people, go to a religious service, and understand the connection to God that a member of each religion might feel. For a short period of time, I wanted to become the religion.

As you can imagine, this brought up a lot of questions in my mind about Hinduism. If I was so satisfied with my own religion, why did I feel the need to become so immersed in others? It was at this point when I realized that every faith had something that attracted me to it: its practices, myths, or rituals. However, the more I thought about it, the more I realized that Hinduism was the religion whose values were engraved in my head. It's what I grew up with. **Learning about other forms of spirituality wasn't betrayal—it was a way for me to appreciate my spirituality. I was finally able to learn about other religions but still know that my religion was the one best suited to me.** Hinduism is one of the world's most inclusive religions, and in a way, I was illustrating that tenet by accepting and wanting to experience so many different religions. I was fortunate; this test of faith didn't cause any permanent damage. In fact, it only strengthened my connection to my religion, my faith, and God.

SICK OF SALAD: WHAT TO DO WHEN CAMPUS DINING DOESN'T MEET YOUR NEEDS

Three days in a row, you've tried to eat lunch in Quad Commons, a.k.a. the cafeteria, and given the vast array of pork options (bacon cheeseburgers, ham-and-Swiss sandwiches) and spaghetti with meat sauce (who really knows what the heck is in there), three days in a row, you've ended up eating a poor excuse for a salad—wilted romaine lettuce, sorry tomatoes, tiny remnants of cucumber, and nasty, nasty dressing.

So, even though it's going to take you more time—and will be a tight fit between classes—you try the food court over in the student center. There you find a sandwich shop, a pizza/pasta bar, a salad bar, and oh, yes, a hot pretzel stand. The meat isn't going to work given your religious dietary guidelines, the salad bar is only one step above the let's-not-even-talk-about-it salad over in the quad, and pretzels just aren't going to cut it for lunch. What to do?

If you have tried all of the dining options on campus and they all feature menus that will rarely, if ever, allow you to eat a decent meal that follows your religious guidelines, then it's time to take action.

- Identify and connect with any religious groups on campus that share your dietary guidelines. Talk with a member of the group and see what others are doing. Perhaps they have a building on campus that includes a dining room and you can eat there.

- If you don't find a student group that shares your religious identity, consider other groups that may share the same rules. If you are Hindu and thus vegetarian, but there isn't a Hindu group on campus, contact a Jewish student organization and see what the students who keep kosher are doing.

- If you encounter other students who share the same frustration and haven't solved the problem, then identify the proper campus channel to pursue this issue. Your student government may have a campus food committee—you could file a complaint with these student leaders and they should advocate for you. Or campus dining services may have a student advisory group. If you can't find any other potential advocates, make an appointment with your dean of students or someone in the student affairs office, and they should be able to help you resolve the situation.

- Be prepared to educate your dean or other representative regarding the dietary guidelines that you follow.

- You may also need to offer suggestions as to how they can solve the problem. One of the easiest solutions is to find an off-campus catering company that could provide food on campus. Many campuses have had success with an off-campus caterer who will gladly prepackage a variety of meals and sell them through a campus outlet. They keep a range of selections in stock and rotate the menu for variety. Often a kosher caterer can provide food that meets the needs not only of Jewish students but also of students from a variety of religious traditions, including Buddhist, Hindu, Muslim, and Seventh-day Adventist.

- If there aren't any local caterers who can meet your needs, then request that campus dining services solve the problem internally. Perhaps a small kitchen and serving/dining area can be built (or an existing area renovated) to meet your requirements.

Make sure that whatever solution you arrange is covered through your campus meal plan—you shouldn't have to pay any more for a good meal than any of your classmates who are chowing down on the standard campus cuisine.

A TALE OF TWO ROOMMATES
LAURA CARROLL

My roommate and I are polar opposites. She's an engineer, I like humanities; she watches TV, I don't; she eats meat, I'm vegetarian; she wakes up early, I stay up late. Our religious views are also very different. She is Catholic, and I am Unitarian Universalist Pagan. Surprisingly, this hasn't been a major source of conflict for us. Although we have had our differences, for the most part we have found ways to coexist peacefully in a small space by respecting each other's beliefs.

When we first moved into our room at the beginning of our first year, both of us independently put up objects that had religious meaning for us. **She hung the cross from her first Holy Communion over her bed; I created a small altar to the elements on my windowsill. And even though I think we were both a bit perturbed at first ("Oh, no, she'll think I'm evil" and "Oh, no, she's not Christian" were some of our respective reactions), it was a chance for both of us to inquire about each other's faiths** and share a bit of what we believed.

For her, one of the important things about her faith is that it helps bind her family together. Her heritage is Mexican, and Catholicism is an important part of the culture in which she was raised. For me, on the other hand, my religious beliefs are very personal. Although I was raised Unitarian Universalist and both my parents ascribe to the Unitarian Universalist principles, our individual beliefs are all different because our religion leaves a lot to personal exploration and interpretation. I embraced Paganism because I liked the idea of a female deity, and I liked the connection to nature. Seeing each other's religious displays helped create an avenue in which we could talk about our different beliefs and gain respect for one another's views. And respecting and understanding one another's views made it easier for us to get along.

That is not to say that we haven't had conflicts. Although I was familiar with Catholicism before going to college, my roommate had had almost no exposure to Paganism before she met me. At one point I was speaking with a mutual friend and housemate about clearing her room, because she thought that her room was cursed. She asked how I would go about clearing it, and I told her that there are several different ways, from the simple one that I used in my room every night to more complex methods. My roommate overheard and was freaked out that I was manipulating energy in our room every night. Granted, it does sound a bit scary if you're not familiar with the idea. But once I explained to her that what I was doing was simply meditating every night before bed and visualizing any negative energy leaving the room, she calmed

There is no enlighten-ment outside of daily life.

—THICH NHAT HANH

down. Once she knew that I wasn't calling on demons, the idea seemed much less scary. Talking to one another when we had questions or concerns helped us maintain good relations even when we were less than sure about where the other was coming from.

By keeping our lines of communication open and talking about our faiths, we were able to overcome the differences in our religious beliefs. We respect each other's viewpoints, and we don't try to impose our individual views on the other. By talking about our beliefs we created understanding, and understanding is the key to any good relationship. Before the first day of class, my roommate gave me a glass flower and a note wishing me luck. I put it on my altar to symbolize friendship. Its twin hangs next to my roommate's communion cross. Despite our differences, we've managed to be friends and get along well during our first year of college. And next year will be even better.

LIKE THE ONE YOU'RE WITH: MAKING THE MOST OF LIFE WITH YOUR NEW ROOMMATE

Dear Resident Assistant:

My roommate and I are at different ends of the religious spectrum. I won't get into details about that, but our problem is that we both want to hang up things in the room, and these are things that are going to make the other person uncomfortable. How can we both grab some space for ourselves and deal with the fact that we are so different?

Dear Student:

Well, I'm glad that you are ready to "deal" with the fact you are both different. It's one thing to disagree, and it's another to be disrespectful. But I'm going to assume that since you're writing to me in the first place, you are indeed ready to value your roommate's opinions and respect each other.

Okay—with all that heavy stuff out of the way, we can now

address the problem at hand. Here's the thing—you both have equal claim to the room, so, in theory, both of you have the right to put up whatever you want on the walls. *However,* it is a different story if one person is uncomfortable. So the best road to take here is simply to talk to your roommate (yeah—easy to say, hard to do, right?). If your roommate is hanging up stuff that offends you, explain why the stuff is offensive and the relevant aspects of your belief system. And if I were you, I wouldn't leave anything unsaid here—don't hold back. Try not to let anger or frustration rage out of control, but do try to say everything you need to say. This way neither of you will make any assumptions in the future about what to display in the room.

Now for the flip side of the coin—your roommate's wishes. As I said before, the room belongs to you both; I know you want to hang up things that are meaningful to you. But if you do that without any regard for your roommate's feelings, she might think that you are unwilling to compromise and have no regard for other faith traditions. Religious beliefs are very personal, and people can be very passionate about them. Besides, debate is healthy! Don't try to change your roommate, but try to learn from her.

Ideally, you two will be able to come up with some sort of compromise. I don't know what you can do to make things more comfortable, but you definitely need to work it out—you don't want this issue to separate you two for the rest of the year. Learning to respect each other will be harder than decorating the room, but it'll be worth it.

Dear Resident Assistant:
I get up early on Sundays to teach at a religious school. My roommate brings friends back to the room on Saturday nights and they are pretty noisy. This makes it hard for me to get to sleep and then get up on Sunday. This is also sometimes a problem during the week when I'm trying to study. What should I do?

Dear Student:
Honestly, this is a pretty common roommate issue, and it can be worked out easily, just as long as you both are willing to compro-

mise. You will have to talk to your roommate about this, preferably during the day. Trying to talk when the problem is occurring at night isn't really the greatest idea—attempting to have an effective conversation in the heat of the moment never works for me (but maybe you can stay calmer than me, a typical redhead!). Wait for a time when you aren't both rushing out of the room or in the middle of something. Then say something such as, "Hey, I know that you like hanging out with your friends in the room, but I'm having a problem studying or I need to get up early some days. Do you think we can come up with a solution so I don't prevent you from hanging out with your friends and I can still study?" (*Negotiation* and *compromise* are key here.) Come up with some sort of schedule for the week. For example, Sunday through Wednesday you can have the room to study, and then Thursday and Friday nights your roommate can chill out with friends. Those nights you go to the library or a lounge to study. Ask your roommate to find somewhere else to hang out on Saturday night as you need to get up early on Sunday. The roommate gets Friday night to chill in the room and you get a quiet room on Saturday night—and you've split the weekend.

For readers who have not already experienced this problem, I would suggest a preventive measure. Roommates should have some sort of meeting where you spell out all the practicalities of living (ideally, this should happen on one of the first days of moving in). For instance, ask your roommate what his morning schedule is like (you need time to shower, eat, whatever). Talk about who is a morning person and who a night person, and other topics such as sharing food. And one of the questions you should include is, "How do you plan to use the room—will it be a 'social room' or a 'study room'?" After finding out what your roommate intends, you can then proceed from there, so ideally this problem never arises. Believe me—getting all this stuff out of the way first is the best thing to do; trying to figure it all out using your assumptions might take a month or two of irritation!

Dear Resident Assistant:

My roommate belongs to a religion I know nothing about. I'd like to learn more about it, but she seems very private about things and I feel like I would be intrusive to ask. I think it would bring us closer, though, if I could get to know her better. Do you have any advice?

Dear Student:

Well, I must admit—you don't seem to have too bad of a problem here. I think the best way to start the conversation would be to say exactly what you wrote to me here—that you're really interested in her religion, and that you think it would bring the two of you closer together. It's pretty flattering when someone asks you about *you,* know what I mean? And believe me, it's always easy to talk about yourself. . . .

But if she still seems to be a little apprehensive after your initial inquiry, ask her if perhaps you could read up on it first and then have some sort of conversation about it. Maybe that would make her feel more at ease. And after that, if you *still* can't get through to her that you just want to get to know her better, then ask her about her other interests. Hopefully then she'll realize that you have a general curiosity about her and who she is outside the dorm room.

—JOANNA LOVERING, COMMUNITY ADVISOR,
CARNEGIE MELLON UNIVERSITY

UNCERTAINTY
CONOR CASHMAN

I

I do not know the face in the mirror. Those sky-blue gemstones mounted on bloodshot eyes, the sharp early morning beard, cigarette tar on lips, a pale complexion—a stranger's bewildered face from behind the window of an unknown world. I do not know what it is thinking. I do not know what it wants. I do not know who it plans to be or what it plans to do. I do not know who or what if anything it believes in. I do not know if it has faith. I do not know if it has experienced true love or if it even knows where to look for it. I recognize the face, though, and I think it recognizes me. I see it all around me. Store windows, puddles, my cereal spoon, a lover's eyes, the ocean, the moon. I feel as if I am being watched, judged, and yet guided at the same time. It is as if this image is leading me somewhere that I do not understand, somewhere outside my realm of senses, somewhere godly.

Attempt easy tasks as if they were difficult, and difficult as if they were easy; in the one case that confidence may not fall asleep, in the other that it may not be dismayed.

—BALTASAR GRACIÁN

Someone once said that each man's faith leads him on a path up a mountain and that no two paths are the same. On the mountaintop rests God, and when one reaches the divine presence, one understands the world. One knows what God knows. One knows the secret behind the mystery of the universe. Thus, one comes into union with God and his divine knowledge. Someone else once said that God exists inside each and every person and that to love another person is also to love God. So by branching out, meeting people, caring for others, and loving, one actually strengthens his or her relationship with God. Needless to say, whether one climbs a spiritual mountain or develops meaningful relationships with others, it is obvious that people aspire to unite with God in some way. We must recognize this.

II

I do not know the face in the mirror. I do not know why the face is stained into glass, carved out of wood, or chipped into stone statues. I do not know how he not only represents a mortal man but also a trinity of immortals. I do not know how my parents, my family, and some of my peers have faith in such ridiculous beliefs that are not founded in reason. I do not know why I go to church. I find it boring and I cannot understand the mumbling priest half the time. I do not know why I am not supposed to bite the Eucharist. Would I really be biting into Jesus? Am I a cannibal? I have bitten it a few times before and nothing has happened. I do not know why I pray. No overwhelming feeling or deep voice inspires me. I say the Our Father and the Hail Mary before I go to bed and try to mean what I say every time. I ask him to help heal sick friends, comfort those who have lost someone, and lend me a hand in my own predicaments. Some things I pray to happen. Others, I do not. I want to believe in him, in prayer, and in heaven, but there remains, sitting in the back of my head like a cancer, a feeling of doubt.

A time comes in a person's life when you must stand back and calculate the meaning in your life—where and who it comes from and what makes it important. These calculations usually come during transitional periods—a marriage, a death, a move, a new job, and so on. For many, the transition from high school to college acts as the first major shift in life. Childhood friendships are tested. Family members who were once everyday characters in life now call once a week. Other smaller characters, such as favorite high school teachers, the soccer coach, or old neighbors, sometimes disappear completely. Ultimately, we wind up placing importance on the characters who remain. Meanwhile, we must also awkwardly force our way into the social atmosphere of college and rebuild a new structure of friends. At such crossroads in life, we must believe everything will work out for the best. Friendships that were not meant to be will cease. Things will change, we will change, the world will spin out of orbit and sink into the black of space. We must look past the seeming chaos of changing surroundings and focus on the dim wavering light, a match alight in an empty universe, the light at the end of a long opaque tunnel, and we must chase after it.

III

A face in the mirror. I know I am its owner; I know my name is Conor Cashman, but I do not know what that means. I like sports, reading, women, movies, but that does not mean anything. **I go to church every Sunday, yet I do not know what I truly believe. Yes, I received the sacrament of confirmation, but I constantly struggle with my faith every day.** My name, my religion, these words, these labels only attempt to make sense out of the nonsense that is my self and my beliefs. Simple vague generalizations for the unexplainable. Moreover, since we ourselves are unexplainable, we certainly cannot understand the complex workings of the world around us. In this world, uncertainty rests around us as thick as a fog. The only thing we can do is keep moving, keep believing, keep praying, keep edging forward over the unseen ground, hoping that each forward step won't lead us off a sharp incline. We pray our plane won't crash. We pray the dying will die peacefully. We pray the cancer won't grow back. We all know what we pray for. We all know what we don't understand. We all know our present world lies uncertainly below us and our future unknown ahead.

As we step into a new day, whether it is to move into a dormitory or a new house, we are stepping forward into this thick fog. Anything and anyone could be lying in front ahead. T. S. Eliot, a wife, computer science, a best friend, a business partner, Shakespeare, spiritual guides, run-ins with police, drug addicts, long-lost relatives, alcoholics (just to name a few I have encountered). Although this may seem scary, we must not be intimidated. We must have faith in the uncertainty of the world. We must have doubt. We are not God. Humans are by definition imperfect. We make mistakes. We make wrong turns. No one walks a certain path. We wander in unexplored forests with our faith as our compass. Obstacles will come, and our faith will waver, but we shall overcome. So when you find yourself lost in the uncertainty of this foggy universe, follow your faith, which guides like a lighthouse, and you will find your way.

LOOKING FOR HELP IN ALL THE RIGHT PLACES

Perhaps your dilemma is a good one . . . for instance, you want to start a new student organization and you don't know how. Or maybe your situation is much more serious, such as a member of your faith group commits suicide and you find that you can no longer focus on your academic work, or really much of anything. Regardless of the nature of the challenges, dilemmas, and difficulties you face in college, there are a number of professionals on campus who are available to help.

Campus Faith Leaders. If your dilemma or crisis is spiritual in nature, and you want to talk with a leader from your faith tradition, then there are a few options for you to seek help. Many campuses have local spiritual leaders who are on staff either full- or part-time, and they meet with students individually, as well as run services, study groups, and programs. If you don't know how to find the appropriate leader on campus, contact the campus multifaith center or campus ministry center, and staff there will refer you. If no leader from your tradition works on your campus, then seek out a leader in the local community.

Resident Assistants. Resident assistants are student staff members who are trained to be helpful to you, their peer. Students take these positions because they are dedicated to supporting you and other students. They are often more accessible on evenings and weekends than professional staff are, and they are trained to respond appropriately. Resident assistants are good people to start with to get help, and if the scope of the problem is beyond them, they are connected with a number of other resource people on campus and can refer you to the proper professional.

Health Services and Counseling. Your campus should have both a health center and a counseling center. These departments employ professionals who are particularly interested in working with college-age clients. They should have firm policies on confidentiality so you can get competent professional help without having to get your parents involved.

Student Life Staff. The student life staff includes everyone from the full-time professionals who work in residence life and housing to the student activities, athletics, and career center staff. Again, these people have chosen to make a career at a college campus because they like working with students. In most cases, they are often guided by firm confidentiality commitments. They should be effective problem solvers, so if campus dining isn't providing enough options for you to keep kosher, or if your prayer or mediation group can't find a place to meet, these are the folks to ask for help.

Academic Advisor. Your academic advisor will help you with procedural matters, such as signing up for classes. He or she can also be a valuable resource if you wish to pursue religion-related courses or a major or minor. Your advisor can help you understand the process and implications of taking courses outside of your major, as well as potentially cross registering for classes at another school.

Dean of Students. When you don't know where else to turn, make an appointment with your dean of students. Whether you've tried other channels and they haven't worked or you simply don't know whom to ask for assistance with a specific situation, the dean of students is the person who can always help.

Understand that you can and should approach your dean for positive as well as negative situations. Perhaps you'd like to attend a leadership conference and want to see whether the school will fund part of your trip; your dean is a good person to ask. If you are meeting with your dean to solve a problem, just follow the obvious rules of respect and professionalism. Call ahead for a meeting, and show up on time. Be prepared to clearly articulate the problem and, if possible, suggest solutions.

Although deans are often involved with discipline, most chose the position because they are committed to making the campus community a better place and they love to see individual students grow and succeed. The dean's job is to look out for your well-being and support you in your endeavors. Even if you have screwed up but want to change your ways, your dean may be able to help you out of a mess, if you are honest and show a sincere effort to improve.

Although college is a time of welcome independence, it's also an important time for you to get help when you need it. Asking a professional for help is not a failure of your ability to remain independent; it's actually an assertion of your independence because you are taking care of your own business.

2

READING, WRITING, AND RELIGION: SPIRITUALITY IN THE CLASSROOM AND BEYOND

The comment was an aside. Half the students in class probably didn't even hear it, because they had already stood and headed toward the door. But you heard it.

It was something your professor said right at the end of the lecture. It followed the discussion about immigration. The comment was based on an assumption that you've heard many times before, about "your people." You've just never heard a professor say it.

Later in the day, you start to think that maybe you misheard the professor. You hope that you misheard. But another comment a week later confirms your instinct. Your professor harbors a bias against people of your faith tradition. You know this already, and it's only the second week of classes.

The convergence of religion and academic studies, as well as the academic line that keeps spirituality out of the classroom, are two very different issues that may confront you with challenges during your college career. Should you choose to study religion in college, you may find yourself frustrated by the academic approach to a subject that is very emotional for you. Or you may find yourself in a classroom with a professor who seems to be teaching from a religious perspective that conflicts with your beliefs. Or perhaps you may be troubled by the way in which academic study rarely makes room for the discussion of spiritual beliefs and values.

From the Front of the Class

If you find yourself at odds with what a professor is teaching, then your first challenge is to consider whether the ideas you are hearing in the classroom are disturbing simply because they are outside of your current framework. Or is the material troubling because it comes from an uninformed or excessively biased position?

When you find your core beliefs challenged, how will you react? Will you seek to understand new and confrontational ideas before deciding whether to hold on to your existing beliefs? You might seek out additional readings that will further inform your position. Or will you attempt to filter out the new ideas to keep your core from being challenged? If you find that this experience is shaking your foundation, don't be alarmed. Understand that having your assumptions challenged is a normal part of intellectual exploration. Consider talking with your professor or a spiritual leader about your struggle. Other students—both from the class and from your faith group—may also be helpful.

Many of us get very nervous about these challenges, as do our parents and others who are invested in us holding on to the beliefs with which we were raised. We, or they, believe that if new ideas are presented that confront our beliefs, we will abandon all we have held to be true. In some cases, new ideas will ultimately bring about a shift in thinking, sometimes subtle and sometimes more drastic. Just as often, though, a thorough examination of new ideas will lead us to more thoughtfully evaluate our own faith and then hold on to it more strongly with a newfound understanding and appreciation. Either way, this journey is an important one, one that requires an openness to new ideas and an ability to hold on to the core values that make you who you are. Although the challenges can be stressful, they are imperative. You will not grow, even in your own faith, if you are not challenged.

If you are a humanities, business, science, or arts major (with arts broadly defined to include any creative field), you can be sure that you will encounter ideas in class or through readings that will challenge your beliefs. If you are a technical student, you may hit these challenges if you take core (humanities) classes or classes on ethics or leadership. Finally, group work, in any discipline, often presents issues relating to collaboration, including fairness, inclusion, and the assumptions that we make about others—all ideas that tap into our religious ideas and ideals.

Even if we have no interest in challenging our own beliefs, at least learning about other traditions has become an ethical imperative in the post-9/11 world. Before 9/11, many argued that with increased globalization, understanding cultures other than our own had become a key ingredient for success in almost any chosen profession. After 9/11, we also know that increased understanding among different peoples is profoundly important for creating local and global peace. Further, understanding how religious beliefs (our own and those of others) impact political beliefs is now a key to understanding events on the world stage.

What if a professor exposes a bias against people of your faith tradition or clearly seems to discriminate? At this point, you should seek advice from your academic advisor, campus spiritual leader, dean of students, or other appropriate campus official. You may be faced with deciding whether this is a battle you want to pursue. You may decide to confront the situation, though obviously you are in a delicate dilemma, as you will be receiving a grade from this professor. Or you may decide to dismiss the professor as uninformed and not worth your time. Regardless of your course of action, you should seek a campus official with whom you can have a confidential, purposeful conversation.

We should take care not to make the intellect our god; it has, of course, powerful muscles, but no personality.

—ALBERT EINSTEIN

33

Too Much Theory, Too Little Faith

In many college classrooms, religion and spirituality remain among the most taboo subjects, far more off-limits than race, politics, gender, and sex. If this is true in your academic experience, then you may feel that your studies are failing to help you understand how your spiritual and religious beliefs shape your thinking about your chosen field of study, and thus your evolving perspective as a professional. In addition, if your academic program is designed to push your thinking, it will likely present ideas that challenge your core beliefs, many of which may be tied to your spirituality and religion. How will you integrate your spiritual beliefs with all the other knowledge and skills that you are developing as you prepare for your chosen career? How do you resolve these conflicts, when spirituality and religion are not brought explicitly into the discussion? When is it appropriate to bring your spirituality into your academic work? Or is "appropriate" a moot question, as perhaps your spirituality is always present and the question is when do we get real about discussing it?

You may have a desire to bring your faith more directly into your studies, and there haven't been any signs that this is acceptable. If this issue has emerged for you in regard to a specific class, visit your professor during office hours and discuss your interests. You may be pleasantly surprised, and your professor may have specific ideas about how additional readings, a twist on an assignment, or even a future independent study might allow you to explore the convergence of your spiritual beliefs and the course material.

If you wish to bring your faith into your studies and the professor is not open to the idea, then you must consider how compelled you are by this situation. If you feel that you simply cannot address the course material without tying it to your beliefs and the professor has balked, then you should talk with your academic advisor for help in resolving the situation. With the help of your advisor and perhaps a spiritual leader, explore why you feel so strongly about tying the two together. If the professor is refusing, the question remains whether the professor is afraid of a difficult class discussion or has good reasons for omitting faith from the discussion.

If you remain compelled and can't resolve the situation with this professor, you have two options. If the class is an elective or if another professor teaches the class concurrently or in a different semester, perhaps you can drop the course or change to a different section. If you must remain in the course, or wish to for reasons outside of the faith discussion dilemma, then consider keeping a journal in which you can explore faith-related aspects of the course. Or perhaps you can have regular meetings with a spiritual leader or other students from your religious tradition to discuss the course material in the context of faith.

If you are attending a denominational college or university, then you may encounter a different set of issues. Courses may be taught from a distinct religious perspective. By choosing to attend a denominational school, you have agreed to study within a particular curriculum. If you wish for a more broad perspective, consider cross registering for classes at a nearby college or university.

Majors, Double Majors, and Minors

Another approach to exploring faith directly through your academic pursuits is to major or minor in religious studies. The first thing to understand about majoring in religious studies is that in most cases this will not offer you four years in which to explore your spirituality. Religious studies as an academic field typically includes in-depth exploration into the historical, sociological, and political content of religion. Religious studies is an intellectual pursuit, not an emotional or personal journey into religious connection and spirituality.

If, after understanding the intellectual nature of this academic discipline, you wish to pursue a religious studies major, one question that you (or your parents) may have is where that will lead you in terms of a career. If you are interested in working within your faith tradition after graduation, then this won't be an issue. If ultimately you want to do something else professionally, however, then you may be concerned that a religious studies major will leave you

*Those in a hurry do
not arrive.*

—ZEN SAYING

unprepared or at a disadvantage in terms of a job search.

If you also have an interest in a business, science, or technical field, and particularly if that interest is tied to your career goals, then you should consider a double major or a minor. Science and technical careers in particular require specific training, and if you forgo that for a religious studies major you won't be as qualified for those respective job markets. This is also true for the more quantitative areas of business, such as finance and accounting. Your academic advisor can help you understand the implications of these courses of studies in terms of requirements, scheduling, and other practical issues.

If you don't want to work in a faith-related career and don't have career goals in the business, technical, or science fields, then there is no reason not to major in religious studies if this is the academic area that you find most compelling. One concern that some students (and parents) have is that religious studies, like other humanities, doesn't prepare you for a specific career. The good news is that religious studies and other humanities do give you a tremendous skill set that is indeed valued by potential employers. Problem solving, research and writing, and critical thinking are just a few of the marketable skills you will develop. These are the skills that employers in many fields look for in potential employees. Keep in mind that if you plan to apply to medical school or pursue some other specialized professional or graduate school program, you'll need to research the prerequisites and work them into your undergraduate program. Also consider doing summer internships that will give you on-the-job experience to complement your studies. Summers spent in an ad agency, a law firm, a nonprofit organization, or another professional setting provide a nice balance to a humanities course of study, as you will gain practical experience in your area of career interest.

Independent Studies

If you are unable or choose not to pursue a religious studies major or minor but wish to further explore your faith, then think outside the academic box. Many faith communities offer adult education classes and retreats to help you learn more about your tradition and increase your sense of spirituality. In fact, if you are on a personal spiritual search, these sorts of endeavors may be more suitable than an academic course of study. Retreats, in particular, typically focus on personal spiritual growth rather than on the academic side of religion.

In addition, you may want to consider starting a study group on campus. First explore and make sure there isn't an existing group that would meet your needs. If not, then start your own (see chapter 3). Bible studies and prayer groups usually involve students from a single faith tradition; however, multifaith groups can be equally, if not more, powerful.

LOOKING TO SCRIPTURE
DALE JOHNSON II

During my final semester of college, I had the absolute pleasure of enrolling in a course titled "Christian Prayer: Practice and Understanding." This course presented a new challenge to me within my religious studies major, a challenge that made me a bit hesitant, because it stepped outside the academic arena of historical and social criticism and concentrated on searching for one's own experience of God in a semipublic forum. I was extremely nervous about enrolling in such a course at my school, which is a Jesuit college with a predominately Catholic student body, because I was raised in the Lutheran Church and I was unsure whether the other students in the course would welcome my tradition's perspectives on the subject matter. It was with this hesitancy that I entered the course, which ultimately helped put my four years of college into greater perspective.

From the very onset of the course, our professor asked us to constantly reflect on the nature of our personal relationship with God. As I sat one night pondering this question in the dark, lonely book stacks in the library, I realized that although I had a strong faith in God and adhered somewhat faithfully to the teachings of the church, I did not know how to categorize my relationship with God. Needless to say, I found this revelation to be extremely upsetting.

Christianity, like Islam and Judaism, is a religion that seeks spiritual answers from what is believed to be divine text. Therefore, I decided to turn to Scripture to see the types of relationships my tradition's mothers and fathers had with God. What I found was that each person experienced moments of great vulnerability and weakness, including Jesus. As a matter of fact, vulnerability seems to be an overwhelmingly common theme in the Bible, due primarily to its experience as one that defines all of us as humans.

Having had this revelation, I soon realized that it would be a better exemplification of Christian values to apply the practice of sharing my own vulnerability with the other students in my class. This was achieved by openly discussing my upbringing and viewpoints in class with the professor and the rest of the students. I soon found that my hesitations and nervousness left me when I expressed a differing opinion or understanding of the course material. The same class that at one time had made me uncomfortable was transformed into a forum of respect and interreligious dialogue.

This is not to say that we all agreed on every single point. Quite the contrary, we often disagreed. However, instead of feeling outnumbered or that I might be "ganged up on," I felt more confident in discussing my own insights and beliefs. I truly felt there was a sense of respect in the classroom and a genuine searching for truth. No longer did we discuss only the "Catholic approach" to spirituality, but we discussed multiple Christian approaches and the limitations that each tradition's approach has.

The result of this was remarkable! All too often, Christians of every denomination choose to discuss religion solely with those who believe the same things they do to avoid confrontation or debate. Most Christians never take the time to evaluate or discern what they are told by their church to believe. The result of this lack of differing viewpoints is narrow-mindedness, a sense of superiority, and, often, being less than well informed. All of this was voided from our classroom because each member of our special group made a conscious choice to listen to what others had to say and respect them for having the courage to say it out loud. By doing this, it is my belief that we all were able to learn more about what we believe and, therefore, were able to grow spiritually.

The intelligent man who is proud of his intelligence is like the condemned man who is proud of his large cell.

—SIMONE WEIL

Sitting here now, shortly after the completion of my four years of undergraduate study, I can honestly say that my Christian prayer course was one of the most rewarding experiences that I have ever had. By recognizing our vulnerabilities, a human characteristic that we so often try to hide or get rid of, the class was able to learn so much about each other, our faith, and our relationship with God.

WHEN ACADEMIC IDEAS AND FAITH COLLIDE

The teaching and learning that you encounter in college often tend to emphasize the so-called rational and the explainable. The emphasis is on learning about external things that we all can agree upon or at least argue about "objectively." In many courses, you are expected to leave issues of faith, or "subjective" topics, outside the classroom. Even courses on religion examine the rituals and historical and social processes rather than ask you to reflect on your faith. This usually avoids conflicts about and challenges to beliefs, and it may be considered the only academically correct way.

I remember Sean, a student in a course on environmental issues, who told me that he would like to add one more attribute to those we were discussing as sources of environmental problems, but he said it was a concept that I—the teacher—might not want to discuss in class. I responded that the only type of discussion that I do not allow in class is one that knowingly hurts a member of the class. Despite this assurance, Sean would not discuss the concept—which he later identified as "love"—until the course was finished. In response to my question about why he was so reluctant to talk about the role of love in preserving the environment, he said that he had been told in at least two courses that concepts such as love are too personal and subjective and outside the scope of academic discussions.

So it is with the topic of faith. There should perhaps be more occasions in learning situations where you have to reflect on your faith and think about how some of the concepts learned in the classroom and matters of your faith fit together. This might help you articulate better the foundations of your faith, and understand yourself and the core of your being more clearly. Is this type of discussion appropriate for an academic setting, particularly a formal course or class? Your teachers may hold widely differing views on this. At least one relevant issue here is whether academic learning is only about building your professional and scholarly identity or also for helping build your authenticity.

What is authenticity and what does it have to do with faith or academic learning? Charles Taylor, a philosopher at Harvard, in his wonderful little book called *The Ethics of Authenticity,* talks of authenticity as "self-determining freedom." He writes, "It is the idea that I am free when I decide for myself what concerns me, rather than being shaped by external influences." He points out that listening to and understanding the "inner voice" requires that the moral ideal one lives by also come from self-reflection.

Our rather artificial partition of the internal and external in academic learning does not give much room for self-reflection. This partition is also an attempt to distinguish the public from the private. Our society, with its scientific bent and respect for privacy, thinks that faith and personal religious beliefs are private matters and should be left alone. It is an extension of the paradigm of separation of church and state. But this can cause a schism in your thinking, even the belief that you need not—and maybe cannot—be a whole person in the classroom.

Although extended discussions of faith and personal beliefs may distract the class from its main agenda of imparting a certain domain of knowledge, you can find appropriate venues for discussions about faith. This makes learning richer and gives you room to integrate your selves—public and private—with greater clarity and conviction. It gives you room to develop your authenticity.

You may be led to reflect on your faith even when the learning environment does not explicitly ask you to do that, if you just allow yourself to think of matters of faith in things academic. For example, a rabbi's son had to read Daniel Quinn's *Ishmael: An Adventure of the Mind and Spirit* in my course on science, technology, and ethics. *Ishmael* challenges common worldviews and calls on the reader to think beyond conventional assumptions. I give detailed instructions on how to read the book. The instructions say, "If it makes you angry, lay the book aside and come back to it later. If you think it is trivial, you are not getting the point, or are not ready to read it yet," and so on. This student told me that he was glad I had provided those instructions. Initially, he did get angry because he thought, at first reading, that the book challenged the tenets of Judaism, but on rereading it, he realized that it was consistent with Judaism and his own beliefs! He said the book clarified things for him, forcing him to articulate his own faith and examine his beliefs more closely.

So my advice and fond hope is that as you go through your college education, as you discuss and exercise other people's visions and ideals, you allow yourself to reflect on matters of faith and the place of faith in your life. This reflection is not antithetical to academic learning; it can help you integrate the body of your knowledge. It will be a lifelong, dynamic quest, and one that makes you whole.

—Dr. Indira Nair, vice provost for education, Carnegie Mellon University

POLITICALLY INCORRECT

NATHAN BLACK

When I was looking at colleges during high school, I came across a guidebook that judged each institution largely on how politically incorrect it was. The author described political correctness as one of the main scourges of modern higher education, and accordingly he ripped into the intellectual climates of some of the country's top schools.

At the time, I thought this was a rather odd and fairly unhelpful way of comparing colleges—until this past year, when I was *in* college.

I love Rice University, but overly zealous political correctness is definitely a problem. As opinion editor of the newspaper, I am subjected every week to submissions that hide behind euphemisms for fear of writing something controversial. And as a student, I sit at lunch-table conversations and see other students terrified to express unique perspectives. Those at the university who do spark controversy through their words or actions usually regret it, as they are overwhelmed by reactionary cries for "diversity," "task forces," and other buzzwords behind which students and faculty hide. It is no wonder that, as a result, true diversity of opinion is so discouragingly rare.

Probably the last place I expected to experience a departure from the politically correct climate of Rice was in my introduction to religious studies class this past spring. Even at a less wishy-washy university, why wouldn't a 120-person class giving a broad overview of the world's religions be a bit on the politically correct side? At the beginning of the semester, I couldn't think of a non-PC way the professor might present the material without offending someone—and at Rice, that's the kiss of death.

But one of the course's two professors had a refreshing approach. **Instead of timidly tiptoeing around the core beliefs of the faiths we explored, she chose to passionately defend each creed as if it were her own.** Although this approach meant that the negative aspects of the religions we studied were generally either ignored or glossed over, she nevertheless managed through her defenses to bring the faiths and the class to life.

When we studied Taoism, she presented the central attitudes of balance and nonpassion as being analogous to the attitude of a professional athlete while he was "in the zone"—when his mind was at peace and everything was going well. For Judaism, she emphasized the potency of a religion that dictates many of the practicalities of daily life, strongly advocating the comforting power of such an involved creed. For fundamentalism—perhaps the only type of faith about which the PC community will state a strong opinion—she explained the rock-solid sense of self and God that such an unbending religion instills in its believers and how these strengthening effects were far from purely negative. Then, when we studied the antireligion of secular humanism, my professor cried out in a frenzy, "It's not religion that got us to the moon and back!"

When she first began these passionate defenses—she initially covered Judaism—I, at least, was a little confused. "Is she Jewish?" I thought. "And is it really appropriate that she is promoting her faith so enthusiastically?"

In time, of course, I realized she was giving the same treatment to each creed we studied (and that she was a former Pentecostal Christian). She was not proselytizing; she was expanding our minds.

For when she chose the approach of equalized passion over that of bland political correctness, she gave us much more than a watered-down, easily forgotten snapshot of the faiths we studied. She helped us, through her fiery, direct style, to appreciate how each religion was so appealing to lonely, confused, and helpless mortals such as us—such as *all* mortals.

As a result, when the semester ended, I did not think of Taoism as a strange, spooky religion that was embedded in another culture and deserved a passive nod of respect for that reason alone. Instead, I saw Taoism—and fundamentalism, and Judaism, and secular humanism, and more—in universal terms of why their followers followed.

Because of this perspective, the followers did not seem so strange or spooky either. Their views, while assuredly not mine, made sense—so, thus, did they. And making sense of other people—not hiding behind PC-driven euphemisms—is what cultural awareness should be about.

I hope my professor's style is emulated across the university community, and especially at schools such as Rice that have gotten a bad (and well-deserved) rap for political correctness in recent years. When the hunger for true understanding trumps the fear of giving offense, we have stepped away from sickly-sweet courtesy and stepped toward enlightenment and acceptance.

WHEN FINALS FALL ON A HOLY DAY

One of the more difficult dilemmas you may face is what to do when an exam, important presentation, graded activity, or even a major campus event such as a job fair conflicts with your spiritual commitments. We aren't talking about your regular meditation practice or the services you attend. You should have already planned your meditation or worship schedule around your classes. Rather, we are talking about when you have a conflict with a major day of observance, perhaps one that forbids you from working or requires you to fast or spend the day in prayer or meditation. The best strategy for dealing with these potential conflicts is to be proactive.

- Check all syllabi after the first day of class and note any conflicts that you will encounter between class and faith commitments.

- Talk with your professor after the second class, noting the conflict that you anticipate later in the semester.

- If the time you will need to miss class is during a lecture, assure the professor that you will be responsible for the notes and get them from a classmate.

- If a paper is due during your absence, assure the professor that you will submit it to him or her prior to your absence or on the due date.

- If you will not be able to submit the paper early, make arrangements with a classmate, roommate, friend, acquaintance, mail carrier, yoga instructor, waiter at your favorite restaurant, or anyone else you absolutely trust to deliver the paper at the appropriate time.

- If your faith commitment means that your absence will take place during a scheduled exam, propose alternatives. The first option would be to offer to take the exam early. Be aware that there are situations in which an instructor would rather not make that accommodation.Occasionally, the fear exists that letting the exam out of the hermetically sealed vault before the assigned time may lead to problems, for instance, the exam appearing on the Internet, in the school newspaper, or posted on the bulletin board in the student center. Other alternatives may be the traditional "makeup" exam, a paper in lieu of taking the exam, or possibly a presentation.

In the majority of cases, faculty members are understanding and will work with you, particularly when you explain that you have faith commitments that are not accommodated by the school calendar. Remember the key is to be proactive and make arrangements as far in advance as possible. With the exception of not being registered in the class yet, it is never too early to deal with a future conflict.

Uh-oh! You've done it all, and your professor will not accommodate your needs. Don't panic or become discouraged. There are still steps to take.

- Check your student handbook. These are usually given out during freshman orientation or may be found at the beginning of the year in strategic offices at the student center. It may now be under your bed or being used as a doorstop or possibly a coaster. The majority of students and faculty don't read it. Among other valuable information, it may have a written policy for your school's philosophy on religious holidays and observances.

- If you cannot find a formal policy, it is time to start climbing the ladder. The first rung is the department chair. Make an appointment to speak with him or her and bring along your concerns in writing.

- If the results of a meeting with the department chair are not acceptable, the next step is to meet with the dean of that particular school. Follow the same procedure. If you are not successful with the dean of the school, then meet with either your dean of students or the vice president for academic affairs.

- Finally, when you have resolved your immediate conflict, you may wish to pursue this on a larger scale. Meet with your dean of students and ask that a committee be formed to publish a list of religious observances during which professors should avoid giving exams and otherwise scheduling graded activities. This committee should include representatives from as many faith traditions as possible, staff from your campus spiritual organizations, and students. This committee won't be able to "protect" all days of religious observance, but a thoughtful committee can develop a list of priority dates for the campus community to consider. This list should be sent to all faculty and staff at the end of the spring semester, to be used in planning graded activities and major campus events the following year. The list should be sent with a cover letter from a dean or vice president, urging faculty and staff to avoid scheduling on these primary days of observance.

—BOBBIE KOPLOWITZ, ACADEMIC/LIFE SKILLS
COORDINATOR FOR THE MEN'S BASKETBALL TEAM,
CENTRAL CONNECTICUT STATE UNIVERSITY

AT THE SAME TABLE
LEAH RACHEL BERKOWITZ

Whenever I meet a new person, I like to ask, "What's your favorite book?"

All people have a favorite book, even if they have to think really hard, reaching way back in their memories to the books that were read to them as children. I find that I can discover so much about people by learning what words have spoken to them and what stories they have truly connected with over the course of their lives.

If someone asked me this question, we might be talking for quite a while. I enjoy reading so much that I have trouble choosing a favorite.

Someone might find it surprising that I chose Near Eastern and Judaic studies as my major in college instead of English. But as I moved from my secular high school to a university where Jewish students were in the majority, I found myself completely overwhelmed and fascinated by the depth and breadth of the religious community.

Although I continued to read and write, I kept my literary interests on the back burner as I developed my identity as a leader in the Jewish community. I never expected that the two pursuits would end up overlapping.

The most difficult thing about the religious community at Brandeis University was finding common ground. Even within the Jewish community, people come from a variety of backgrounds and traditions. Coming together to do anything was a challenge. Some students studied a page of Talmud, a difficult Jewish legal text, every day between their academic classes. Others had never set foot in a religious school.

My religion places a high value on learning, both in the classroom and around the table. As a Near Eastern and Judaic studies major, I was doing plenty of learning in the classroom. So when I became the education coordinator of a liberal Jewish group on campus, I began to ask myself: How can I bring together the various groups of students in my community to study at the same table?

With this challenge in mind, and knowing that the way to most people's minds is through their stomachs, I started a program called "Books and Bagels." I picked out a few novels and memoirs for students to read over vacation.

Discussing these books over bagels and lox, students of different religious backgrounds began to open up to each other about their families, spiritual identities, and the unique, often tragic history they carry on their shoulders and in their hearts.

Our first two books were *The Sunflower,* by Simon Wiesenthal, and *The Jew in the Lotus,* by Rodger Kamenetz. A Holocaust survivor, Wiesenthal tells the story of a dying Nazi soldier, whose final request is to be forgiven by a Jew. Kamenetz, a nonobservant Jewish journalist, describes the voyage of a group of Jewish leaders to India to speak with the Dalai Lama, in exile from Tibet.

While in the privacy of my dorm room, these books seemed as different as night and day. It was only when we came together as a group of Jews, Christians, and Buddhists that we were able to find the similarities at the heart of the texts.

First, we realized that Judaism is not the only religion that pairs studying with food. In *The Jew in the Lotus,* everyone in the room is given a sweet mixture of nuts and raisins before studying with the Dalai Lama. Likewise, children in a Jewish religious school are given a drop of honey as they learn each letter of the Hebrew alphabet. There is a psalm that says that the words of the Bible are "sweeter than honey."

But while our religions share the idea of sweetness in learning, they also share the bitterness of oppression, persecution, and exile.

In spite of the different backgrounds of the authors, and the different ideologies of the readers, the two books raised similar questions for our discussion group: Can Jews and other persecuted minorities forgive the Nazis for the

I shall allow myself to be perplexed time and again perhaps, in order to arrive at greater certainty.
—ETTY HILLESUM

crimes of World War II? Can Tibetan Buddhists forgive their Chinese oppressors for taking away their homeland? And, looking at a wound that had occurred only months before our discussion, can we forgive the September 11 hijackers for their acts of terror?

Many of our religions encourage us to embrace this anger and channel it toward improving the world; the understanding of Buddhism we gained from our reading suggests that it is best to let go of this anger completely. Kamenetz writes that there is a Buddhist teaching that being angry at an enemy is like stabbing yourself through the stomach with a sword to hurt someone standing behind you with the tip of your sword.

Because each religion has its painful memories, we often got stuck discussing the negative aspects of our histories rather than the positive aspects of our survival and our growth. For many of us, pain and anger have been driving forces in our religious lives. We are encouraged to maintain a spiritual identity, if only to spite those who tried to take it away from us. How do we, as Jews, Christians, Buddhists, and human beings, remove the sword from our stomach and heal the wound?

In the midst of one discussion, a student said simply, "You can't forget a hurt, but you can cover it with something better." We cannot ignore the fact that we have been persecuted in the past, but we can refuse to let our anger keep us from making the best of our lives.

By sharing stories that caused us pain, we were able to recognize that there is no religious tradition on Earth that has not been at one time oppressed or persecuted. But we also realized that, **in a world where so many people practice a religion based on anger and hate, each of us has the potential to create a religious life, and to continue writing our own story, based on something better.**

SINGING IN DIFFERENT LANGUAGES
VARUN MEHTA

I do not know which came first: my deep affection for music or my keen interest in religion. All I do know is that both of them have been complementary. Through a deeper study of one, I have become more enlightened about the other. For instance, I got really interested in *quawallis,* an intently devotional style of prayer taken up by Muslims to aid them in converting Hindus in the sixteenth century. The music is very strong and upbeat, dealing with a variety of writings and poetry by famous Islamic leaders and prophets. The lyrics are powerful. They command the listener to pay close attention to the beauty that the poet has incorporated in his work, in order to get the true sense of what is being sung. My amplified interest in this genre of music changed my life in two momentous ways: First, it forced me to become familiar with Islamic culture and some of the popular mythology of the religion, and second, it intensified my interest in bringing this type of music into Hindu prayers. While I have no interest in converting anyone, listening to such music has enticed me to strive for knowledge, understand others who are different, and love the uniqueness in each, all keys to becoming a better human in the Hindu religion.

Quawalli lyrics have motivated me to learn more about my culture, increase my vocabulary in Hindi and Punjabi, and interact closely with my parents on a totally new level. Singing in different languages, I have been able to ascend the culture barrier, and sometimes even religious barriers. Although I read and understand only Hindi and Punjabi, I am able to sing in Urdu and Farsi, which are close in nature to Hindi and Punjabi.

Not much has been sung about the unity that humankind should bring about in the world, regardless of differing religions. In recent months, I have begun to compose original material. This has helped me send the message I want to express philosophically wherever I am singing. My lyrics articulate a unity that can cross the barriers of all religions. I try to include the names of not only the

Indian deities but also that of Allah, Buddha, and Christ into my lyrics. Being that they are names, I feel as though I should respect all of them equally. It has been a fulfilling experience to see the acceptance of the message in my audience's eyes during my performance as well as in the conversations that arise from it afterward.

It is my strong belief that only two means of refuge exist from the distress that life can sometimes become. They are music and religion. Totally different in composition, polar opposites in the type of support they provide, the two are still the only things that can assist one in escaping the troubles of everyday life. In music, we are allowed to reflect true feelings without having to find the right words to express our thoughts. Where words fail to elicit the accurate emotion, music takes over. It has the power to express that which cannot be spoken. Music has such a command on us that it is able to heal the plagued heart, mend a battered relationship, and wash away from the soul the dust of everyday life.

As a trained musician and enthusiast of all music, I can personally vouch that not just any type of music can have such a soothing and serene effect on a person. Chiefly, devotional and religious hymns are particularly able to inject a dose of life into a person and drain the stress away. When singing, I must make an informed decision in regard to selecting the perfect *raag* (a set of musical notes of a particular scale), at the proper time of day, with the optimal mood. I have kept my performances simple, amplifying my *alaap* (a slow introduction of notes to a particular *raag* that a singer/musician is about to dwell in). By approaching the music in this way, I let that Almighty lead me to the next note I hit, its duration, its tonality, as well as its manner of conclusion. For accompaniment, I play the harmonium, which is a unique combination of an accordion and a piano, the only difference being that it is usually tuned closer to a singer's voice. Especially through Indian classical music, I have been able to discover and express a side of myself that neither I nor other people close to me knew I even had. Without any doubt, it has kept me from dwelling too much on the unnecessary evils presented before others my age.

51

Music has kept me focused in demanding circumstances, yet relaxed in stressful situations. My faith has taught me to keep busy with things that are good for me, personally and as part of our society. These two things have been gifts that have kept on giving. Whether in utter despair or extreme ecstasy, I have been able to lean on my music and faith for comfort and support. Fortunately, I have seen that the audiences have been affected similarly; they are provided the same hypnotic results. I personally have developed a deeper understanding of music by delving into my faith, and vice versa. Though I might not be able to recall which of these interests I pursued first, in the end, I am thankful that I discovered them both.

CHAPTER **3**

THE CLUB SCENE: MEMBERSHIP AND LEADERSHIP IN CAMPUS ORGANIZATIONS

"You should be our campus coordinator next year," says the outgoing leader of your faith-based service organization.

"I'll think about it," you reply.

Fact is, you've been thinking about it for most of the semester. As one of only five juniors in the group, and the one who has led most of the service projects for the past two years, you are the logical choice to run things next year. However, you know that you have begun to take a more progressive view of your spirituality. You expect that many members of your group still hold more conservative views. Should you take the coordinator position and try to broaden the other students' thinking? Or would it be misleading for you to take charge when you know your agenda isn't entirely what they expect? Perhaps you should start a new group.

They want you. Campus faith and spiritual groups want you to join, and they make themselves known. They hold events with free food, chalk the sidewalks, poster the campus, and advertise in the student newspaper. They may even send mail to your parents, trying to get them to get you to join. Indeed, they want you.

So the question is, do you want them? If you are in a religious minority and are looking to connect with a community, the answer may be an easy yes. You may also be clear that you plan to join if you are in the religious majority and want your primary campus connection to be faith-related. If your campus has more than one group based in your tradition, then your only decision may be about which group to join. Are you looking for a group that provides a prayer or meditation community? Or are you looking for an opportunity to learn more about your faith? Perhaps you seek to do community service with others from your tradition. Or maybe you are seeking a social group. Are you looking for a group that is narrow in its membership, attracting students who are clearly similar in their beliefs, or would you prefer a group that builds a diverse membership based on a shared tradition? Of course, you may be seeking a group that combines several of these elements.

Try a variety of groups—some of them may not be what they seem, so it may take time to decide which is the best fit. Moreover, you may find as your spirituality evolves, you will decide to look for a different group that is a better match than the one that first appealed to you. And what if you don't find a group that fits? Then start your own.

Creating a new student organization inherently puts you in a leadership position. You are just as likely, though, to become a student leader by rising within an existing organization. As a student leader you will face a variety of challenges, including issues with and among members, rapid increase or decrease in numbers of members, and funding and fundraising.

Some of these issues will overtly include an ethical dimension that will connect with your spiritual beliefs. For example, as editor of the student newspaper, you may wish to challenge your university president on policy decisions. If your president is also a member of the clergy, however, and your faith prohibits challenging spiritual leaders, then you may be torn between confronting behavior that appears to be unethical and taking a stand against a leader of your faith tradition. This kind of dilemma provides a profound test of your faith because you are required to examine thoroughly your own ethical code, understand the tenets of your faith, and then process all this information to make thoughtful, ethical decisions.

Many other issues won't have such a clear faith-related element, but your spirituality will keep you grounded during stressful times. Perhaps a few members of your organization quit, and thus the workload on remaining members is magnified as you carry out commitments. Praying or meditating will get you through the stress of running the organization, keeping up with school, and managing your day-to-day life on campus.

FINDING FELLOWSHIP
ALICE CHEN

I was going to begin with a dramatic retelling of my experiences with a faith-based college group, but the question is really about you. Should you join a faith-related group in college? And if so, which one and how will you know which one? Aren't there cults around, or what if you don't really know how involved you want to be? The great thing about college is that, for most people, it's a place where you can develop an understanding of what you really want to do. You're away from familiar faces and environments. You'll probably change your mind about everything from your major to your significant other.

So should you join a college fellowship group? If you're not sure whether you want to go all hard core, I'd say you should still take the time to meet the groups at school-sponsored activity fairs. Five minutes of your time will show you who's around, just in case you ever do want to get involved. Who knows? Two years down the line, you could be down and out, flunking your classes, and feeling as if you don't belong, and you just might want someone to pray for you or bring you cookies. You're not signing your life away to the group by asking for help, and, depending on the group, you might even get a free meal out of it (and who doesn't like a free meal?).

If you are someone who devoutly practices your religion, you should join a college faith group. Faith and religion need support and teaching in order to grow. A faith-based group offers opportunities to learn more about your faith, fellow classmates to encourage you, a connection to local religious services, and, oftentimes, trained staff workers who provide support. It's like this—if you decide to become a chemistry major, you would need to take courses to learn about the topic, talk to professors in the chemistry field, and build relationships with other chemistry majors who might help you with studying and research. You do this because it's what interests you, and it, in some way, defines you. You learn the vocabulary, the terms, and the concepts, and eventually, you can advise new students on how to get the most out of the major. In the same way, your faith in God needs the same time, dedication, and effort because it's what you're interested in, and it, to some degree, defines you. Faith doesn't just spring out of nothing. It takes effort.

Once you've decided how involved you want to be, the next question is, what group should you seek? After all, you don't want to approach the one creepy group on campus and get harassed for a year. (Actually, if that happens, report it to your school's student life office.) On my campus, there were a number of Christian groups, an active Jewish community, a smaller Muslim population, and a Hindu group as well. Granted, if you can find only one school group that's of your faith, that might be your only choice without going off-campus. I was lucky and could choose from six different Christian fellowship groups. I couldn't make up my mind, so I joined three fellowship groups my freshman year—partly to check them all out and partly to avoid being responsible to any one of them. I wouldn't suggest this as a long-term method, but I did learn a great deal about what faith-based groups have to offer.

Although it sounds obvious, sometimes it takes a while to realize that every group has its pros and cons. One group was mostly Asian and, being Chinese American, I felt it offered a great sense of community. However, I eventually couldn't reconcile myself with its teachings. Another group offered a deep and intellectual approach to faith, but it also met sporadically and was very small. I didn't feel like I belonged there. The final group I seriously considered was a national organization, Intervarsity Christian Fellowship (IVCF). It was multicultural and relatively well sized for my preferences. However, I didn't feel it offered as much community or as

The power of a man's virtue should be measured not by his special efforts, but by his ordinary doing.

—BLAISE PASCAL

much depth as the other two. Not all faith-based groups will fall along these lines—some of you will find a group you absolutely love—but it depends on what you value. I eventually chose Intervarsity because it offered a little bit of both community and depth, it was multicultural, and it showed signs of growth.

Be forewarned, though, because joining a multicultural group (or, for that matter, engaging in activities with different religious groups) is hard especially if you are the minority. Whether you're white in an all-Asian group, black in an all-white group, or a rural student in an all-suburban group, your minority status will often put you at odds with the way the organization is run. I doubt that it's an intentional slight on the part of the leadership. If the people in your group grew up thinking a certain way about your faith, religion, and God, they're going to act according to their background, because that's what they know. When I joined IVCF, I absolutely *hated* the music that they played at meetings. Apparently, so did a lot of my black brothers and sisters, but I didn't know this. I thought I was just weird or picky, but it also made me consider not going to those meetings. Eventually, the band purposely began to play music from more diverse sources. So what should happen but that a couple of my fellow worshipers who were white began to hate some of the music. You'd think that it was a lose-lose situation because everyone hated some of the music, but at least everyone also liked some of the music.

The truth is that belonging to a multicultural group doesn't ensure that you dialogue about race and culture. You'll find that it takes a conscious effort to truly address the topic. We once had an event called "Race Matters" and invited the campus and specifically the gospel choir to join us. At one point during the meeting, all the whites, blacks, and Asians split off into their own racial groups to discuss their experiences. After some time, we came back together to talk with the whole group. The black students had experienced a lot more racism and were vocal about it, the white students were generally vocal but less racially aware, and the Asians didn't speak unless called on. We basically fell back into stereotypes of how we, as different races, deal with issues of race and culture. The point is not the stereotypes, however—it's the conversation. At least Race Matters gave us a chance to confront race issues in the United States and come to the conclusion that we believed only Jesus could change people from the inside. In so doing, we recognized differences but also acknowledged a similar faith.

Joining a faith group or involving yourself in cross-cultural/faith activities can and should teach you more than you ever expected. Somewhere in the middle of my time at college, I realized that I felt more comfortable with the Asian people in my fellowship, and that forced me to examine how I communicated with others. What did politeness look like to me? How do I give and receive criticism and praise? Multicultural faith groups don't just offer you the chance to learn about other cultures. They give you the opportunity to learn who you are; what it means to be part of your race, culture, and history; and also how your history influences your view of God and religion. You're forced to see and evaluate what truly makes you yourself.

Your vision of God also expands and changes because you begin to see God without your own cultural lens. My friends showed me that God values prayer and outreach in a way that was never fully realized in my Asian American church at home. I came to understand that God shows grace and forgives more than I had believed. Once you've eaten,

Experience is what we call the accumulation of our mistakes.

—YIDDISH FOLK SAYING

studied, played, and served with someone of another cultural group, you're reminded that God loves that person even when you are disagreeing with each other. I've enjoyed showing my friends how to make wontons and experienced smashing Mexican confetti eggs at Easter, but what I've loved most is that I got to love my friends. When you love someone, you begin to want to protect him, to show mercy toward him, to teach him, to forgive him, to understand him, and you are suddenly willing to suffer for him. Or at least, that's what happened to me (and I'm not talking romantic love), and it expanded my understanding of how much God is willing to do to love and forgive others and me.

Maybe you're not ready for all this thinking and loving. Maybe you just wanted a yes-or-no answer. Or maybe there's no such group on your campus. No fear. Joining a non-multiethnic group is perfectly fine. You'll find that being raised in either a city or in the country can often bring about the same culture differences as race. You can still visit other groups or encourage some interfellowship group activities for the different ministries on campus. The point is that **a college fellowship should help grow your faith, expand your vision of God and love, and make your faith your own. To do all this, you've got to challenge yourself and your faith.** You've got to ask what it is that you believe, how do you know, whom do you trust, and why. Good fellowship groups can help you ask and answer those questions. Multicultural faith groups will force you to learn even more because you won't have the normal habits of culture to rest upon. What you get in return is solid—it's knowledge and faith that have been put through the fire and come out refined. So, for your own benefit, challenge yourself and join a fellowship group.

WHAT YOU NEED TO KNOW ABOUT
CULTIC BEHAVIORS

College can be a time for exploring many aspects of life, and religion is no exception. It is common for young people to become frustrated or disillusioned with their religion—maybe you've experienced it yourself. Maybe you realized that your religion didn't make your life easy or take away the struggles of everyday life. Maybe you did everything your religion told you to do, but something bad still happened. Maybe you had questions about God that no one could seem to answer. Maybe you were hurt or offended by a spiritual leader or a member of your religion. Maybe you saw people who professed something but didn't live up to it as you thought they should. Or maybe you just got bored.

And in the midst of all this searching, many groups—from traditional religions to the newest cults—will promise to deliver what you are looking for: protection from suffering, a community that really cares, easy answers to difficult life questions, leaders and followers that live holy lives, and, of course, new and exciting forms of prayer and worship.

But with so many groups trying to get your attention and offering so much, how can you tell the difference between a trustworthy religion and a dangerous cult? Well, sometimes it's not easy, but here are some things to watch out for if you think a group may be a cult:

- **Control of thought and action.** Telling you what you can or cannot do. Limiting your options in a way that denies you any real freedom to choose. Not allowing opposing ideas or thoughts. Not allowing you to have certain information.

- **Isolation.** Limiting your contact or conversations with others within or outside the group. Separating you from your everyday life and your existing relationships.

- **Physical or emotional manipulation.** Keeping you physically or emotionally exhausted or confused. Subjecting you to constant activity, sleep deprivation, public humiliation, or intimidation. Inducing fear or anxiety about what might happen if you do or do not do certain things.

If you feel yourself getting pulled into a group that you are unsure of, you can be careful by doing some of the following:

- **Keep in touch.** Stay actively involved in your existing friendships and family relationships. If the group does not allow you to do so, they may be attempting to isolate you and control your interactions.

- **Ask yourself whether it is too good to be true.** Is the group promising no problems, no struggles, or no suffering? If so, it's probably not everything it's cracked up to be.

- **Ask others.** Talk to friends, family, or other people you trust and get their feedback about the group—they may provide a more objective outlook. A spiritual leader from your own religion may be able to explain things that have left you confused in the past.

If someone you know is getting pulled into a group that may be a cult, you might be able to help him or her:

- **Keep your friendship active.** Ask questions and do things together. And be sure to listen—not every conversation needs to be a debate about religion.

- **Get others involved.** Get your friend together with other friends or family members and strengthen those connections of real and true community.

- **Ask why.** Ask your friend why he or she is exploring this group: what was missing in the "old" religion, what is beneficial about this "new" group? If it doesn't sound right, a friendly challenge to your friend's thought process is okay, too.

In the end, don't fall for any group telling you it has the easy solution to life. False religions often teach that if we do the right thing and trust completely in a particular God or person, things we fear will not happen to us. On the other hand, true religions teach that things we fear probably will happen to us, but that we will be okay when they do. The struggles, confusion, suffering, and fears you experience during your college years are part of a deeply lived life, and true religions will help you find faith, strength, and spiritual connection in the midst of them.

—DAVE EBENHOH, DIRECTOR OF CAMPUS MINISTRY,
FONTBONNE UNIVERSITY

DHARMA BRAT
LODRÖ RINZLER

No one ever told me that I had any responsibilities as a young Buddhist. I am what is known as a dharma brat, raised by Buddhist practitioners, and as a result I got involved in my practice at a very young age. I took refuge in the three jewels when I was six, went on retreat for the first time at eleven, shaved my head and took temporary ordination as a monk at seventeen, and have maintained a daily practice ever since. Never did anyone tell me while I was on retreat, while I was sitting meditation in my college dorm room, while I was doing prostrations to my teacher, that I am a member of a rising generation of Buddhist practitioners, teachers, and meditation instructors. I, and other young people my age, never entered into Buddhism with the knowledge that we would have to step up to leadership roles and inherit the job of carrying on the teachings that have made their way to the West, but we're in the position to do it and we know that we're needed. Our predecessors and teachers will one day pass on, and we will have to fill their shoes.

On June 6, 2003, in a rural retreat center based in Barnet, Vermont, Sakyong Mipham Rinpoche addressed two hundred young people between the ages of eighteen and thirty. He had called them together for a four-day conference, revolving around the notion that they are responsible for carrying on Buddhism in America today. To begin the conference, this powerful teacher leaned over and very firmly stated, "I am going to try to change the world. And I need your help. Now." Everyone in the room was shocked. We knew he could do it, but us? Most of us thought we had all the time in the world to practice, study, and maybe eventually give a few introductory talks on Buddhism to a roomful of friends. That day a seed was planted in everyone's heart, and that seed is already ripening for some of us. Young people left inspired and are forming Buddhist practice houses in Boston and New York City, getting trained as meditation instructors, and fighting any preconceptions that people confront them with; on the whole, we are stepping up to leadership positions in our daily lives.

The small performance space was packed last year when Wesleyan University hosted its first Sacred Slam. The performers rocked the house, doing hip-hop, space awareness performance, and spoken word. They were people of all different backgrounds, ethnicities, and ages, all bound together under the banner of slamming preconceived notions of spirituality. Afterward, one performer began free-styling about all the different religious experiences he had had, and I had to ask my friend, one of the spoken-word performers, "What *is* he?" "Akim?" my friend replied. "He's everything." I watched Akim in amazement and realized that, as religion takes root in the hearts of my generation, we strive to look beyond the notions of spirituality that we were brought up with and reach out to other religious traditions, to be everything and try to understand everything. Last year we had professionals lead Sacred Slam; this year the students feel inspired and want to host it.

Right now I live in Buddhist House, a program house given to the Buddhist group on campus as a space to practice

You must watch my life, how I live, eat, sit, talk, behave in general. The sum total of all those in me is my religion.

—MAHATMA GANDHI

meditation and explore the dharma, or teachings. As far as I know, we're the first Buddhist house ever to exist on a college campus. In our few months of existence we have already had some rough times: an emergency trip to the hospital for a diabetic whose blood sugar dropped too low; an empty keg picked up outside someone's door. I was saddened by these events, but I wouldn't change a thing about our house because, whether they know it or not, the eighteen people living here are all leaders in bringing Buddhism to America. None of them was at the youth conference where Sakyong Mipham Rinpoche talked about becoming leaders, and few of them may end up taking refuge, or "officially" becoming Buddhist, but they are doing something amazing. We sit down once a week and talk about our responsibility in creating an uplifting space for meditation on campus, one that inspires people to practice and connect with this path, and it's a task that takes eighteen leaders to do—trust me. I'm surprised all the time by how seriously people here take it, and without knowing that they are doing it, the people living in this house are creating an enlightened space.

No real leader starts off striving for leadership, but qualities manifest themselves in different ways at different times, and all of a sudden more and more young people are finding themselves leading religious student groups on campus, leading services at the local church or temple or center, or leading their lives in a way that empowers them and others to pursue spiritual paths. It's different for everyone. Some of us may not consciously recognize that we're being leaders in a religious community, or we may not be leaders at all right now, or we may have no interest in filling the shoes of our religious predecessors, but **a time will come when we young people have to come to terms with our future, and someone has to carry on our beliefs for future generations. We might as well get started**.

We bring our beliefs to music, to dance, to our artwork, our writing, our knowledge of how the world works (or doesn't), to everything that we put our minds to. A new generation of religious people is here, sneaking into church late with hangovers, counting mantras while walking across campus, leading services that the rabbi at home would never approve of. We do things differently, but we do them well. We're just learning right now how to adapt our beliefs to different sectors of our lives and incorporate them fully into our being, but we have started a process that will change us and, ideally, the world.

My favorite book right now is Sakyong Mipham Rinpoche's *Turning the Mind into an Ally*. I read it shortly before the youth conference where he commanded us to step up to leadership roles, and I am rereading it now. The book is autographed. Every time I pick it up I flip to the page on which he wrote to me. He left a simple message, but it haunts and inspires me whenever I think of it. On the signature page is a single word: "Now."

AN ORANGE ON OUR SEDER PLATE
MICHELLE MANDELSTEIN

I grew up in a fairly secular, Jewish home. My family celebrated the "major" holidays but never attended synagogue or studied Judaism in any great depth. Naturally, this lack of religious participation ignited a curiosity about religion in me, and I decided that my college years would be the best time for me to find my faith. When I began my freshman year, I attended my first High Holiday services at a synagogue and began going to the campus Hillel center. However, as I explored my religion I realized that in practice (but not in theory) it conflicted with my modern beliefs about women's equality. As I began to research the contradictions between the teachings and the actual practices of Judaism, I stumbled across the monthly women's holiday, Rosh Chodesh. Rosh Chodesh is the celebration of the new moon, coinciding with women's menstrual cycles. On the holiday, groups of women meet and discuss women's issues, whether intrinsically Jewish or just female oriented. I became interested in the idea of a Rosh Chodesh group and was pleased to discover that one existed on my campus.

However, I was very disappointed in what I found after researching the Rosh Chodesh group that existed at Tulane. The group was led by an ultra-Orthodox Jewish woman, who used the occasion to reinforce traditional gender roles/stereotypes and search for the relationship between traditional female roles and the weekly Torah portion. Every so often, the group took part in an activity such as arts and crafts or baking bread. I understood that some women found these activities fulfilling, but they just weren't cutting it for me. I felt that there was so much more to being a Jewish woman than how we related to Torah passages or whether we kept a kosher home. I also felt uneasy about a group that focused solely on the teachings of one of the various Jewish denominations. There are so many different types of Jewish women of different ages, denominations, and backgrounds, and I felt that these differences should be celebrated. I also thought that by examining these differences, women would find many similarities with each other that they hadn't previously considered. In my mind, a multigenerational, multidenominational group was a necessary addition to the spiritual offerings available to Jewish women on campus.

I discussed my idea with advisors at the campus Hillel center, and they helped me research the history and rituals of Rosh Chodesh. They also supplied me with a database containing the e-mails and phone numbers of the majority of the Jewish women on campus. I posted some flyers, sent out an e-mail, and made some phone calls advertising my vision and inviting other women to come to a "brainstorming meeting" to help me see not only my vision but also theirs take form. About five women came to this first meeting, and we decided to have a discussion about mother/daughter relationships at our first official Rosh Chodesh event. The discussion was held at a campus coffeehouse so that it would be accessible to students and members of the community. We used excerpts from the hilarious CD *Amy's Answering Machine* to jump-start the conversation and selected quotes from the CD to use on our flyers. Twenty-six women ranging in age from eighteen to seventy-five, who were Orthodox, Reform, secular, and so on, came to the discussion. Almost everyone participated, and the discussion flowed freely without my guidance.

Word of mouth helped spread the news of my Rosh Chodesh group around campus and the greater New Orleans community. Some months were more popular with certain age groups than others; for example, an outing to see *The Vagina Monologues* was more popular with students than with older women. Another evening about "women's roles" in society created conflict between more traditional students and feminist women's studies majors. But it was nights like these that showed participants that maybe there was a need for another type of Rosh Chodesh group as

When you see that you're grasping or clinging to anything, whether conventionally it's called good or bad, make friends with that. Look into it. Get to know it completely and utterly. In that way it will let go of itself.

—PEMA CHÖDRÖN

well. Non-Jewish women also started to attend the meetings and discussions, because they were interested in women's issues, or Judaism, or just wanted to check it out.

The most successful event of the year was a Women's Seder for Passover. Frustrated with a few months of sagging attendance in the group, I sat down and thought about why I had started this Rosh Chodesh group in the first place. I decided that the last meeting of the year should be a Women's Seder for Passover, and rather than make it a "women only" Seder, I was going to create a Seder geared specifically toward women. Disappointed with the traditional and gender-neutral Haggadahs (the ritual book of Passover) I found for the Seder, I wrote and arranged my own female-oriented Haggadah. I changed many traditional passages, such as the Four Children and the Ten Plagues, to be specifically female oriented (i.e., the Four Daughters and the Ten Plagues of Women). I also continued Susanna Heschel's tradition of including an orange on the Seder plate as a symbol of including groups who are traditionally disenfranchised within the Jewish community. I asked for input on the service and Haggadah from regular Rosh Chodesh–goers of various backgrounds, and although some of the more traditional women didn't always approve, I went ahead with my feminist vision. More than forty women from the Tulane campus and greater New Orleans community attended the Seder, and only two were offended by my liberal take on the holiday. **It was so gratifying to see that my quest for my own spirituality had filled a void for so many other women.**

So for all of you college students out there exploring your spirituality and finding your options unfulfilling, my advice is: If you can't find it, found it on your own. All it takes is a little research and dedicated PR to see your vision take shape. Help and input from others should not be feared; it can help your idea grow in ways you never thought possible. Your spiritual quest may help others who are looking for the same thing you are or even inspire them to branch out and form their own organizations. With seemingly little effort, your vision for religious life on campus can provide a lot of people with a spiritual outlet of their own, and what could be more spiritually fulfilling than that?

CAN'T FIND A SPIRITUAL GROUP THAT WORKS FOR YOU? START YOUR OWN!

Being an active member of a student organization can be one of the most rewarding and challenging experiences of your college life. Your involvement provides you with opportunities to develop your leadership skills that will benefit you both now and in your future career and community responsibilities. Being active in an organization is not only a learning experience but is also rewarding and fun. It's an excellent way to make friends and to relax. Most important, student organizations give you the opportunity to share similar interests with other students.

But what happens when there isn't a group with similar interests? Should you simply sit back and give up? NO! It's time for you to put your thoughts into action by creating your own student organization! By following these ten simple steps, you'll be well on your way to creating your own special group.

Explore the Process. Go to the student life department and get a copy of your school's student handbook. It will outline in detail the steps you need to take to start or "charter" a new student group. There may be a lot of paperwork along the way, but the student life staff is there to help you negotiate the red tape. Students at public institutions are protected under the U.S. Constitution and have a right to form organizations; private institutions, on the other hand, may more closely regulate their groups with specific guidelines. It's important to research the process at your school so you are fully aware of the responsibilities you'll have in creating a new group, including the minimum number of students needed to start a new organization.

Find Your Niche. This may be the most critical part of the process because often special interest groups come and go with the passing of campus fads. You want to make sure your new group will have something to offer that can't be found in an existing group. Spend some time thinking about what you'd like your student organization to be; if someone asked you what identifiable need your group would meet, how would you answer?

Conversely, you may find during your research that it would be a better idea to start a committee rather than an entirely new group. For example, let's say you have a Muslim Student Association already on campus, but you're looking for a group to study the Qur'an. You may want to approach the group first to see whether you can chair a committee specifically for this purpose; the advantage is that you'll be entering into a group with an established structure and history, name recognition, and resources. Starting a new committee within an established group can be a shortcut to meeting your needs.

Generate Interest. You've researched the process and identified what makes your new organization unique. Most universities grant limited organization privileges to groups that are trying to form.

These privileges normally include reserving meeting space for organizational planning purposes, advertising for the recruitment of members, and announcing planned meetings.

Your student union will allow you to use its meeting facilities for free; ask a student life staff member to help you make a room reservation early in your planning, so you have the correct date, time, and place of your first meeting for your advertisements. A few suggestions:

- Post flyers on campus. Don't be afraid to get creative with placement—for example, ask whether you can insert flyers on the cafeteria trays or post them in the bathroom stalls!

- Hang banners in the student union or residence halls.

- Use sidewalk chalk.

- Attend other student organization meetings or stand up in class to announce the formation of a new group.

- Post messages on web-based discussion boards.

In general, you're more likely to generate interest by targeting certain students in areas where they are likely to see or hear your message. For example, post heavily near the campus faith office or ask that your announcement be read at the end of religious services.

Hold Your First Meeting. Prepare an agenda ahead of time. After the welcome and introduction, review the purpose of your group. Give other students "ownership" in the group by soliciting their feedback and input. Here are some other tasks:

- Brainstorm future activities or events you'd like to sponsor.

- Identify a potential faculty or staff advisor.

- Get names and contact information from the members.

- Set your next meeting time.

Select an Advisor. Having the right advisor can make or break your organization. Select a professional who has the time necessary to dedicate to the newly formed group. Negotiate the role of the advisor before you commit to this relationship—who has final say about organizational decisions? Does he or she need to be at every meeting and event? Who will manage the budget? Clarifying the role of the advisor and the student leaders early in the process promotes a positive working relationship from the start.

Create a Constitution. You want to create a living document that will guide the group in the future. One that is either too vague or too inflexible will cause problems. A good constitution outlines:

- Statement of purpose

- Membership qualifications and selection process, including required nondiscrimination clauses

- Election of officers, their duties, responsibilities, and removal process

- Procedure for the selection and removal of an advisor

- Voting rights

- Committees and committee structure

- Meeting times

- Constitutional amendment process

Seek Formal Recognition. Submit your paperwork to the appropriate university body. Most student government associations are empowered to grant recognition to new groups and may require your presence at their meeting. For religious groups, it's important to know whether the approval of the campus faith office is required or simply taken into consideration. Research the organizational relationship that must exist between your group and the campus faith office. For example, is there a larger umbrella organization for religious groups for which you must have a representative? If not, what are meaningful ways the campus faith office offers support to various groups?

Apply for Funding. Recognized student organizations may be eligible for funding by student government from money paid to the university as part of a student activity fee. Although the nature and criteria for funding will vary from campus to campus, generally student organizations must demonstrate that expenditures will directly benefit the campus community (such as by sponsoring a speaker or an alcohol-free event) or the organization itself (such as through conference attendance). A quick call to the activities office will help your group understand the criteria and deadlines when applying for funding.

Secure Office Space. Some student unions have dedicated community office space for student groups. A student life professional will be able to inform you of the application process. Likewise, you may ask your campus faith office to assist you in identifying office space on campus.

Develop Future Leaders. The strength of the executive leaders will carry your group into the future; therefore, it's important to take advantage of every opportunity now to develop leaders from within your group. Participation in campus, regional, or national leadership conferences can act as both a reward and a motivator for younger members. Find out whether your university offers an academic course in leadership and enroll in it. Take advantage of student life professional consultation services and maintain a working relationship with your advisor.

—Chris Cameron, director, Danna Center and Student Activities, Loyola University, New Orleans

CHAPTER 4

SEX, DRUGS, AND ROCK 'N' ROLL: SPIRITUALITY AND YOUR SOCIAL LIFE

"Do you want a beer?" asks one of the students you remember from intramurals.

"Maybe, in a minute," you reply as you slip into the crowd, walking further into the apartment.

You need a moment to think. To drink or not to drink. You partied last weekend and ended up with a major hangover. To make matters worse, you felt lousy when you realized the next day that you had been so ripped that you woke up your roommates when you got home, despite their tired pleas to keep quiet. Deep down, you know that your actions are inconsistent with the values you talk about in your more spiritual moments.

"Hey, do you want a beer?" shouts another voice from across the room.

Few areas of college life push spiritual questions to the forefront as much as parties, dating, and the search for someone to love.

Chances are, at some point in your college life, you will feel social pressures from one direction or the other. That is to say, if you don't consider yourself to be someone who likes to party you may feel overwhelmed by students who do. Or you may be a social animal and find that the friends you connect with spiritually don't support that kind of expression. Or perhaps your ideas about dating and intimacy conflict with the teachings of your religion, passed on to you by parents or spiritual leaders. Whether we're talking drinking or dating, spiritual dilemmas abound.

No Parties Allowed

If you are fundamentally sure you don't want to be anywhere near a party scene, then you probably want to find out whether your school has a 24-hour quiet residence hall or floor. Many students are going to let loose on the weekends, maybe with drinking, probably with loud conversation and music, and if you simply don't want to be anywhere near that, a 24-hour quiet zone is the only way to go. You may want to consider your views further before you make this decision, though. Are you concerned about not being able to get work done? Do you believe you are better off not being near any parties? If so, is that because you don't trust other students or you don't trust yourself? Is a 24-hour quiet zone the best way to resolve these issues? For some students, a quiet hall is the best option. Other students come to believe that there are lessons to be learned by living in a more diverse setting.

Wait a Minute, This Looks Like Fun

Let's say you have come to campus knowing that you don't want to be involved with the out-of-control party scene. But what happens if you walk into your suite one Saturday night and your roommates and their friends are having a little party and it actually looks like fun? People are eating pizza and talking, others are dancing, and you realize that it looks like a good time. How will you integrate this with your previously held beliefs about "partying"? What kinds of problems will you run into with friends in your spiritual community who may judge you if you decide to socialize more actively outside their circle? Are you concerned that your parents would flip out if they knew?

The most important thing you can do is to clarify and integrate your thinking about the idea of taking part in a new and different kind of social life. If you can get clear on your own values, this will give you the foundation to make good decisions and deal with friends and family who may not understand.

How can you clarify your thinking? First, consider your fears. Are you afraid that everyone who parties just gets wasted, loses their lunch, and then passes out? Good for you for not wanting to do *that*. Perhaps you are afraid you won't make the best decisions when faced with the opportunity to drink. Clarify your values in relation to drinking. Does your spiritual tradition forbid alcohol? Does your tradition call on you to honor and respect your body— if so, how might that influence your decisions about drinking? Reflect on your past and consider what kinds of pressures have led you to make counterintuitive decisions. How can you deal with those situations differently in the future?

Perhaps you've decided you really don't want to drink or you are committed to a spiritual tradition that forbids it, but you want to be part of the party scene anyway. Go to a party, enjoy the conversation and dancing, and drink nothing but soda. That's right— it's been done and you can do it, too. If someone offers you a beer and you don't want one, just say, "No, thanks, I'm good" and keep enjoying that cola. Be confident in your spiritual commitments. Anyone who is worth talking to will respect that you are making your own choices.

(Oh, and as far as drugs? They're illegal.)

All Revved Up with No Place to Go

What if you are both social and spiritual and the two seem to be in conflict? You may have two distinct groups of friends. The friends you meditate or pray with may be telling you that you party too much. Before you write them off as uptight, consider what they are saying. Is your party life compromising your spiritual life? Are you making social decisions that put you or others at risk? Think about your friends' motivations. Do they seem genuinely concerned with your safety, or do they seem to be judging you based on their own standards, which don't allow for an occasional safe party night out? If you consider these questions and determine that you are making thoughtful decisions, that you are having good, safe fun—then perhaps you want to look for a more liberal spiritual group, one that allows for an active social life and a strong spiritual practice.

If, on the other hand, your party friends are the ones who are criticizing your spiritual life and commitments, then you should again look at your friends and look at yourself. Are they critical because you are proselytizing? Or are they giving you a hard time because they just don't understand your spiritual side? If it is the former, then consider how you talk about religion with your friends. How can you talk about your religious commitments without making others feel judged or recruited? If it is the latter, then you should find another social group that includes people who are also more active spiritually. A third alternative is to start a social group within your spiritual circle. Perhaps your prayer group can stay together after Friday night prayer for pizza and music. Or your meditation group can plan a Saturday meditation in the park, with a picnic afterward.

This Party Thing, It Isn't for Me

Finally, keep in mind that there are many, many opportunities to have an active social life outside of the party scene. If you try parties and don't like them, or decide you don't want to be anywhere near an open keg, then look for other places to connect with students. Community service, intramurals, performance groups, cultural organizations, campus media, student government . . . most campuses have hundreds of student organizations where you can not only pursue a common interest but also develop a close and important group of friends.

The Deal with Dating

No exploration of spirituality and a social life would be complete without considering the influence of parents and spiritual leaders, particularly around issues of dating, sexuality, and intimacy. Maybe you have been forbidden from dating someone from outside your religious tradition. Or perhaps you have come to know that you are gay, lesbian, bisexual, or transgendered. You may anticipate that your parents will oppose this on religious grounds.

If you feel pulled in directions that conflict with what you have been taught, again, you must explore your thinking and feelings more closely. Examine readings from your tradition, seek input from spiritual leaders you respect, and talk to others who hold strong to their spirituality while maintaining an active social life. See whether you can find a way to hold on to your spiritual values and pursue the social life you imagine for yourself. You may choose to find a more liberal group within your spiritual community, one that accepts that you are dating outside the faith or that you are coming out as gay, lesbian, bisexual, or transgendered. Or perhaps you wish you had more support for your commitment to date people within your tradition, and so you might seek a campus group that is in line with that principle.

Always remember: joy is not merely incidental to your spiritual quest. It is vital.

—REBBE NACHMAN OF BRESLOV

Another issue that develops for some students as they date more actively in college is that of sexual intimacy. If you come from a religiously conservative family, you have probably been taught that people shouldn't have sex until they are married. If you have now fallen head over heels for someone and believe that your relationship is based on trust and love, you may want to develop a more sexually intimate relationship with your partner. This is another time when you should review the teachings of your faith. Do the teachings specifically say that sex is forbidden outside of marriage? If so, does that idea still work for you? If you have grown more liberal in your spiritual involvements, you may begin to take a different view of intimacy and sex. You may come to believe that sexual intimacy is an important expression between two people in love, but only in committed, trusting relationships. This means you don't want to drink and lose your ability to make thoughtful decisions, and you want to date only someone who is willing to move slowly in terms of intimacy. If you remain committed to waiting for a sexual relationship until you are married, then keep in mind that you aren't the only person out there who holds those beliefs. Chances are there is someone wonderful who would love to date you and maintain that same value in a relationship.

Out and Spiritual

Coming out as gay, lesbian, bisexual, transgendered, or questioning (GLBTQ) can evoke many questions related to spirituality. You may be concerned that you will be rejected by your faith community. Or you may wonder whether you can find a place for spiritual expression and connection within the GLBTQ community. Some traditions are increasingly open to GLBTQ members, including Reform Judaism, some Christian denominations, Unitarianism, Paganism, and Buddhism. Within most traditions, even ones that do not officially accept openly GLBTQ members, there are formal or informal groups of people who support each other and worship or meditate together. Your campus GLBTQ resource center or local GLBTQ community center can refer you to groups where you can be openly gay and explore and practice your spirituality.

MOTIVATION ON A FRIDAY NIGHT
LODRÖ RINZLER

I spent the summer before my freshman year of college at a Buddhist center in Barnet, Vermont. Even though I was happy with my quiet summer schedule of work and meditation practice, the moment I got to college I was ready to party. After living the typical "I'm finally on my own" week of parties, women, and rock 'n' roll, I realized that my meditation practice was waning, that I would cheat myself into thinking I had only so much time to practice, yet have a lot of time for friends and social life. I then went in the other direction and somehow managed to sit a three-day silent retreat in my dorm room during my first semester. It was chaotic and poorly planned, but it gave me a lot of time to sit meditation.

Finally I decided that I had to find a balance. College wasn't the ideal retreat center, and at the same time I wasn't ready to party mindlessly. I struck up a schedule of sitting a half hour every morning and worked it perfectly so that at the end of my session I received a knock on the door from my hallmate, coming to get me for our 9:00 a.m. class. I went to classes during the day, then after my last one I sat for a half hour more, often getting distracted by my hallmates' music, before going to dinner and relaxing. On weekends, I continued to get up before anyone else and sit meditation, but there were times when I woke up and feeling yucky from the previous night, I would get disheartened and not practice at all.

Conscience is the soul of freedom, its eyes, its energy, its life. Without conscience, freedom never knows what to do with itself.

—THOMAS MERTON

The solution in my case came down to two things: mindfulness and motivation. I consulted with friends who were Buddhist practitioners and other people within my lineage of Tibetan Buddhism and came to the conclusion that I think a lot of people may find helpful. If one maintains mindfulness in partying, in drinking, in whatever a Saturday night might throw at you, you may find yourself catching things that go against the current of your faith and that you may regret later on. Remaining mindful of the actions of the present moment is a surefire way not to get lost in the moment and do something stupid. I found that what I was checking in with, in those moments of mindfulness, was my motivation for each action that I was doing. Why was I kissing this girl? Was it because I really liked her and wanted her to know that, or because I was caught up in the moment and had had too much to drink? Was this something I would look back fondly upon, or was I about to upset her boyfriend, subsequently her, and maybe me if he was on the wrestling team? A lot of my decisions, when I was mindful enough to think them through at the time, came down to "Would this be helpful to other beings, or is this just something for my personal, short-term happiness?"

I realized that if I totally let myself go, I would act in a way that would hinder my practice. Half of my meditation practice is developing mindfulness while on the meditation cushion; the other half is taking it off the cushion into my daily life. This isn't to say that I'm not stereotyped in a way that is inappropriate. If people who knew that I was Buddhist saw me but didn't know that lay practitioners can drink, they would turn their nose up at me. This has happened before, and nonpractitioners have thought that I might be considered "the wrong type of Buddhist." I quickly get over these scenarios, however, as it is my own knowledge that I'm working with the college life experience that matters, and more often than not, someone else's preconceptions of what a Buddhist should be are 100 percent wrong.

These days, I enjoy my social life in a way that directly reflects my practice and enables me to feel that I am staying true to my faith. If I couldn't go out on a Friday night and have a good time while maintaining some sense of awareness of my actions, then I wouldn't consider my practice to be helpful to me. In bringing mindfulness off the cushion and putting it on the motivation for my actions in my daily college experience, I have found a perfect balance in living the life of a college practitioner who loves to sit meditation and loves to party.

HOW TO HAVE A MEANINGFUL SOCIAL LIFE
WITHOUT SPIRITUAL COMPROMISE

- Don't let anyone stereotype you in a way that makes you feel that you cannot act like a nonreligious college student.

- It's important just to be mindful of what you're doing and why you're doing it. Other people's interpretation of your actions is entirely their neurosis.

- Sometimes the best time to really connect with certain

aspects of your faith is when you're hungover and still struggling to practice them.

- One way to check in and make sure you're not compromising your values is to think about the motivation behind your actions.

- Relax; when you meet your maker, it probably won't care what you did last Saturday night, only how you handled yourself.

- Don't be afraid to explore new things. If you wake up in the morning and regret it/her/him, then you've found out what you DON'T want in your social life.

- If you can't have a social life without feeling like you're disrespecting your faith, then you probably want to look at your interpretation of your faith and see how harsh you are with it.

- Although it may be helpful to date or have friends within your faith, you can always learn a lot from people who hold drastically different beliefs.

- Don't feel like you have to hide your religious beliefs in social situations; people may be really interested to hear about them.

—LODRÖ RINZLER, STUDENT, WESLEYAN UNIVERSITY

FREEDOM AND CAUTION

I, for one, perhaps erred on the side of extra caution in trying to live a life of integrity during my undergraduate years. I was quite conservative in my approach toward campus social life. In an attempt to live a life worthy of the calling I had received and the spiritual values

I had adopted, I voluntarily set up strong parameters and boundaries that effectively precluded me from many activities that are the essence and highlight of the lives of many college students.

Although I had good intentions, I passed up parties, lectures, and social gatherings that may have been, for the most part, harmless and beneficial. I may have even passed up situations that, though not presented in a specifically religious context by fellow men and women of faith, would have been beneficial in that they would have challenged some of the misconceptions I held regarding the nature of faith in action.

One instance of a boundary that was perhaps too constricting prevented me from attending a performance of Eve Ensler's *Vagina Monologues*. It may have been a very powerful and informative experience. When I finally read the text, almost as an afterthought because I made reference to it in one of my works for a class, I found the collection of monologues to broaden my understanding.

That said, the freedom and independence associated with college life does not mean that we ought to run amok. Independence, or even confusion in discovering an identity you can proudly claim as your own, does not warrant being—or serve as an excuse for being—wild and careless. The freedom of college life, during which many of you will be free to pursue your own interests, including social and religious ones, for the first time also offers a unique opportunity to develop your intrinsic values and self-discipline.

Balance is a key concept. I know that the approach you decide to take may be entirely different from mine. In your pursuit to define the niche that campus social life will occupy in your life, you will have to tinker with the sensitive formula that we dub balance. The spiritual values you possess, and will likely further develop in college, are indeed part of the very essence of who you are. They should, and will, have an influence on the decisions you make.

College may prove to be a time of utter destruction and reconstruction of the faith and beliefs you possess or may serve only to further solidify your faith. As a young man or woman of faith, know that you are not alone in obsessing over what is the right approach or attitude you should adopt regarding the pleasures of college life. Nevertheless, I am sure that your attempts to balance your emerging spiritual values with the freedom of college life will be an exciting endeavor. While being wise and deliberate in your choices, do not be afraid to err into wisdom and a more mature faith.

—RANDOLPH ROMERO JR., STUDENT,
UNIVERSITY OF PITTSBURGH

DIVINE INTERVENTION
HANNAH BEERBOWER

Guy meets girl. Guy likes girl. Girl ignores guy. Guy woos girl. Girl likes guy. Guy and girl get married. They have 2.4 children, two dogs, and a cat—happily ever after. And it takes only two hours from start to finish before the credits roll across the screen, the lights turn on, and you throw your popcorn container in the overstuffed trash can at the door. If only real life were that simple!

I can't remember ever *not* being in the church. My father was a pastor of a rural Protestant church when I was born. He left the ministry shortly thereafter, but my family was always active in the church and its activities. I was in elementary school before it ever dawned on me that there were other religions in the world. Naïve, yes, but I can't say that I have ever had to search for religion in my life; it was always a given.

I embraced the environment I grew up in, and I am certainly better for it. However, all the religion in the world doesn't change adolescence. By high school I wanted what every girl I knew wanted—a boyfriend! I had my high school "crushes," but none of them ever amounted to anything. My parents made it clear that I wasn't to date until I was sixteen years old. But they never had anything to worry about, because I made it through high school without ever getting a date. From there it was off to college, with hopes of new prospects and new beginnings.

By the time I went to college, my head had started to come

back to Earth, and I was more realistic about the whole dating scene. I knew that my religion was important to me, and someday I wanted to be able to share that with my future husband. Because dating tends to be the most popular way of meeting one's future spouse, I knew that I didn't want to date anyone who didn't share the same religious values that I did. So I spent my first semester making friends, joining organizations, and doing homework until the wee hours of the morning. At Christmas break, I returned home with my new experiences and embraced independence, ready to conquer the world.

When I went home that Christmas, I was eager to talk with my old friends from high school. I visited with one of my friends, and we swapped girl talk about what was going on in our respective lives. I described my friends to her, trying to make comparisons and analogies so that she could get a good picture in her mind. I kept mentioning one of my college friends, and she finally asked, "Who is this 'John' guy?" I tried to describe him, saying that he was the nicest, sweetest guy you could ever meet, the kind of guy that every mom wants her daughter to bring home to marry. My friend looked at me and asked, "Why don't you marry him?" I looked at her very matter-of-factly and said, "Well, I can't do that. He's Catholic!"

Now, to some people, that may seem like a perfectly silly statement, and it is. **I was never one to have the "us" and "them" mentality with people from different religions; I have friends from many different faiths and treat all of them with the same respect. However, dating is a different category from mere friendship, and I simply would not entertain the thought of dating outside of my religious boundaries.** The problem was that I knew precious little about religions other than my own. Furthermore, I knew even less about the differences within the denominations of my own religion. I grew up knowing what I believed, but I was not really aware of the distinctions that other people make within the realm of Christianity.

Second semester began, and I continued to foster the relationships that grew the previous fall. Not too long after, I had a conversation with my friend John. He and I were quite good friends and talked about anything and everything, from relationships to God to homework to what the cafeteria would be serving the next day for dinner. One evening, the conversation was about relationships, and to make a long story short, he asked me out on a date. I don't know what came up within me or what thought process I was using, but I gladly accepted the invitation.

The next day I was, for lack of a better term, "flipping out." I had never been on a date before, not to mention that it was with a boy whom I had said I would never date. But he was so nice, and we had so much in common! He was very involved with his religion, and I was involved with mine. What was I going to do?

The months to follow were a time of learning and a time of growth. The relationship started out slowly, but when it was time to go home for the summer, we had to decide whether we were going to keep our dating relationship or call it quits. We kept dating, and I came to the realization that if we kept on dating, either (a) it would eventually end or (b) we would get married someday. No one likes to think about potential breakups, so I focused on choice (b). I needed to decide what was important to me and what religious qualities I found essential in a relationship.

That summer and the following fall was a time of questioning. I questioned what I believed. I questioned why I believed in that way. I questioned what and why he believed what he did. We had many conversations about religious issues, and over time we came to realize that our two schools of thought were not as different as I had once understood them to be. I had always known that Catholic and Protestant beliefs were similar, but I never really knew what the difference was. The more we talked, the more we found that our religious traditions were quite different but our personal beliefs were almost identical. When it came to the big picture, we had the exact same view on religious essentials. Don't get me wrong—we did have disagreements, but they were over things that people in the same church building would argue about. We were far more alike than we were different.

During this time, our families were very supportive of the relationship. Both his family and mine came from mixed traditions, and good conversations came from our blossoming romance. Both families were in favor of a marriage, and both were interested in the spiritual direction that we would take. In the end, everyone was supportive of the religious direction we have chosen, and we are conscientious to include as much of both traditions in our relationship as we can.

I learned a lot over the course of the several years that I have known John, who is now my husband. I learned that religion is much more than just the traditions that your family shares with you when you are young. I learned that you do not know what is truly important to you until you are forced to question. I learned that you do not know how different or similar you are to someone else until you make an effort to find out. And so I married the guy who took me on my first date. You could say that it was divine intervention. Sort of like something you might see in a movie—happily ever after.

YOU AND YOUR CRUSH

Dating is such a complicated issue. You've got the guy, the girl, the emotions, the baggage, the friends, and then you add faith into the mix. Even for people with super-strict parents, the questions still come up: Whom can you date? Whom will you date? Does faith have anything to do with dating?

Faith has a lot to do with dating, but only if faith has a lot to do with you. Let's face it: If you don't care about how your honey dresses, his clothing isn't going to be an issue in your relationship. Same with faith—if it's not important to you or to your possible significant other, it's not going to be a major concern. But if you have an everyday faith or a particularly strong love for special holidays, then your faith and religion will influence not just your romances but also all that you do.

When considering how faith influences your love life, look at how it influences all of your life. Consider what values you hold and what convictions you keep. What are the most important core issues that you hold on to? And how important are these issues to your crush? Think of convictions, faith-related or not, like this: You have a vegetarian and a meat eater. If the vegetarian doesn't care whether others eat meat or whether meat is cooked in the house, and if the meat eater doesn't mind vegetarian fare, they're probably going to do okay together. Meanwhile, if the vegetarian holds deep convictions that all meat eating is evil or the meat eater believes that vegetarian eaters are crazy, that relationship is going to the dogs. So if you firmly believe one thing and your crush quite the opposite, you might want to hold off on the smoochies.

This issue of convictions pertains to same-faith romances as well as different-faith romances. One of my friends' grandparents believes that Baptists should marry only Baptists—no Presbyterians or Methodists and definitely no Charismatics. They obviously weren't going to marry outside of their very specific beliefs. On the other hand, my mom believes that, although Christians should preferably marry other Christians, it's not terrible for a Christian to marry a non-Christian. She didn't feel as though she was disobeying God by marrying my agnostic dad. If your beliefs cause you to feel like dating a particular person will separate you from God or your religion, don't date. Either wait for the person to change or wait for yourself to change, but don't date until one of you changes. And if you can't—if these are deep convictions—don't date. Have a clear conscience before your God and yourself.

Clearly, however, we aren't supposed to serve conscience over God, even though our consciences help us in our faith. So do consider what your faith tradition says about dating. Don't take it blindly but weigh it, see whether what is being said makes sense, consider the cultural influences, ask a religious advisor for advice, and talk to your trusted friends. Not everything they tell you will be wise, but you'll have considered different opinions. Pray or meditate about dating. If you have issues with picking bad partners, praying may reveal to you a need to abstain from dating for a while.

I realized a while ago that my feelings of wanting a boyfriend came during times of uncertainty or pain. I began to see that those feelings indicated a want of security and love, two things I professed to believe that only God provides completely. Did I trust God? Did I believe that he loved me? I began to work on my faith in God before addressing my desire for a significant other. Ultimately, this is actually an act of love for any future boyfriend because I won't expect him to be perfect, read my mind, and always know what I need. What you expect of another person is crucial to dating, and if you expect perfection—white knight or curvaceous bombshell— you're gonna be disappointed a lot. If you believe your partner should support you spiritually, you want to pick someone who can do that.

This is where different-faith romances get sticky. I am the product of a different-faith marriage, and I can tell you that my mom gets little spiritual support from my dad. They have a good marriage that has lasted twenty-five years already, and my dad goes to church every week for the sake of my mom. But it's lonely because my mom believes that whoever accepts Jesus as his or her savior is saved, and, well, my dad hasn't done that. My mom isn't going to change her belief and not because she wants to think ill of my dad. Faith is defined by deep-seated beliefs, and my mom can't change her faith any more than she could start believing that she has three feet and five nostrils.

Influenced by their contrasting faiths or nonfaiths, my parents have different ideas on what a purposeful life looks like and con- sequently argue over the direction of their children's lives when- ever faith-related decisions are made. Even healthy marriages are lonely at times, but to add another layer of spiritual distance is not something I'd wish for anyone. I've had numerous friends break up because their different faiths led to conflicts of purpose. One friend dated a guy whose parents would disown him if he dated outside the religion. She was outside the religion and it was an on-off relationship partly because of his inability to deal with his religion, his parents, and his emotions. So, please tread very carefully when considering dating a person of a different faith. It's better to wait for one of you to change than to get embroiled emotionally in something that you already know won't pan out.

Treading carefully goes for considering a same-faith dating relationship as well. Make sure you both share an understanding of faith and its influence on your lives. It's one thing to think being Hindu is only a cultural identity and another to go to a temple every week. If you have the patience to deal with a partner who is unwilling to worship with you or who wants to worship more than you, then give it shot. But remember that, as with different-faith romances, if you don't move toward one end or toward a compromise, this sort of coupling can end up in frustration and resentment. Once again, it comes down to convictions and core values. You can be from different cultures and backgrounds and still work out because you both have similar core convictions that are expressed in similar ways. Value diversity in your friendships, of course, but when it comes to a long-lasting union, don't compromise on your convictions, whether the person is from the same faith or a different faith.

When you do date, talk to each other, love each other, and share your faith with each other. Go with what makes you comfortable while still challenging yourself. Date within a community of trusted friends so that they can give you a clear picture of your significant other and vice versa. Worship together. Know what matters to you and to your boyfriend or girlfriend as you aim to share your life, religious and otherwise, together.

—ALICE CHEN, STUDENT,
JOHNS HOPKINS UNIVERSITY

HEY, BABY . . .
WHAT'S YOUR RELIGIOUS BELIEF SYSTEM?

BETH KANDER

I've never been good at knowing for sure who should date whom. Should you ever encourage a friend to date your ex? Should a Sagittarius date an Aquarius? Should a nice Jewish girl date a nice Catholic boy?

I'm still learning, but I can tell you that in my experience, encouraging a friend to date your ex is a bad idea. I don't really believe in astrology, so I have no answer to that one (but for anyone out there who is a believer in such star-crossed predictions—I'm a Sagittarius, and I did have a truly horrible breakup with an Aquarius once, so if you like you can file that away for future reference). It's the last one that seems to present the most difficult dilemma.

Being a nice Jewish girl myself, I've been trying to figure out as I go just how important it is to me to date someone within my own religious community. This has been a question for me ever since I started dating. My mom, funnily enough, is the one who really hopes I marry someone Jewish—I say funnily because she converted to Judaism, and her relatives are the Christians in my family tree! Still, while she hopes that I will marry Jewish, she also loves and trusts me, and therefore goes along with my decisions.

My dad doesn't express a strong opinion about intermarriage, but he is certainly supportive of nice-Jewish-boy prospects. Okay, so "supportive" is putting a nice spin on it. He still maintains I shouldn't date seriously until I'm thirty-five.

I know that I won't be disowned by my family for interfaith dating, or even intermarrying; that's not my concern. I'm lucky, in that sense. But my concern is still pretty important: Who am I comfortable dating?

At first, my stance was, "I don't care about the religion of whoever I date." I prided myself on my open-mindedness and didn't want to discriminate. (Also, there were no Jewish boys in my hometown. But I digress.) My first boyfriend, in high school, was the aforementioned nice Catholic boy. He was cute and sweet, and we were both in the same drama group. Disappointed when we weren't cast opposite one another as romantic leads, I got over it when we started dating midway through the show's run. We were fifteen, which made dating a pain because neither of us could drive anywhere on our own. Other than that, for the first month or so, it was a pretty idyllic relationship. We saw each other at rehearsals, went out with friends afterward, and went to the movies on the weekends. Then one night, when we were out to dinner with our drama friends, he cracked a Jewish joke. I'd actually heard the joke before—from a Jewish friend. It was funny when she made the comment. Somehow, it wasn't so funny coming out of my Catholic boyfriend's mouth.

We didn't break up over the comment, but it bothered me even more than I let him know. I started noticing that whenever I mentioned that Passover was coming up or I had to chant Torah at services this Shabbat, he didn't really know what I was talking about. After we had been dating for about four months, I went to a Jewish youth group summer camp. Hearing stories of my friends and good times at camp, he jealously referred to my youth group as "a cult." When I tried to tell him it wasn't a cult, he would hear none of it, and we pretty much stopped speaking. Needless to say, we broke up shortly thereafter. (I then encouraged my nice Catholic friend to date him when she admitted she had a crush on him. This was about a week after my breakup. I won't get into those details, but I will reiterate: bad, bad idea.)

My stance on dating shifted a little. Was it really a problem to date someone from a different religious background? What would it be like to date someone Jewish?

My next boyfriend was Jewish, but the relationship was pretty short-lived. Outside of being Jewish, we had nothing in common. I liked theater, writing, travel, learning new things. He liked football and video games. He also lived an hour away. Not exactly a recipe for success.

My first two dating experiences left me confused. Was being Jewish really the issue here? Or did a relationship come down more to having common interests and being able to relate to each other? My Catholic boyfriend and I had managed to keep dating for four times the length of time my first Jewish boyfriend and I had dated. What was that telling me?

It was shortly before my high school graduation that I started dating my third boyfriend. It was one of those fall-in-love-with-your-best-friend situations: We were best friends, and then suddenly, we were more. He liked football, just like the last one—but he also liked traveling and learning new things. We discovered even more shared interests in summer camping trips, volunteering for community service programs, and talking everything to death.

And—he was Jewish.

It was incredible to have a romantic relationship with someone whose religious views were so in line with my own. When I left for college, our relationship became long distance, but whenever we were in the same state, we went to services together. I loved spending Shabbat with him, sitting beside him in services. When he spent a holiday with my family, he knew the blessings to say along with us; when I spent holidays with his family, their traditions were familiar to me.

I realized how important it was to share my Judaism with the person I was dating, to be able to discuss spirituality, to be open about my enthusiasm for debating theology and wrestling with ideas of the Divine while incorporating Jewish tradition into my life. I love learning about other religious traditions, but I would never want someone else's forced on me and would never want to force my beliefs on anyone. It was so comfortable to just already have religion in common.

Unconditional love means that regardless of the conflict we might have had with our friend, regardless of whatever still lies unfinished between us, we can honor our deep connection of Spirit.

—STARHAWK

The initial comforts of an already-established friendship and a shared religious background laid the foundation for something wonderful. Loving, fun, supportive—two nice Jewish kids doing so well together. Everyone thought we were the most terrific couple, and they were right. We had a great relationship for nearly three years. It was great up until the very sudden end, which came during my junior year of college. We didn't break up for reasons of difference in religion or lack of common interests. We broke up, basically, for reasons of immaturity. I was devastated. (I'll skip the details on this one, too—but let's just say, this guy was the Aquarius I mentioned earlier).

One man cannot do right in one department of life whilst he is occupied in doing wrong in any other department. Life is one indivisible whole.

—MAHATMA GANDHI

I swore off dating for several months. I had plenty of other crap going on in my life and had no interest in pursuing another relationship. Even when most of the other crap was dealt with, I continued to focus my attention on anything and everything that would help keep me out of the dating world. I came to college with a boyfriend; I hadn't had a "first date" with someone since I was seventeen. The prospect was terrifying.

I shot down the first few boys who were fool enough to approach me during my mourning period. My first date post-Aquarius actually wound up being a setup—I said no several times to the girl who wanted to set us up, but she was very determined. I finally agreed to a double date. My date wound up being a nice Argentinean guy. He was musical and charming, but I just wasn't ready. The girl who set us up didn't believe me and gave him my phone number. He called me the next Friday evening as I was heading out to services.

"Hola!" he said.

"Hi," I said, feeling ill at ease. "How are you?"

"Very good! I wanted to call and talk with you." I could hear his grin through the phone lines. He was so cheerful.

"Well, now's not the greatest time," I said. "I'm actually heading out the door."

"Where are you going?"

"Um, services. Religious services." I said, twisting the phone cord and glancing at the clock.

"Services? Like to pray?"

"Yeah," I said.

He was confused. "Who goes to services on a Friday night? Nobody goes to services on a Friday night! Services, that's for Sundays! Who goes on a Friday night to services?"

"Jews do," I said, closing my eyes and waiting to hear his response.

I was expecting a sheepish "oh, yeah," or maybe even an interested "oh, really?" Instead, there was silence for a minute, and when he finally spoke his voice was no longer so cheerful. "If you didn't want to talk to me, you could have just said it."

With that, he hung up the phone.

I couldn't believe it. He actually thought that I had *made up* that "Jews go to services on a Friday night" in order to get out of talking with him! I felt terrible, but I also felt overwhelmed with the realization that, clearly, a relationship with him would never have worked out. How could I even consider dating someone who knew so little about something so important to me?

That phone call was really a wake-up call. I had already had one relationship that made me realize how comfortable I was dating someone who shared my love of Judaism. It took a nonrelationship to solidify for me just how important it was to me that my relationships support and contribute to that other love, the love of my traditions.

Although perhaps it should have been obvious before, it wasn't until that phone call that **I truly realized how important it was to me to be able to share my whole self, including my spiritual self, with my partner.**

I wound up dating a few more people in college, no one seriously. But even casually, I found myself dating Jewish guys, without even really thinking about it. My campus had a large Jewish population, which made a Jewish dating pool more readily available than in other places. Still, there were non-Jewish boys I could have dated. I just didn't date them.

There is a difference between friends and relationships. Okay, there are a lot of differences, but one of them is how close you can become when you have religious differences. I love and respect my friends who are from religious backgrounds other than my own. Our beliefs and traditions may differ, but rarely has that affected one of my friendships. It's a different story when it's someone with whom you might consider spending the rest of your life. Not sharing the same holidays with a friend is not such a big deal. You can learn from one another, and it's not an issue when your friend wants to go to church and you want to go to synagogue, or a mosque, or some other house of worship. It's not a death sentence for a friendship if one person believes in God and the other doesn't. But it is an issue when you want to go to synagogue and your significant other wants to go elsewhere. When you know you want your family to be brought together by religion, rather than be divided by it, shared beliefs become a huge issue. Some people can resolve this issue or work around it. I wound up deciding that I can't.

The decision is not always foremost on my mind, but it somehow manages to play out in the choices I make now. I don't want to make the blanket statement that I won't date anyone who isn't Jewish. Never say never. However, I do know that I can't date anyone who doesn't love me all the more for my spirituality. I can't date anyone who can't share my appreciation of traditions, and specifically Jewish traditions—Seders and *Havdalah* and a *mezuzah* on the doorpost. My partner needs to relate to my interest in the larger Jewish community, in Hebrew and Israel, in working to make a difference in the world because I feel culturally and religiously

> *To accept the ups and downs in human relationships and to see them as positive features, not as causes for sadness.*
>
> —ETTY HILLESUM

obligated to do so. When I get married, I want to stand beneath the *chuppah*, the Jewish wedding canopy. I want my kids to be Jewish.

Maybe there is someone who exists who can share all this with me, and who isn't Jewish. I'd certainly rather date someone open, accepting, and in touch with his spirituality, regardless of religious affiliation, than someone completely uninterested in matters of the soul. Maybe my spiritual life partner is out there and isn't Jewish, but will embrace me and my Judaism with a whole heart. If I find him, I'll let you know, because hey, maybe that could work. Unless, of course, our astrological signs aren't compatible, in which case, the relationship is clearly doomed.

Just kidding.

CHAPTER 5

TURNING POINTS: SPIRITUAL AWAKENING
OR CRISIS OF FAITH?

You feel as if the whole world has come crashing down. You had this belief system, this faith, and you followed it. And it seemed as if others did, too, in one form or another—or at least enough people followed it that the world kept spinning. But then something fell apart.

Perhaps it was another person who let you down. You are wondering, if I can't trust this person, whom can I trust? If I can't trust anyone, can I have faith?

Or perhaps your God has let you down. Something so awful, so seemingly unfair has happened. Would a compassionate God let this happen? If I can't believe in this God, whom can I believe in?

Or perhaps you have let yourself down. Maybe you have made some bad decisions and feel as if you can't trust yourself. Or maybe, for the first time, your faith isn't getting you through a difficult time. And if you can't count on your own faith, what can you count on?

That crisis of faith—it hurts. It hurts in the pit of your stomach. It gives you a headache. It makes your muscles tight. It hurts.

It hurts because your faith is what gets you through all the other hard stuff. You struggle with loneliness; maybe you miss home or don't quite feel like you fit in at school, but when you pray or meditate, you connect with something greater and you are less alone. You deal with failure, perhaps not achieving a goal you worked hard to accomplish, yet you reconfirm your self-worth in connecting with your faith, believing that as one door closes, another will open soon. A loved one dies and the ache to have him or her back is excruciating, and yet your faith gives you some amount of solace.

So when your faith is rocked, you lose your foundation. It is often during that time of deep despair, however, when we do our most profound soul-searching. Or it may be a time when we realize our faith is stronger than we could have imagined, because all logical reasons for our faith have disappeared and all that is left is faith at its essence, a trust, a commitment to believe.

Fortunately, we grow spiritually not only in the darkest hours but also during better times. Maybe we connect with someone who is strong in faith, and that example inspires us to explore, practice, and connect with our own spirituality. Or maybe through action we come to connect with something greater and feel a sense of being centered and trusting, a sense that was previously unknown. Or perhaps through community, a sense of commonality and mutual care, we come to feel more strongly a shared faith.

So how do you survive a crisis of faith?

Take good care of yourself physically. Eat right. Exercise. Get enough sleep. This may all sound like stuff you know, but even though you know it, these are often the first things that drop away when crisis strikes. Crisis time is often when we skip meals, lose sleep, and forget to move around. This is a time where we need to make conscious choices. Be sure to eat at least two nutritious meals a day. Make sleep a priority—if you are having trouble sleeping, try taking a shower or sipping tea or meditating before going to bed. And get some kind of exercise at least three or four times a week. Whether it's an all-out game of basketball or a vigorous walk around campus, get yourself moving. These things sound both obvious and at times impossible to do when you are stressed, but if you eat, sleep, and exercise, you are taking good care of your physical self, which in turn gives you a much better foundation to deal with the spiritual challenges you are facing.

Find a place to call your own, a place to get centered. This place doesn't have to be anywhere fancy. Sure, if your campus has a garden or a pond, that would be ideal. But if not, a quiet spot under a tree should do just fine. Or you

I have not lost faith in God. I have moments of anger and protest. Sometimes I am closer to him for that reason.

—ELIE WIESEL

might choose a location indoors, perhaps the chapel or a corner in the library or an alcove in one of the academic buildings. What you need is a place where you can go day after day when you need quiet, a place that will become familiar. This quiet and familiarity will eventually help you get a bit more centered or grounded. Just make sure that if you go there at night, it's also well lit and safe.

Identify a few people you can rely on for support. These could be friends, an R.A. or some other student leader, a spiritual leader, a coach, an advisor, or anyone else you trust. Keep in mind that you aren't looking for someone who will solve your problems or give you the answers. Rather, you need someone who will be a good companion, will be available and consistent, will support you emotionally, will help you recognize the questions, and can help you develop your own answers. Ideally, this is also someone who will challenge your thinking when that is what you need. If this companion is being too directive or seems to have his or her own agenda, you may want to reconsider whether this person is really there to help you or to further his or her own cause. Once you have identified one or a few support people, establish an agreed-upon way of communicating. Can you call this person at home? Should you have a regular meeting time? And so on.

Consider all that is on your plate. If you are in crisis, you need all the physical, emotional, intellectual, and spiritual resources available to deal with it. If your academic work is suffering, meet with your academic advisor and seek advice about resources, academic coping strategies, and even extensions, if necessary. As a last resort, you may need to consider dropping a class. The most important strategy regarding your academic success is to be pro-active and prevent your spiritual crisis from also causing an academic crisis. Most advisors and faculty understand that personal circumstances impact academic performance; they are more understanding when you take the initiative to talk with them in the early stages of a problem. You will have a much better chance of finessing your schedule or getting an extension if you talk with your advisor or professor as things are getting more difficult, not at the end of the semester when everything has already fallen apart. The worst thing you can do is just to stop going to class and wish it would all go away. Find an ally on campus and get help.

Likewise, if you are involved in clubs, sports, or the arts on campus and have commitments that are getting difficult to keep during this crisis, talk with the other members of your organization, the coach, or an advisor to see how you might adjust your involvement. Clubs are the easier situation to deal with, because you may be able to take a leave from your leadership position and have someone else fill in. Sports and performing arts are more complex. Taking a leave from these activities may have a significant impact on you and the team or group, and it may also have a tremendous financial implication if you are an athlete on scholarship. Nonetheless, talk with your coach, director, or some trusted member of the organization. If they know your situation, that alone may help you feel more comfortable about staying involved. Also, keep in mind that being part of a team or group may help keep you going during a difficult time, so don't bail too soon.

Consider seeing a counselor at the campus counseling center. Counseling can be helpful for anyone in crisis or transition. You don't have to enter deep psychotherapy and spend years talking about your parents. A counselor is someone objective—totally outside of your regular circle of family and friends (who may have an agenda

The longest journey is the journey inwards.

—DAG HAMMARSKJÖLD

for you)—who can help you look at your situation and understand what you bring to it and how to find a way out.

Taking good care of yourself, identifying the members of your support system, and evaluating your academic and nonacademic commitments lay the foundation for you to take on this crisis of faith. Exploring your experience and being present with your emotions—this is the real work.

Give yourself time and permission to feel your feelings. Many of us were raised in families where painful emotions were not allowed, and we carry that idea into adulthood. That message may have been tied to ideas about "God's will" or simply the result of parents who couldn't cope with their own emotions. Either way, it's a difficult dynamic to undo. Nonetheless, feeling sadness after a painful breakup, or anger at a mentor who turns out to be unethical, or an overwhelming sense of helplessness in response to violence among nations—these are all natural emotional responses.

Before you can begin to cope with the loss, anger, or fear, you must share your feelings with someone you trust. Let yourself cry or find a safe way to express your anger. After you express some of your initial emotions, try to clarify those feelings. Are your emotions tied to a specific person or incident, or are you making generalizations and attaching your emotions to something bigger? For example, to be angry, disappointed, and sad because a spiritual leader has done something unethical makes sense. To assume that no spiritual leaders can then be trusted throws you into a crisis of faith that may not be based in reality. To feel angry, sad, and helpless because men and women are committing violence in the name of religion is understandable and real. But to assume that religion is no longer a positive force in the world discounts the reality that it is a source of strength for millions of people.

Likewise, consider whether one aspect of your faith community is causing you to write off the entire tradition. Perhaps there has been a ruling from your spiritual leaders that contradicts your sense of fairness and commitment. You may be tempted to distance yourself from the entire tradition. And ultimately, you may need to do that. But perhaps your faith tradition allows for disagreement. If not, perhaps there is a community within the tradition that adheres to an ideology more like your own.

When you have clarified your thoughts and feelings, and have been careful to avoid generalizations and other sweeping decisions that distort the reality of your situation, you are left with the core of your crisis. What does your tradition say about dealing with doubts of faith? Read, and read multiple perspectives, if you can find them. Talk with spiritual leaders, perhaps someone you know well and perhaps a leader you don't know as well. Each may be able to offer helpful insight, or at least buoy your faith. Look for spiritual connections and evidence of aspects of your faith that are still working. Even if you feel alienated from your spiritual community, you may still feel a connection to something greater when you pray or meditate alone. If a spiritual leader has let you down, explore other communities within your tradition; perhaps you can connect with a more solid leader. If you find prayer difficult, spiritual song may still empower you. If you can find these cushions of faith, hold on to them, lean on them, let yourself rest in them.

In addition, this may be a good time to reflect on the reasons you first felt compelled by your faith as well as your most intense experiences connecting with your tradition. Memories of meaningful prayer or meditation experiences, holidays and festivals, and moments of sharing and growth with others may counter current doubts and frustrations.

Sometimes, when nothing else makes sense and you know you want to hold on to a belief in meaning, a trust in the ultimate good, you may be able to find comfort in an abstract faith. This may contradict everything going on

I don't think prayer for me has always been connected with sadness and misery. I have prayed when I have felt low and tired and worried. But when I have felt joy and fulfillment in this world I have always wanted to say thank you. I just can't believe there isn't someone to thank.

—DOROTHY DAY

around you and bring doubts from people you love. But if you can hold on to that optimism, it may strengthen you until you can see the other side of your crisis. Sometimes holding on to your faith is possible only because it is better than the alternative: giving up.

In addition, consider how this crisis can motivate you toward positive action. If you are grieving the end of a relationship, consider what you might do differently next time. If you are dealing with despair over the state of the world, think about how you could contribute your time and talent in your local community. And so on.

Finally, keep in mind that even if you are in the middle of a spiritual turning point that is the result of something positive, rather than a crisis, change is almost always stressful and challenging. Pay attention to all that eating, sleeping, and exercise stuff outlined previously. Find that good friend or trusted advisor with whom you can share your thoughts, enjoy your new community, and revel in this time of growth and discovery.

MY TRUTH
MERRITT BAER

For me, religion has never been a given. I envied those who could be so unquestioningly confident in their faith—I tried, but in the end, I just could not keep from doubting. I couldn't understand how there could be so many different religions, all believing in different manifestations of the Divine. Yet by the same token, I wondered how they could all be so similar, too—so many civilizations, developing independently, have acknowledged some form of spiritual existence. I still question my belief in God and religion as a whole. But I think I've started to realize that that's okay.

My little brother, Lyle, is Lakota Sioux. He is the youngest of my three brothers, and we adopted him as a foster child four years ago, when he was four. Through him, our family has enjoyed the unique opportunity to join the Native American community. A common American Indian saying is "*Mitake oyasin,*" which loosely translates to "We are all related." This phrase got me thinking. If we are all

103

related, then perhaps there is no right or wrong religious sect; perhaps we are all simply grasping at the same truth. I have never been able to reconcile the fact that there are a million different religions in the world, each claiming to be the right way, the most truthful faith. They can't *all* be right . . . right?

My father was an ardent Christian Scientist. He loved his God passionately, and he followed Christian Science beliefs with a dedication anyone would admire. He never drank a drop of alcohol, never took an aspirin, never even sipped caffeine. For him, it was important that he remain true to these dictates so he could demonstrate his belief in the immaterial, his confidence in the power of love.

My father was diagnosed with terminal cancer last summer. It was hard being at school in Massachusetts while my dad was dying in Denver. I wished I could be home, even though I knew that my dad didn't want me to leave school, and even though I knew there wasn't much I—or anyone—could do for him at home. Walking around Cambridge, I wondered how no one knew; couldn't they see the pain in my eyes? Didn't they know what was going on? But they couldn't, and they didn't, and so I went to classes and parties with this secret, silent pain flowing like a current through the back of my mind. Had I been a religious person, I felt I would have relied upon it strongly at that time. But I was not, and I did not.

The Sunday night in January before my dad died on Thursday, I walked to Memorial Church, across the campus from my dorm. I sat on the steps and leaned on the huge white pillars, my mind churning with emotion. It was the closest I came to a religious encounter. It wasn't until a few months later, when I was writing my mom a letter, that I realized that somehow, sometime, during Dad's illness, his death, and our grief, I had begun to find my religious awareness.

The next message you need is always right where you are.

—RAM DASS

Having struggled all my life to find a religion that matched my convictions, I was now okay with the fact that there probably wasn't one that preached *exactly* what I had come to believe. I had been angry with Christian Science because it was the reason my dad hadn't had a medical checkup that might have caught the cancer early. It was also the reason he had sat downstairs, reading and praying through the pain of what we would later learn were tumors on his spine, shoulder, and leg. When we finally convinced him to seek medical care for the sake of our family, his guilt was acute. And I hated Christian Science for it.

I no longer do.

I have realized that Christian Science was a part of him—and not simply a part of his religious identity, but an element of his entire personality. In addition to the medical restrictions, Christian Science also provided him with an overwhelming faith in love and an emphasis on the immaterial world, which influenced all aspects of him and were evidenced in all he did. I could not love him without loving the Christian Science part of him, too—the two were one and the same.

I still have questions. Things are so much more complicated than they seem—I have begun to wonder whether religion is a way of grappling with a truth that we can only begin to comprehend. The other day, my mom asked me where Dad's memories went. Did they all just end with him? I sat at my desk in my dorm room and thought about this. Certainly, that seemed too superficial an explanation—too simple. Memories were not "alive" before; how could they now be "dead"? It seemed so arbitrary to label them thus, and I realized that though I had not articulated it before, I did believe that Dad's soul, his consciousness and its ability to interact with our consciousnesses, is not "dead" any more than it was "living" when his heart beat and his lungs breathed.

I have begun to discover my sense of the truth. There are so many questions—about God, about religion. How much of religion is real and how much is just in response to people's needs? And is there even a difference? But I have reached a sense of peace with my questions, and I guard them carefully—for questioning never hurt something true. I don't fear the questions anymore. I don't panic at the thought that everyone else has "got it" and I've been left out. I'm not sure whether I will go to church next semester; perhaps I will. For now, I just keep grasping, as we all do, for a glimpse of that core reality, and all the freedom that understanding can bring.

RELIGION, POLITICS, AND PEACE OF MIND AFTER 9/11
SHADI HAMID

It was a day that changed my life. I remember hearing the news that planes had crashed into the twin towers and thinking to myself that things would never be the same again for American Muslims. The first thing that came into my head was the U2 song "Sunday Bloody Sunday," when Bono sings, "I can't believe the news today; I can't close my eyes and make it go away." And I couldn't make this go away. Before that day, we could afford to be innocent and carefree but, for me at least, the days of innocence had ended abruptly. In dramatic fashion, the violence in the Middle East had spilled onto our own soil. In one sudden and unforgettable explosion, we were awakened from our short-lived state of post–Cold War peace and prosperity. I had to wake up, too.

In the days and weeks after 9/11, I struggled to make sense of it all. I read every day about how Muslims throughout America were being harassed, attacked, and even killed. I knew Muslim girls who wore the headscarf (the *hijab*) and were afraid to even walk outside their dorms. This wasn't the America that I knew.

I had been in college for only about two weeks when 9/11 happened. It was hard enough adjusting to a new and challenging environment. But 9/11 made things even more complicated and confusing. I found myself asking, what kind of person did I want to be in college?

During those times of trial and tribulation, I found myself turning more and more to religion for solace and strength. Late at night I would walk over to the Muslim prayer room and just sit back and reflect. I needed to sort things out for myself. I couldn't afford to drift anymore.

In a way, I experienced a political, spiritual, and religious awakening all at once.

I had started at Georgetown thinking I would major in international economics and perhaps go into investment banking (and make a lot of money) after I graduated. **After 9/11, my focus began to shift. As a Muslim, I felt an extra burden. None of us could now afford to stay on the sidelines. More and more, I felt that I wanted to dedicate my life and career to something that mattered**—to helping my fellow Muslims and, more important, helping America become the place I always believed it could be. I wanted to convert my passion for politics into real action that could make some kind of difference.

What followed was a flurry of political activity on my part. I took on a leadership role in the Muslim community and in the greater campus community. As I became more politically active, I found myself becoming more religious as well.

The events of 9/11 showed how religion had become part of the problem. Some of the most ungodly acts that had been committed in recent memory have been committed in the name of God. So, I thought to myself, if religion was part of the problem, then surely it would have to be part of the solution as well.

I couldn't help but think that there was so much suffering, poverty, hatred, corruption, bloodshed, and hopelessness in the world because people had forgotten God.

We had forgotten God's message of compassion, mercy, tolerance, and peace. And in God's place, we had fallen in love with a whole hosts of false gods—capitalism, nationalism, and technology, to name just a few.

The evil actions of the terrorists on 9/11 pushed many Muslims away from Islam. But at the same time, it also caused many Muslims to become more religious. In the aftermath of the tragedy, I, along with millions of other Americans of all faiths, found strength in faith and religion. The only way I was able to make sense of it all was by looking at 9/11 as a test from our creator. Would 9/11 be the start of a descent into a never-ending cycle of violence, revenge, racism, and hatred? Or would 9/11 awaken us all to the importance of interfaith and cross-cultural dialogue and understanding? Would 9/11 bring out the worst in us, or would it bring out a common humanity in us, regardless of our religions?

Growing up in the thick of so much political, spiritual, and cultural turmoil is quite a challenge. It will continue to be a challenge as we try to feel our way through an unpredictable, violent world. We, the young people of America, are struggling to make sense of the very complicated world in which we now live, post-9/11. Because of this, many of us have felt a need to turn to something. Some people turn to the fleeting pleasures of life—drinking, sex, and drugs—but these pleasures can provide only temporary respite from the pain and suffering of life. Or we can choose to face our difficulties head on and use our faith to help guide us. The choice is ours.

FIGHTING WITH GOD
MEGHAN MUELLER

I was a junior in college when I began fighting with God. Well, fighting is a bit of an overstatement, considering I was the only one who was angry. In any case, I had a severe falling out with God and a traumatic loss of faith. Maybe if I hadn't been so connected to God and my faith before this spiritual crisis it would not have seemed so bad. But my beliefs and values were intertwined with the faith I had grown so accustomed to. I was raised as a dutiful Roman Catholic, attending Mass every Sunday and participating in all of the sacraments. When my friends began struggling with their faith in high school, I still felt very connected to God and continued to grow in spirituality. Even at the beginning of college, my faith provided a foundation that gave me constant support and guidance as I made the transition to college life. I was grateful for my growing relationship with God and the beauty I found in my faith. In fact, I was arrogant enough to believe that I was one of the few who really understood spirituality; I was a model of faith. Little did I know that my faith would be challenged beyond anything I believed possible.

Everything changed on September 11, 2001, when terrorist attacks killed thousands of Americans in New York, Washington, and Pennsylvania. It was amazing how the country pulled together during this tragedy, caring for one another and inspiring hope in the human race. This nightmare also led to churches overflowing with people who longed for solace and hope during this difficult time. With fear, sorrow, and anger, people looked to their faith to put the pieces of their lives back together. No one really knew what to do, and so we prayed. Well, others prayed. **I began to feel doubt creep into my heart, as I questioned how the God I believed in would allow such a tragedy to occur.** While my friends and family urged me to trust in God and pray about my anger, I continued to withdraw from my faith, ignoring prayer and refusing to attend Mass.

In the following months, my pain and anger grew, and I was diagnosed with depression. The chemicals in my brain no longer wanted to function properly, and I lost interest in everything I once loved. It was a struggle to get out of bed each morning, and eating even one meal a day was a good sign. As I began to spiral into despair and sadness, my anger toward God grew stronger than ever. Why would God let me suffer so much? Why did I have to deal with depression at such a young age? Most of all, I wondered why I had wasted so much time believing in a God who apparently cared nothing for me or the rest of the world. At least this is what I thought as I watched my life crumble before me. I remember telling my campus minister, Dave, about the pain and doubt I was feeling and how I thought things would never get better. He told me that I would eventually see grace in all of it. I was terrified that he would be wrong.

As the weeks passed, I slowly began to feel better both physically and emotionally. And as I felt the goodness and beauty of myself trying to break through the mess of my depression, I realized that I would never be the same. Through my pain and suffering, I had experienced a transformation, and I could never go back to being the person I once was. I regained confidence and strength and became committed to caring for myself and my emotional well-being. Not surprisingly, I also began to feel a strong urge to reconnect with God and my faith. I wasn't sure how to do it, but I knew that my belief in God was essential for me to continue to remain healthy and happy.

Slowly, I began to talk with others about my struggles with spirituality. And what I learned was that my anger at God was okay—that where I was in my spiritual journey was where I needed to be. There is a Catholic Eucharistic prayer that says, "When we were lost and could not find the way to you, you loved us more than ever." God didn't love me any less because I was angry or depressed. In fact, God loved me more than ever during those rough times in my life. I began to rebuild my faith through prayer, discussion, and the guidance and support of friends and family.

My faith is not perfect; in fact, it will never be perfect. But God does not expect that from me. God expects me to find my own sense of spirituality through my own journey, no one else's. I know there will be bumps, rough patches, and moments of pure joy. I will embrace these things as part of my spiritual journey, knowing that where I am and where I am going is enough.

WHEN FAITH FAILS

It happens. Sometimes we have those moments, days, or longer spans when we lose faith. We've lost our anchor and are drifting; whatever faith we had seems far away, or fallen away, and our footing groundless. No matter which metaphor we use to describe the state, each of us has had the experience, and chances are pretty good that we'll have it again. That's the way with relationships.

Faith is a relationship, not an accessory like our car keys or cell phone. Else we could press a button, follow the chirping sound, and locate it again. Or retrace our steps, turn the house upside down, pray all the more fervently for divine guidance, or do whatever it is we do to track down misplaced items. To lose faith is to lose trust, to falter in relationship. That's why we feel the way we do when it happens—not like we've misplaced the keys but more like we've lost someone, not like we miss some convenience but more like we miss a friend and companion.

Living in relationship with another living being entails ups and downs, togetherness and apartness, and a host of other opposites and every subtle gradation in between. Knowing and accepting this reality is mature faith and a comforting strength when the fallow times come.

The sensible, experienced hiker knows that when lost, panic isn't helpful. Stop, stay put, settle in. Even if you're hiking by yourself, you're not alone; someone who knows you, loves you, is in relationship with you and will be looking for you.

When faith fails, that's the time to remember the relationship, to recall the Divine. Someone knows you, loves you, is in relationship with you, is looking for you. This is not the time to panic, to rush or flail about in search of what's missing or who's to blame. In that posture of patient waiting, attending to one's own care and safety, a different constellation of perceptive gifts is exercised.

The hiker lost in nature discovers resources for shelter, food, water, and warmth. Self-pity gives way to creativity; the fear of vulnerability and want gradually shift to an awareness of belonging and abundance. A rock crevice or richly leafed bough becomes shade and house. Plants yield nourishment and protection. Even dead wood and grass, sun and glass, or simple friction grant fire. Wild creatures offer companionship and encouragement. The alien becomes familiar, and long before one is located, one can in a far richer sense be found.

When faith fails, the posture of patient waiting opens to a deeper awareness of self. The believer separated from the beloved may discover precious resources within. Grief gives way to perception; fears of inadequacy and failure open to a more profound acceptance of gifts and abilities. The difficult people and challenging responsibilities offer new friendships and accomplishments. Common tasks and familiars taken for granted yield new nourishment and companionship. Even dead relationships and old hostilities are kindled and burst into flame, offering new warmth and insightful light. Those dismissed as wild or strange become prophets and friends, guides and mentors. The distant draws near, the weird becomes wonderful, and long before one is restored to faith, one can be brought to a richer awareness of relationship.

When faith fails, a space opens. The Other in whom we have placed our trust, in whom we have faith, seems distant or absent. Don't be quick to fill the space. Let it be a place of hospitality into which others are invited, a place where one sits quietly in comfortable conversation with others. Invite trusted advisors into this place; sit there with your most valued spiritual guides, your most intimate friends, your closest family. But invite the opposition, too, the ones who bring the wisdom of wider perspective and the corrective of criticism. Invite also the strangers; sit there with the ones who see differently, think differently, sing and pray differently.

When faith fails, make yourself a home in the wilderness, make yourself at home in the wilderness. Keep the door and the space open and hospitable. The Beloved knows the way home.

—REVEREND SAM PORTARO, EPISCOPAL CHAPLAIN, UNIVERSITY OF CHICAGO

THE JOURNEY OF A PILGRIM
JOHN NEWTON

I would call myself a pilgrim. What I mean is that I have "embarked upon a quest for something conceived of as sacred," as one dictionary defines the word. This definition should help you if you are still defining yourself in terms of spirituality, what I call being a pilgrim. I like this definition of the word *pilgrim* because it introduces the two most important aspects of my own unique journey: the "quest" that is embarked upon and also that which is seen as sacred, or the inspiration behind the journey.

My quest began my junior year of high school, the day before my seventeenth birthday. I borrowed a book titled *The Journey* from my religion teacher, and, looking back, the book's title has proved to be symbolic of these past few years. I do not remember why I asked to borrow it or, better yet, what urged me to read the entire 128-page book from cover to cover that very same night. All I remember is that I borrowed and read close to twenty other books on religion throughout my junior year, I began to read the Bible and attend church with an unimaginable zeal, and for the first time in my entire life I felt true joy. My joy was no longer dependent on things such as popularity or a new car but arose solely from a new-felt relationship with a God I was very interested in.

It was not long before senior year rolled around and it came time to worry about applying to college. My major concern in choosing a college was to find an environment where my newfound faith would grow. I was accepted to two universities, and I was convinced that one of the two colleges was "God's plan for me" and it would be my fault if I chose the wrong one. If I did not pray enough or consult other Christians who could help me with my decision, maybe I would choose a college that God would not approve of. It is such a funny thing looking back. Seriously, what nonsense! Nevertheless, I was troubled over the decision and my lack of clarity. If I chose one university, I was destined to join the same party fraternity my father and all my friends were part of. If I chose the other out-of-state university, maybe I could get away from such college "distractions" and concentrate on what really mattered to me, or so went my reasoning at the time. To make a long story short, I committed to the state university at the last minute and joined the party fraternity.

The following year is when I faced my first real challenge on my quest. I found me a new bag, and that was college life. With college came new friends and new interests, and suddenly I did not have as much time to spend "searching" for God. Everything I feared seemed to unfold right before me, and I could not help thinking I had made the wrong decision. I drank a few nights a week and became determined to gain popularity within my fraternity. I no longer went to weekly Bible studies, and I only went to church whenever a fraternity obligation did not get in the way. This was a real challenge. I wanted to grow in my faith and deepen my understanding of who God is, but there was just no time.

As it happened, the Episcopal chaplain at the church I attended had been a member of the same fraternity at the same university several years before. He left after my first year at the university, and his replacement was yet again a former fraternity brother from my university. Now, most of the dues I pay to be a member of my fraternity go to a "social" budget, and it would be wrong to assume that our fraternity is one big seminary. This was a big coincidence. Meeting these two guys, who I could talk to with zero fear of being judged, was just what I needed. I could relate to them. They had experienced similar dilemmas and understood my concerns. It soon became easier to balance "the college life" with activities that I felt nourished my faith, and more important, I learned that a balance should exist! Now, after three years of college, I am involved in two different Bible studies within the fraternity I once feared would ruin my faith, one of which I lead, the other of which is led by my friend and fraternity brother/priest. I have also become a program leader within the church, but most important, I have support for my journey from the people and the environment I once feared would hinder me.

I mentioned earlier that one of the two things worth considering is the journey itself, and this story is a perfect reminder of perhaps the most important lesson I have learned. The quest can't be predicted, charted, or planned out! You can't look forward, only backward, and you need to focus on the present. It was so foolish for me to think that by going to one university over the other I would be fulfilling God's will. Maybe it was God's will that I attended the college I did, but I was wrong to think that God would not have been with me either place I went.

Muddy water, let stand, becomes clear.

—LAO TZU

I know now that if you want to find that which is sacred, you must open your eyes and your heart and live one day at a time. It is pointless to worry about the future and what lies ahead on the journey.

This brings us to that which is sacred, the reason for the journey itself. One theologian said that the most perfect way to know God is to know God as unknowable. Basically, the longer you search, the more you come to know God as an "absolute mystery."

When looking for friends to help you along the way, stay away from those who claim to know exactly what God is like and what he thinks about this and that. It is fine to feel conviction for whatever beliefs you have, but it is also okay to have doubts. If there is no doubt, there is a good chance that you have stolen someone else's beliefs and pawned them off as your own. It is critical to find people to talk to, people such as the two priests I mentioned, with whom you can share your feelings or doubts and not be met with judgment. However, if people are not open and listening to you, and are so sure of who God is that they judge you for thinking differently from them, they will not help you. Such people will harm you. Your faith will not be nourished, it will become mechanic, and you will pawn off the beliefs of others as your own.

As I have come to know God as unknowable, I believe that I make progress. Now, after several years, I consider what a blessing it was that I went to college and got "distracted" from the path I was on. Why? It made me think. I might still believe in the same God in the sense that I identify with the Christian faith, but to claim to know God's essence is foolish.

Do you want to embark upon this journey? Open your mind and drop what you think you know. Only then can you begin to truly experience God and give worthwhile advice to others on your very same path. As I said, I am a pilgrim and looking for something sacred. I am sorry to say I cannot describe God, because the human mind cannot comprehend the sacred. I can't even tell you about the future of my journey, because I can't look ahead to something I don't have the capacity to see. What I will say is this: As I strive to concentrate on the present, I look back and see I have moved forward. As I continue to define myself in terms of spirituality, I can now see that the quality of my life has changed and that the quest has made all the difference.

OUT OF THE CLOSET, IN THE SPIRIT
JEREMY D. POSADAS

If I think about it, I can remember exactly how it felt, before, during, and after. I can remember the nervousness and fear the week before, right through the walk to the office. I remember the stillness of the moment—as though time had paused—once I'd actually started to explain what I was doing there. And, maybe most of all, I can remember what it felt like to start breathing again, as though my lungs and body and soul were new.

This moment, which defines a significant Before and After in my life, was the moment I first decided to be honest with another person about the fact that I'm gay. But almost as important as *what* I had to say was the person to *whom* I was able to admit this thing about me, which at the time had seemed so terrifying and alien and now feels as natural and comfortable as wearing glasses or being left-handed.

For I had found someone to whom I could be open about my sexuality *and* who would still accept me as a fellow member of our faith community (in my case, Christian). I had found a minister who knew just how hard it can be to remain true to yourself—*all* of yourself—and true to your faith at the same time. More important, I had found someone who knew that faith, religion, and spirituality could help me discover and affirm who I was just as powerfully (and tragically) as they could be used to repress people's sexual identities.

And wow, did I know the damage religion could inflict on those who considered themselves gay, lesbian, bisexual, transgendered, or queer (GLBTQ). I had grown up in an extended family whose religion was a strong source of unity. We lived and believed with a fairly fundamentalist orientation to the faith. In fact, one of the worst forms of spiritual violence against GLBTQ people when I was growing up was that they were simply invisible in my family's religious world. Homosexuality would be mentioned in church as a sin and sign of cultural disease, but it was never discussed among family members. I had no chance to meet gay people, to see them living as regular human beings, to witness them sharing love and care and joy in their families just like we did in my family.

In fact, I began to embrace a new faith long before a sexual identity was clear to me. The legalistic structures with which I'd been raised had become menacing, not comforting. I found it harder and harder to believe that God had such a narrow vision and voice for human beings—that God couldn't be present in human life in many different ways and speak in many voices to all people. Changing family circumstances brought me to a different church, a more open-minded one, where I began to find other ways to encounter and express my God and my faith.

When I decided to become a member of this newfound church, many in my extended family were openly opposed. Thus, I had my first chance to learn the survival skills that would later be part of my coming out as gay *and* Christian. I learned to trust my heart when I felt God's presence in a new way. I learned how to hold my ground in my new understanding, though not without many painful fights. Most important, I learned that once I had chosen to be honest and authentic about an important aspect of my deep being, I was *not* responsible for how others would choose to respond. For the first time, I had to trust that being my authentic self was worth more than the relationships I might lose in doing so. I actually lost some relationships, but fewer than I'd feared. But in all the time since, the rule of self-authenticity has always brought more fulfillment and peace than any attempt to hide or compromise the seed of personhood I believe God placed in me. All these things are as much a part of claiming a new spiritual identity as they are a part of coming out.

Such growth, theological and emotional, helped prepare me for the vast discovery, experimentation, and testing of self that is college at its best. This, however, is different from saying I was *ready* for the experience! I wasn't—and few people are. I was thrust into a set of peers who had all sorts of backgrounds and perspectives along every axis. For the first time, I met people who fully accepted gays, who had grown up knowing GLBTQ people, and even some who themselves were exploring sexualities other than straight.

This isn't to say that there was no anti-GLBTQ prejudice. For every person who had an accepting attitude, there was another who came from just as conservative a background as mine, if not more so. But again, nothing is certain in college, nothing is set in stone; that's what makes college so exciting and, at the same time, one of the most challenging and scary periods in life.

I guess I lucked out in finding someone who was both in the same faith tradition and welcoming toward GLBTQ people. More and more, there are folks on every college campus who are allies for students grappling with their sexuality. Whether they share your spirituality or not, they probably care a lot about helping you feel safe, accepted, and real. That's probably the most basic and important strategy for coming out: Seek allies, and be open to finding them wherever God has placed them in your life. Long before you need to try to convert people in your life who are not ready to accept you (and that *will* come later, for sure), you need a network of friends, mentors, and advisors with whom you can be you and whom you can trust to support you consistently.

Coming out of the closet while also staying in (or even finding) a faith creates a unique set of challenges. Even now, several years into the process, I find myself at times caught by a tension between my faith community and the GLBTQ community. Actually, part of the process is learning that both the world of faith and the world of sexual minorities contain many different communities. The great part is that you are not bound to just one community, or even to one form of connecting communities. You belong wherever you can discover and can live out who you fully are.

I find myself continually having to explain to fellow Christians how being gay is *not* in conflict with being faithful. At the same time, I find myself explaining to gay people I meet—whether as friends or more—that Christianity stands for more than the destructive force that so many people know. At times, I get tired of all this justifying— and then I give myself permission just to step back and enjoy my life. I doubt there will ever be a time when I don't have to keep trying to connect my faith and sexuality more meaningfully, but in

> *Be patient toward all that is unsolved in your heart and try to love the questions themselves.*
>
> —RAINER MARIA RILKE

the process I'm always finding more people who are fellow journeyers.

At a certain point, I got tired of my faith not making sense to my gay self and my sexuality not making sense to my religious self. I wanted things to come together more smoothly and less confusingly, and I wanted that without delay! So one of the most important ways that God spoke to me was telling me to wait for my life to unfold as it would, and to embrace the uncertainty, despite its unpleasantness. Allow yourself time to learn how to affirm each part of yourself as you find it. Remember how long it took to be ready to live openly, then give yourself at least half that time to put together all the new pieces. God has all the time in the world and doesn't need you to rush through anything. So don't.

The more I live openly as a gay man who is committed to my spiritual life, the more I find what faith and sexuality have to offer each other. Both are modes of encountering God, who is love. Faith begins and ends with the assurance that God—however one conceives God—loves every human being and brings all humans into right relationship with one another. In light of this, my sexuality becomes a means to express God's love through my relationships with other people. It can be difficult, painful, and seemingly hopeless to integrate the two—to say nothing of all the other pressures of college life and young adulthood. But the rewards enrich all of one's relationships—with God, with others, with one's own life.

NEVER MIND JOHN BELUSHI, HOW ABOUT A BAR MITZVAH?

BEN HOCHMAN

My childhood was spent in the far northern reaches of California, amid the redwoods and fog. Both my parents were Jewish, so we celebrated Chanukah while my friends were celebrating Christmas; however, we rarely observed the other more significant Jewish holidays. I never learned about the religion that I called my own. My grandmother always talked about how she wanted me to go to temple and marry a nice Jewish girl and how as soon as I got to college I should join Hillel. I had no idea where the nearest temple was, and I sure had no idea what Hillel was. It wasn't until I arrived in San Diego to attend my first year of college at UCSD that I met the people who helped me discover the elements of my heritage that I had been missing.

Welcome week at UCSD consisted of guys in sandals and girls in miniskirts, as well as fraternities and sororities recruiting new freshman to what I thought were their shameless organizations. Images of John Belushi wearing a "College" sweatshirt with a bottle of JD tipped way back popped into my mind when I was handed my first "join our fraternity" flyer. A fraternity was the last thing I was interested in pursuing. Somehow, I attended a fraternity rush event and found myself sharing my sentiments with perfect strangers. We soon had a group of guys sitting around having a blast, enjoying the sun, and talking about college life. Then it hit me, these new friends of mine were wearing Greek letters, but how could that be? I had just met three of my now lifelong friends, brothers of the Alpha Epsilon Pi fraternity.

Alpha Epsilon Pi, or AEPi, is North America's Jewish fraternity. AEPi is not the "frat" that I knew from *Animal House;* Alpha Epsilon Pi is a family, where each and every member shares a history, a bond, and a deeper connection than any I have ever had with somebody close to my age. I first joined AEPi because of the great guys I met, but I soon realized that I had given myself the opportunity to discover the part of my heritage that I had been missing and now had the ability to become the person that I truly wanted to be.

As I have said, I was absolutely not religious at the time and was relatively uneducated about religion in general. I immediately began attending Friday night services with the guys at Hillel and soon became exposed to numerous Jewish events. I began to hear people speaking Hebrew on campus and was able to recognize it as something other than just a foreign language. By this time, my involvement in the fraternity had grown from nonexistent to extremely active. I was recruiting friends with similar interests, attending every fraternity and Jewish event on campus, and having the time of my life. I now had fifty instant best friends and countless other good friends. Events ranged from social parties to serious debates to lounging on the beach. To an onlooker, our common bond could have been anything. But there definitely was something about us, something unique that connected each of us and made our fraternity special. The definitive camaraderie that was formed by our commonality made this organization what it is.

The initial decision to join AEPi was not an easy one. Like most decisions, however, it turned out for the best. Through AEPi I was given the opportunity to gain insight not only into my friends and my heritage but, more important, into myself as well. Most young teenagers who were raised in a Jewish environment have a Bar Mitzvah when they turn thirteen. When I passed this "coming of age" I didn't know enough about Judaism to realize that it was even an option. **I was so inspired by my interactions with AEPi that I decided to have my Bar Mitzvah at the age of twenty. I attended classes and became educated not only about my ancestors but also about myself.** For the first time in my life, I felt a connection to my ancestors and the history I shared with them. I learned what it meant to be truly Jewish and why the connection with my fraternity brothers was so strong. This single decision of joining AEPi has been the greatest life-changing experience of my existence, and my commitment to my friends, my faith, and myself has only grown stronger by the day.

CHAPTER **6**

ASSUMPTIONS, INTOLERANCE, HATE, AND A HOPE FOR SOMETHING BETTER

"Merry Christmas," said the well-meaning checkout clerk at the student union food court.

"Have a nice Christmas, everyone," proclaimed my lit professor at the end of the last class of the fall semester.

"What are you doing for Christmas?" asked that kid from biology as we waited for the airport shuttle.

I wanted to shout, "Guess what, America, I don't celebrate Christmas!"

If you have grown up as a minority in this country, it's quite likely that you have been dealing with people's faulty assumptions most of your life. If you have been relatively lucky, false assumptions are all you have had to face. If you encountered more extreme intolerance, you may have been the victim of a hate crime such as vandalism or violence. Unfortunately, these forces still exist on many college campuses. The difference between having these experiences while you are growing up at home versus while in college is that unless you are a commuter student, the college campus is now your home. The intensity of the college experience in general is notable because you eat, sleep, study, and play all in the same place. If you get harassed in that space, it may feel as if there is nowhere else to go.

You are going to run into assumptions. Some of the stereotypes are downright predictable. People may assume that because you're Buddhist or Hindu you don't let yourself have fun, or because you are Christian you don't want to have fun, or because you are Jewish you own the fun, or because you are Pagan you have too much fun. Or it may get more serious than that, and people may assume that because you are Muslim, you hate the United States. Sometimes assumptions are fairly harmless—for example, the checkout clerk who wishes you a Merry Christmas when you come from a faith that doesn't celebrate the birth of Jesus. She means well, but the problem is that you feel excluded. This clerk doesn't see any possibilities other than her own, and that leaves you on the outside. If you are an outsider, then can you feel at home on a meaningful level? And this is your campus we are talking about.

So do you confront these assumptions? Some people confront everything. Others are more selective, deciding, for example, not to challenge the checkout clerk but indeed to have a direct talk with a roommate whose assumptions are exclusionary. If you decide to confront assumptions, how will you do it? You might have a direct talk about the facts. You might talk with your roommate about the view of Jesus vis-à-vis your religious tradition and talk about the way in which Christmas permeates our society and how that feels to you. Or you might use humor. When she asks what you are doing for Christmas, you might just say, "I'm going to take my bad Buddhist self to the nearest Catholic Church for midnight Mass"— and maybe she'll stop and think.

Your roommate may be offended about having to examine how she celebrates a holiday that is so central to her tradition. Or your roommate may even respond by telling you how she gets frustrated by the overcommercialization of Christmas. Regardless of the response, you will have been true to

A tree that is unbending is easily broken.

—LAO TZU

124

yourself and your experience by confronting the situation.

But what happens when the assumptions lead to discrimination or hatred? What happens when, instead of just forgetting that you don't eat meat, the guys on the floor don't invite you to dinner? Or they get quiet when you enter the room? Or they harass you? These kinds of actions clearly indicate that your hallmates aren't just oblivious but have issues with you, possibly based on your religious beliefs (or in some cases, their assumptions about your religious beliefs, because they may not even know what or how you practice).

The first thing you need to assess is whether you think you can confront this alone. If the guys are excluding you but aren't otherwise bothering you or your stuff, and if you feel comfortable enough, you may want to ask them to sit down and talk. Maybe they just need to know more about you, both in terms of your spirituality and in terms of the other things that make you who you are.

However, if the guys are truly harassing you, you should talk with someone else on campus who can help. The same holds true if you are being harassed and you don't know who is doing it. If you live on campus, your resident assistant is a good person to start with. Explain the situation to your R.A., and he or she will help you connect with a staff member or administrator. If you don't live on campus, or you don't get anywhere with your R.A., then talk with your dean of students.

There are a variety of potential courses of action, depending on the severity of the situation and your comfort level. Your advisor or dean may suggest a facilitated discussion with everyone involved to help you understand each other better. If the situation is more severe, you may be able to file charges under the university's student code. Regardless, a dean or other university official will help you understand your options and choose a response. The campus is your home as much as anyone else's, and you deserve to feel safe and comfortable there.

Another way to confront the uninformed, and perhaps challenge those who hate, is to go on the offensive. Get involved with, or start, an effort to educate others on campus about your religious tradition. Strategies range from passive to active, one on one to campus-wide.

Even without taking on any big organizational efforts, you can impact the culture on your campus. Start by being friendly. Is a simple "hello" going to stop a hate crime? Probably not. But for someone who makes assumptions about "people like you," a simple hello may be the start of a more open mind. Look for connections with students and faculty who come from a tradition other than your own. These relationships can be extremely rich, as you savor the common ground that you share and learn about your differences.

Or you might take a more public approach. Create a poster campaign that teaches others about your tradition. Plan a speaker, panel, or celebration, and invite the entire campus community. These sorts of activities work best when several students are involved and invested, so you will be wise to do this via a student organization that you already belong to or by securing help from a student group that shares your interests. In addition, invite other student organizations to cosponsor these events with you; this will help promote the event and increase attendance.

You can also take a more active approach and invite two or more student groups from different religious traditions to join together for a discussion. This kind of effort is most successful when you have a strong facilitator to establish ground rules, deal with conflicts that may emerge during the discussion, and ensure that everyone gets equal airtime. Finally, you may wish to take on a more ambitious effort and initiate a campus-wide educational program. This is a tremendous undertaking, but with good planning, administrative support (a.k.a. funding), and strong collaboration with other students and staff, you can impact your campus culture.

I DON'T SIT IN FULL LOTUS
LODRÖ RINZLER

I am confronted more with ignorance than intolerance. It's really surprising to see what people expect of a Buddhist college student. I go to a school that continuously fights against all forms of bigotry, yet I'm stereotyped in the most blatant of ways. The Hollywood-created version of Buddhism, complete with monks sitting in full lotus position chanting "om," has, in the eyes of many Americans, become an unquestionable tenet of all traditions of Buddhism. I find myself fighting to dispel this ignorant preconception every time I introduce myself. Perhaps it is because I have chosen to go by my refuge name, Lodrö, a name given to me at the age of six, when I took refuge in the three jewels of Buddhism, that I have found myself explaining my beliefs and practices in an effort to demystify a 2,500-year-old religious tradition that has been solidified and dehumanized by so many scholars and movie directors.

I started to use my refuge name, Lodrö, as my first name when I was seventeen, after sitting a one-month retreat. I had hoped it would serve as a reminder of my experience, so that whenever someone used it I would remember my commitment to my Buddhist practice. Unexpectedly, it also threw me into a situation where, whenever I introduced myself, I had to explain that my name signifies that I am Buddhist and then, more often than not, talk about what Buddhism is all about (because I'm such an expert at the ripe age of twenty, right?). During one of these introduction scenarios, I took a bold step in revealing to a group of students hanging out outside a party that I had been temporarily ordained as a monk for one month. One kid, obviously on his way home to vomit on his would-be girlfriend, yelled, "You were celibate for one whole month? I don't know if I could ever do that!" The kid was obviously a virgin.

In a society that has so many gyms and diets and other ways to take care of and improve our bodies, the notion that I take the time to relate with my mind in a similar way is somehow outrageous to

127

most of my peers. I find that half the battle is correcting different assumptions of Buddhism, such as "Everyone believes in God," and the other half is trying to make the practice accessible to people, so they can walk away with some sense of Buddhism as a very workable tradition. For example, if I were to broach the subject of my observing silence during retreats, people would assume that they would go crazy under a similar situation. Our current society is too speedy to consider not talking, or even speaking mindfully; we're too busy talking on our cell phone to someone we just saw a few hours ago. So the practice of observing silence is something that I try to make appear workable, in the hope that I avoid isolating myself as a practitioner or making Buddhism seem more foreign or confusing than it actually is.

In order to humanize Buddhism and deflect popular misconceptions, I have had to sharpen one tool—my sense of humor. When leading weekly meditation with the Buddhist group on campus, I mock the preconceptions that people may have, catching them off balance and opening the door for them to try something different from what they may normally experience in college. "Hey, Sam," I may joke, "should we show the new kid how to sacrifice the goat?" Although sacrifices take place in many religions, this form of sacrifice is not characteristic of Buddhism, and when I point out the contrast between sitting down on a meditation cushion to relate with your mind and something more labor-intensive, such as animal sacrifice, things become a lot lighter and more human. The message is the same one that I ought to wear on my forehead: Meditation isn't weird—it's just misconstrued and often poorly explained.

I can't get away with "passing" when someone asks me about my beliefs or makes a drastically incorrect assumption about Buddhism. Although I don't feel that I am the prime spokesman for the 2,500-year-old religious tradition, I have to stand up for what I believe in, and I refuse to let people get away with blatantly ignorant remarks about Buddhist beliefs. I don't sit in full lotus, I don't chant "om," and I won't shut up and let you think that I do.

PLAYING SPIRITUAL HARDBALL
DALE JOHNSON II

Growing up on a farm in rural Illinois, I always had the desire to leave my small town and do something extraordinary with my life. Often I found myself waking in the middle of the day from one of my illusions of catching for the Chicago Cubs or practicing law on an important court case in Manhattan some twenty years into the future. It was this daydreaming, this hope for a life that was entirely out of the norm for a small-town kid, that drove me to excel both academically and athletically.

During my senior year at Beecher High School, a letter came to me in the mail from the head baseball coach at a Catholic college located in New England. Somehow the coach had heard about my accomplishments on the baseball diamond and was offering me the opportunity not only to leave my sleepy, old town but also to play Division I baseball.

Needless to say, I was more than thrilled, even though I knew little about the college other than that it was far away from home and that I could play baseball there. I can honestly say that I cannot remember once asking myself, as a born and raised Lutheran, whether I wanted to go study at a predominately Catholic college. Instead, I was just so happy to have the opportunity to do something exciting and to pursue my boyhood fantasies that I jumped at the chance before any such consideration could be made.

Upon arrival at college in the fall of 1999, I felt strong, independent, and ready to face the world. I had little problem adjusting to the new social climate or my new surroundings. Everything was so new, so fresh and exciting, that I just could not get enough. I even excelled on the baseball field, earning the starting catching position in my freshman year.

Life seemed to be going just as I had hoped, until my team's first regular season road trip. It was common practice that after the completion of our Saturday afternoon doubleheader, the baseball team would drive directly to a Catholic church for evening Mass.

Completely unaware of this practice as a freshman, I blindly followed the rest of my teammates into the church. Through the entire Mass I was very uncomfortable, not knowing when to stand or sit, when or what to reply, and it seemed to go on for hours. I found myself concentrating so hard on watching what everyone else was doing that I did not even hear the words spoken during the entire Mass.

Finally, it came time for Communion. I sat and watched each one of my teammates walk past me, shoot me an awkward glance, and then continue on his way to receive the Sacrament. It was this event, this inability to participate in something so uniting, that made me realize I was different from the great majority of the students at school, including my teammates. I sat and wondered how this revelation would affect my relationship with my teammates, including their actions and acceptance of me.

When Mass finally concluded, we all scuttled back to the bus to return to our hotel. Ironically, we all went to Mass together but separated into small groups for dinner. The events of the bus ride are a blur; I was bombarded with semi-innocent questions. Looking back, it was like playing twenty questions about my religious convictions. No one said anything too inappropriate, or at least nothing that offended me. I was, however, becoming increasingly aware that there were differences that separated me from my teammates.

The jokes and the heckling continued and grew worse throughout my tenure of three years on the baseball team, without regard for me or how I was feeling. The relationship that I had with my teammates declined, and I soon began to dread the time I had to share with them. No longer did I spend time with them away from the baseball diamond; I just did not want to have to face them any longer than was absolutely necessary.

The experience with my teammates, though not consistent with my experiences with other students on campus, and especially not consistent with the faculty, was especially painful because the goal of a team is to establish a brother- or sisterhood among team members. The experience of being isolated and subsequently rejected by this brotherhood made me feel excep-tionally lonely because of how much time was necessarily spent around these people on the field, in the weight room, and traveling. Yet, this feeling of isola-tion was balanced by the acceptance of many supportive friends who were not on the baseball team.

The primary reason I no longer asso-ciated with many of my teammates off the baseball diamond was their attitude toward me; however, a secondary reason was the many insecurities that I had about myself. Although I had considered my faith in God to be con-siderably strong when entering college, when faced with this adver-sity, it seemed to crumble right before my eyes. All I wanted to do was fit in, to have the experience of feeling united with my team-mates. Many people, when faced with adversity of this manner, either pull themselves back toward their own tradition or go the opposite route and give in to the peer pressure, converting to what-ever their friends or teammates believe.

I toiled many days and long nights over my options. Probably the easiest response to this situation would have been to return to my own tradition and criticize those who held viewpoints that dif-fered from mine. This response did not seem to be the proper one for multiple reasons, the least of which is that it did not seem to be the moral response. Second, there was no one else on campus that I knew of from my same tradition, let alone someone else on the baseball team, to talk with or to feel that unspeakable bond that is shared when two people have strong, agreeing convictions.

I then considered what it would mean to convert to Catholicism. Amazingly, what I found when asking myself this set of very difficult questions was that the biggest reason I did not want to convert was my identity. Being of predominately Swedish blood and only a third-generation American, I knew that much of my

> *The ultimate measure of a man is not where he stands in the moments of comfort and convenience, but where he stands in times of challenge and controversy.*
>
> —MARTIN LUTHER KING JR.

family's history and our many traditions stemmed from our native country of Sweden and extended to touch all aspects of our culture, especially religion. To convert to Catholicism and deny being a Lutheran would mean more than changing my place of worship—it could be seen as denying my family's heritage. Therefore, converting did not seem like a good option because I knew very little about Catholicism and failed to see the value of converting my faith just to fit in.

I was then more confused than ever and felt as though I did not know what to believe. I decided to research my own, my teammates', and as many other religious traditions as I could. I enrolled in the first of many religious studies courses and decided to add that discipline as a second major. Taking this more proactive route not only allowed me to cope with an increasingly difficult social situation but also led me to the beginning of what I am now sure will be a lifelong journey.

Having the experience of being different drove me night and day to learn about religion on a grander scale. I found an immense freedom in being a minority on campus because I was not bound by the same limitations that one has within any tradition. Because I was already perceived as being different, it was acceptable for me to explore all avenues and ask the difficult questions concerning all faiths (especially my own) that I had always been frightened to ask.

At the beginning of my journey through my religious studies major, I concentrated mainly on my own Lutheran tradition and Catholicism, but my studies eventually extended to include Islam, Buddhism, and Judaism. I had a newfound openness to listen to the teachings of other traditions, one that I did not have before my experience with my teammates. I soon began to realize that without my experience with my teammates, I probably would not have taken such an in-depth look at my faith or at the faiths of others.

You hear me speak. But do you hear me feel?

—GETRUD KOLMAR

Although the realization of being different was something that was extremely difficult for me to handle, it was, perhaps, one of the best things that has ever happened to me. It allowed me to explore religion and motivated me to evaluate what I believe. Furthermore, it also gave me the self-confidence to be proud of who I am and what I believe while still remaining open-minded enough to value what other religions have to offer. In this sense, my teammates played an important role in who I have become, and for that I will be forever grateful.

> *The highest peace is the peace between opposites.*
>
> —REBBE NACHMAN OF BRESLOV

PEACE AND PEPPERONI PIZZA
SHADI HAMID

With the bleak images on our TV screen of endless bloodshed and hatred, I sometimes wonder whether there's any reason to believe that things can get better. I'm tempted to throw my hands up in resignation. Too often, people are pushed away from religion because it seems that the worst things are done by those who also claim to be the most "religious."

Indeed, we live in an era when love for our fellow man has been replaced by a love of worldly things. Hopelessness and despair reign supreme. But every now and then, a glimmer of hope shines through the darkness and despair. It's just a glimmer, but it's enough to make me believe in the good of mankind once again. Every now and then, there are those rare moments when I feel like great things are actually possible. It is these moments that keep me going.

I had one of these defining moments in the beginning of my sophomore year at college. It was quite a revelatory moment. It came by surprise, and it happened in a place usually devoid of intellectual thought—the university cafeteria. I went to get some pizza, but to my dismay, there were only four pans of pepperoni and no plain cheese. You can imagine my disappointment because, as a Muslim, I cannot eat pork. I was left to contemplate my next

We must openly accept all ideologies and systems as a means of solving humanity's problems. One country, one nation, one ideology, one system is not sufficient.

—DALAI LAMA

move when a fellow classmate, who happened to be Jewish, came up to get some pizza as well. We started complaining about how the cafeteria always has too many pork dishes. And before I knew it, we were talking about how in actuality, our two religions have more in common than people usually think . . . because she keeps kosher, she also could not eat pepperoni. Both of us stood there waiting for a new pan of cheese pizza.

It hit me . . . granted, there are a lot of things that Muslims and Jews disagree about. But, I thought to myself, what was keeping us from coming together as Jewish and Muslim students and pushing for the cafeteria to be pork-free? Maybe we could even have a halal/kosher section. But my defining moment in the university cafeteria wasn't just about food; it was about the larger picture—about Jews and Muslims and how they treat (or mistreat) each other.

There was a time hundreds of years ago when Jews and Muslims lived in harmony. Although Jews often found themselves the victims of persecution in Christian lands, they were welcome in the Muslim empire, where they enjoyed the freedom to practice their own religion. In Muslim lands, Jews were subject only to their own laws, giving them a considerable amount of autonomy. As a result, Islamic society, in the words of historians Sydney Fisher and William Ochsenwald, developed into "one of the most tolerant of all ages." Jews who learned Arabic were able to participate in most aspects of Islamic culture.

It is sad to look at where we were one thousand years ago and where we are now. In terms of tolerance for each other, we have certainly digressed. Let us be honest with ourselves. There are large numbers of Muslims who are anti-Jewish, and there are large numbers of Jews who are anti-Arab and anti-Muslim. Why did this happen? It happened because Muslims and Jews have forgotten the essence of their own religions. Islam is indeed a religion of peace, justice, and tolerance, as evidenced by Islamic history; Judaism is a religion that stresses social justice, compassion for others, and equal rights for all. Indeed, there were many Jews marching alongside Martin Luther King Jr. and other black leaders in the 1960s. Jews have often been involved in civil rights struggles for minorities.

In the summer of my freshman year, I went to a conference in Chicago for the U.S. Campaign to End the Occupation. I was surprised to see that perhaps 70 percent of the attendees were Jews. There was one Jewish woman I'll always remember. She was describing how she had been involved in the movement for Palestinian freedom for the past thirty years. She broke down in tears when she observed that, despite the efforts of many, the suffering of the Palestinian people is worse today than it has ever been. After I saw the emotion and compassion in her voice, I knew in my heart that there was hope.

Similarly, I also remember reading an article in *Ha'aretz,* the Israeli daily, about Tariq Ramadan, a European Muslim, who spoke out loudly and forcefully against the growing trend of anti-Jewish attacks and prejudice in places such as France and England.

There are brave voices such as these in both our communities, and they are speaking out loudly for reconciliation and peace between our two great peoples. If we had more people like Tariq Ramadan and the Jewish woman at the conference, perhaps there wouldn't be so much bloodshed in the Holy Land. It is sad that, instead, intolerant extremists on both sides have misrepresented Islam and Judaism. Too often, "faith" in God has been twisted into oppression, but **I believe with all my heart that faith and compassion go hand in hand. It is only through compassion that religion can once again be a force for justice, freedom, and most of all, peace.**

I look around these days, and I wonder to myself what went wrong. It is sad what has become of us. But it doesn't have to continue this way. Many of my Jewish colleagues and I will probably keep on disagreeing about the conflict in Palestine. We will continue to argue passionately and debate the issues. But, surely, we can agree to disagree. And, perhaps we can even find some common ground. Our shared faith in one God can and should be something that brings us closer together. Even if it's just about pizza, at least it's a start. Great things always start small.

SHALOM AND SALAAM
ALISON E. SIEGEL

I saw her
　I saw her.
She had dark eyes.
　She had light eyes.
She had curly hair.
　She wore a scarf over her head.

She had a strange language on her jewelry.

She says, "Shalom."
　She says, "Salaam."
She has light skin.
　She has dark skin.

Her roots are far away.
She reads the Torah.
　She reads the Qur'an.
She goes to the synagogue.
　She goes to the mosque.
She prays in Hebrew.
　She prays in Arabic.
But her laugh is like mine . . .
　And the other day I saw her crying, just like I do . . .
My friends all had told me to meet her . . .
　She actually knows my best friend from high school . . .

I pray on Friday.

Our roots are intertwined
And one day we realized,

We are on common ground.

—INTRODUCTORY SPEECH FOR "COMMON GROUND IN
THE HOLY LAND," SARA BOKHARI AND ALISON SIEGEL

The University of Illinois at Urbana Champaign is the flagship public university in Illinois and is home to roughly 40,000 students. I came to the university in the fall of 2001 and am now a junior majoring in religion with a concentration in Jewish studies. In May 2002, the Hillel Foundation for Jewish Life on Campus brought together more than four hundred North American Jewish student leaders for an Israel advocacy mission. At that point, the University of Illinois was one of a handful of campuses seen as hosting the most volatile and hostile environments for pro-Israel advocacy in North America. Indeed, the campus had been a difficult venue for Israel/Palestine relations and advocacy for several years.

At a school where the Jewish and Muslim communities are of significant and comparable size, the atmosphere on campus was largely characterized by protests, hate speech, inflammatory chalking, and a divestment campaign. Hurt and humiliation fueled anger, verbal assault, and the polarization of students sympathizing with either Israeli or Palestinian concerns. Voices calling for peaceful communication and dialogue were drowned out by those of extremist leaders within both communities. Jewish and Muslim parents alike became concerned about sending their students to the university, fearing that their children would become targets in the campus version of a battle thousands of miles away.

Be a lamp, or a lifeboat, or a ladder.

—RUMI

One year later, the scene at the university has done an about-face. The heated debate on campus has calmed, the divestment movement is now nearly nonexistent, and Middle East–related hate speech has all but disappeared from campus.

Yom Ha'Atzmaut, or Israel's Independence Day, had traditionally been a favorite day for elaborate protests, with hundreds of angry students demonstrating in droves on the main quad, the center of campus. However, four weeks ago, university students enjoyed the first peaceful Yom Ha'Atzmaut celebration in at least five years. For the first time, students began to understand and respect each other's viewpoints.

How was such a dramatic change achieved?

Peace movements had been ongoing at the university for quite some time, each gathering small numbers of dedicated supporters but quickly ending in defeat. Ultimately, these movements would falter and dwindle as their membership grew older and either moved on from the university or became discouraged and focused their energies elsewhere. I had been involved with one of these movements, the Bridges Dialogue Group on Middle East Issues, since my freshman year. Together with two of my close friends, I watched it go from a small cluster of five interested students up to a medium-size gathering of students and community members, then back to a small group of frustrated and tired students. We started to wonder whether we were doing anything to move our campus in a positive direction.

Early in the spring 2003 semester, the university administration requested my assistance in ensuring that all students would be allowed the right of peaceful expression on Yom Ha'Atzmaut. I enlisted a friend of mine, Sara Bokhari, a Pakistani Muslim and student activist, as a partner, and a grassroots initiative was born. Over tea one afternoon, we decided that it was not enough merely to control the actions and reactions of our respective communities. Rather, we needed to encourage them to know and understand each other. Out of this conversation, and because of our belief that no political solution is possible before we reach an understanding of our mutual humanity, "Common Ground in the Holy Land" was born.

In only three weeks, we mobilized fifty university students, representing multiple religious and ethnic communities present in Israel, to create a cultural symposium on Israel/Palestine. Volunteers created displays on demographics, arts, religions, social issues, languages, and peace initiatives in Israel/Palestine. Representatives of the Muslim, Jewish, Christian, and Baha'i faiths offered to share songs, prayers, and folklore with each other. The event took place on Tuesday night, May 6, which was the beginning of Yom Ha'Atzmaut (Jewish holidays begin and end at sundown, and Israeli political observances follow suit), in the Illini Student Union. Common Ground encouraged collaboration and dialogue in the planning and execution of the program, as well as among attendees. We were successful in establishing relationships among previously warring students based on an understanding of personal history and culture and in creating an atmosphere of understanding and appreciation in the place of prior hatred and anger.

What began as a onetime program is now being turned into an ongoing student-run initiative aimed at creating appreciation through education and communication. It is our hope that once solid relationships are established we can begin to explore our political differences from our base understanding of universal humanity. Our goal is to rehumanize and depoliticize Israel in the eyes of University of Illinois students so that true communication and dialogue can take place.

At the University of Illinois, we are learning that true peace will come only when we understand each others' common humanity. The Common Ground program serves as ongoing proof that it is possible to bring conflicting sides

The bond of our common humanity is stronger than the divisiveness of our fears and prejudices. God gives us the capacity for choice. We can choose to alleviate suffering. We can choose to work together for peace.

—JIMMY CARTER

together in peace and dialogue, and that the connection of the human spirit will always triumph over political argument.

While we were planning for the initial Common Ground evening, Sara and I joked repeatedly that G-d, or Adonai, or Allah, was on our side because of how quickly we had been able to pull people and resources together and how staunchly the university administration supported us. The evening of the event, however, I realized that this was more than a joke: I looked around the room and saw something divine in the faces around me, in the conversations and interactions taking place throughout the room. In a reading from the Christian scriptures, my roommate, Lauren Kidwell, shared, "If one part (of the body) suffers, all the parts suffer with it. If one part is honored, all the parts share its joy" (1 Cor. 12:26). If the University of Illinois community is considered to be one body, then that body can be the one that she described. **When we remain divided, each part struggling independently, the community as a whole will continue to suffer. Only when we come together in order to honor and uplift our separate parts does our body, and our community, become one in joy and celebration.**

In the end, Common Ground has had a larger impact than we ever planned. At the end of the evening, Sara and I sat down with a friend of ours and his video camera in order to capture our immediate reactions to the evening. When asked about the communities' responses to the evening, Sara replied, "I think for at least a lot of people within my own community, they were able to see that it's actually possible to do something like this and not have it be an in-your-face, I-have-to-scream-my-point-of-view, conflicting type of situation. A lot of people didn't think it was possible. . . . They haven't seen it work, so hopefully this will start a new trend."

As for me, my heart was overflowing with happiness, pride, and joy at seeing the way people who may never have spoken to each other or looked each other in the eye before had pulled together and put their differences aside to truly search for their common ground in order to make an important and amazing event happen. People walked away that night with big smiles and warm hearts.

They had had conversations, made connections, started relationships, and begun to dialogue. That was a huge step for the University of Illinois community. My cup runs over with happiness when I think back to that night, and I cannot wait for the fall semester so that we can come back together and continue our work. I think that the impact of Common Ground can be accurately summed up by the words of an anonymous contribution to our expression board: "Love flows through the air as bearers of peace champion the cause of unity and harmony. This is the kind of endeavor that brightens the world. This is the kind of effort that brings happiness to the hearts of our fellow human beings."

GRASSROOTS ORGANIZING—MAKE IT HAPPEN

Developing the idea for Common Ground in the Holy Land, a university cultural awareness program, was the easy part. Knowing how to make it happen, however, was a whole different ball game. Once you notice the need for a grassroots initiative to address multicultural issues, here are some steps to make it happen:

Find an Ally. This program could not have happened without Sara's and my cooperation and commitment. Our prior friendship and the trust that we shared were key in ensuring that our program had the potential to succeed. You need to find an ally who is not only staunchly dedicated to your cause and reliable but also active and influential in the community with which you are hoping to work.

Create a Mission Statement. This simple statement, ranging from a couple of sentences to a paragraph in length, should outline your goals and give others a concrete idea of where your community is presently and what you would like the end result to be.

Gather supporters. Sara and I wanted to create the Common Ground program without the use of any registered student organizations at the university. However, that meant that we could not

141

access the e-mail Listservs of any of those organizations. Instead, we brainstormed the names of people we knew who were like-minded and would possibly be interested in dedicating their support, time, energy, or resources to our cause. That way, we ensured that we were targeting interested individuals, and we also were able to make sure that only students we could trust and rely on were brought into the planning process. We wanted to keep our program free from political strife and therefore selected students who were supportive of that goal. Also, by inviting individual students to participate, we were able to involve a much larger demographic than would have been possible if we had only invited preexisting organizations.

Make a Plan. Develop an outline for your program. What are your needs? What materials will you require ahead of time? What type of funding will you need? How much volunteer power will be required? Have this information available for both potential volunteers and potential donors. They will be much more comfortable with signing on to help you, and you'll be much more organized and therefore efficient.

Work the System. Find out who on campus is in a position to help you reach your goals. At the University of Illinois, which is a very large university with a strong bureaucratic structure, Sara and I had a huge advantage because we were both involved student leaders. For example, one of our biggest supporters was the assistant dean of students, who works with the registered student organizations office and was able to help us secure the facilities we needed. Also, because we had originally begun by working with the chancellor of the university, her office was able to give us plenty of assistance. Other resources that might be available, depending on the school, include the dean of students office, campus counseling and mediation programs, campus ethnic and faith groups, university departments that are related to your cause, and local community organizations.

Get Funded. This is a huge one—you can't put a program on without paying for it. Ask different offices and departments around the university for funding. Also, if you can apply for student program funding, do it. Asking for funding never hurts. The worst they can do is say no. Remember, though, that the more organized you are when you ask, the more likely you are to be taken seriously and thus to receive funding. Have details of your program and your budget available for potential donors. Traditional fundraisers, such as car washes, candy sales, and raffles, work too, though they require more time and advance planning.

Get the Word Out. The best events fail when no one attends. Write a press release to send to local newspapers, magazines, and broadcast stations. Submit an advertisement to your campus paper. Create flyers and delegate students to hang them in dormitories, campus buildings, offices, and local businesses. Begin advertising one and a half weeks before the event and continue through the day of the program. The more people who know about your program, the more people who will potentially get involved.

Never Utter the Words "I Can't." Grassroots organizing is hard work. Make sure you have faith in yourself and your partners, and support each other. Even if you don't make your original deadlines, keep pushing for your goal. There's always a way to make it happen, so don't give up. Never take no for an answer, even from yourself.

—ALISON E. SIEGEL, STUDENT,
UNIVERSITY OF ILLINOIS AT URBANA CHAMPAIGN

CHAPTER 7

HEY, WHAT DOES THAT MEAN?
TALKING WITH OTHERS ABOUT YOUR SPIRITUALITY

"Hold that thought," your friend says, as she jumps up from the table to go get more soup. You have a moment to consider how you are feeling about this conversation. She has been asking you questions about your faith tradition for the past twenty minutes. For the most part, you think it's cool that she's interested. Although there have been some moments that stirred some strange mix of feelings inside you.

There was the one question about something that you thought was common knowledge. You felt a twinge of being an outsider as you realized that many people know very little about your faith. On the other end of the spectrum, there was the question that stumped you, and then you felt a bit embarrassed for not knowing the answer. Beyond that, your emotions went back and forth; at times you felt enthused by the opportunity to share, and other times you felt more vulnerable, as if you were giving up something personal.

Talking about faith and spirituality tends to be a rather complicated endeavor. Sure, sometimes it feels good, sharing a part of yourself with others, feeling competent that you know what you are talking about. This process of sharing can be energizing and fun. But more often, it is a bit more complicated. You may feel put on the spot or as if are you being asked to speak for an entire people. Then there is the other side, the side where you are the explorer, endeavoring to learn more about someone else's tradition. This role may hold less stress, but it isn't without its challenges.

If you are a minority in terms of your faith tradition, chances are that other students will ask you questions about your faith, your practices, and the tenets of your religion. And even if you are in the majority, minority students may seek you out, wanting to know more. Then, of course, there is the experience of talking with others who share your tradition. Although there is no way to prepare fully for these discussions, there are some things that you can get clear on ahead of time, which will help you feel more comfortable as you share what you know.

Know what you know and remember that you are only one of millions of people who have followed your faith tradition. Be willing to separate out what you know to be fact about your faith and what is your impression or perspective. People will often ask you to speak on behalf of the entire tradition, and it's fine for you to clarify that what you can share is your experience, that you can't speak for the whole tribe.

Be okay with admitting that you don't know the answer. The range of questions that you may get about your faith tradition is practically endless. Even spiritual leaders occasionally need to look up an answer. So, the dude who stops you after class to follow up on a point you raised a half hour ago can't expect you to know everything there is to know about your tradition.

Set boundaries. You have the right to opt not to discuss certain aspects of your faith and spirituality. It's okay to tell someone that you appreciate his or her interest, but that you are rather private about that part of your practice. There are plenty of topics regarding your faith that won't be at all private, but knowing that you don't have to disclose everything will help keep you from feeling too vulnerable during the discussion.

Set ground rules. You and the people you are talking with should agree on the context for your discussion. Are you simply sharing thoughts and perspectives? Are you all inclined to have a heated but friendly debate? Some people find intellectual banter to be fun and challenging; other people find it threatening. Agree ahead of time on how far you will challenge each other.

Return the favor. If your roommates are asking you about your tradition, then ask them about theirs. This will help balance out the conversation, which again will keep you on steadier ground. It will also allow them to share and you to learn.

Finally, don't hesitate to bond with someone else from your tradition after the conversation. You don't need a whole support group just to share your faith. However, you may find that talking with others who share your tradition and who have likely been through the same sorts of questions can help you feel a little less like a spokesperson and a little more connected.

How about when you are the great explorer—looking to find out more about someone else's faith tradition? Here again, there are some strategies you can follow that will make the conversation more comfortable for both of you.

Check your motivation. Are you really looking to have this conversation so you can learn more about someone else's faith tradition? Or are you posing as someone curious so you can actually try to convince the other person that you and your tradition hold the universal truth? If it's the latter, save it for someone who has asked you to share what you know. Don't spring it on someone in the guise of your own curiosity.

Ask permission. If you want to have a conversation about faith, ask the other person whether he or she is willing to talk. "Excuse me, I was really interested in the perspective that you shared in class, and I would like to know more. Can we talk sometime?" is a lot more respectful than rushing someone after class to exclaim, "I still don't understand why you people do that."

Listen. If you ask questions, you'd better listen to the answers. Don't get preoccupied with your next question or with trying to formulate an impressive-sounding response to what he or she is saying. Really listen so you can hear what is being said.

Don't judge and don't lecture. You asked this person to share something with you. This is not necessarily the forum for you to dispute, unless you both agree that you are up for a friendly debate.

Respect the minority experience. This goes along with "don't judge and don't lecture." If you have never been in the minority, then you can't know what it is like to share something (after being invited to do so) only to be attacked for the ideas that you just put out there. This is a significant point—ask questions respectfully, and check your emotions and motivations before you press too hard.

Get a glimpse of life in the minority. If you are accustomed to being in the majority, ask your friend or classmate about his or her experience as a minority. There is a lot to learn about that experience.

Take risks. If you don't want to have a one-on-one conversation with a student from another tradition, or even if you do, don't miss all the other opportunities to learn. Look out for speakers, panels, and other campus programs. And then when you are ready, take it one step further and attend a service of a faith other than your own.

THEOLOGICAL PAINTING
LAURA CARROLL

As a Unitarian Universalist and Pagan, I've been asked many times what, exactly, I believe. The question has always been a challenge for me, because both my religions are rather unknown, or worse, misconceived, by the general public. I've heard my Unitarian Universalist congregation called an "atheist church," and Paganism is believed by some to be nothing more than devil worship. As a result, I've learned to find ways of explaining my beliefs in a manner that people are willing to accept and understand.

The main thing I've learned is that the most obvious things about your religion are not necessarily the most important things for you to explain. Case in point: Unitarian Universalism is a religion without a theistic creed; it has principles of belief rather than a dogma. As a result, many people in UUism have varying thoughts on theology. Once, in middle school, a Christian student asked me whether I believed in Jesus. The conversation went something like this:

Other student: Do you believe in Jesus?

Me: What about Jesus? (I had heard lengthy discourses about who Jesus may have been, which ran the gamut from "True Born Son of God Who Died for Our Sins" to "Wise Teacher" to "Pretty Good Guy Who Got Too Many Followers and Pissed Off the Romans." I wasn't sure which of these beliefs he was referring to.)

Other student: That he was . . . Jesus. (Said with an extremely puzzled look and a helpless shrug that said quite clearly he had never heard any variations on this theme.)

Me: Um, I don't know. (How was I supposed to speak for all the different permutations of belief that I had heard from members of my church, many of whom were probably engaged in the discussion as an analytical exercise rather than as an exercise of faith? And how was I supposed to say for myself whether I believed in Jesus when I had barely thought about the idea but was pretty sure that it didn't work for me? And how was I supposed to say all this to a boy who was only an acquaintance, before class started?)

Since then, I've learned that this is not the best way to conduct discussions about beliefs, especially when the faiths under discussion are rather nebulous and difficult to define, as mine are. What I have discovered, though, is that when explaining my religions, theology is secondary. The God(s)/Goddess(es)/Spirit(s) that make up individual pantheons are interesting to talk about, but ultimately they are secondary to what the religion is really about. This past year at college, I explained my beliefs, in rather condensed form, to some of

149

my housemates as we sat in the living room. Unlike in the case of the middle school boy, all of my housemates had some idea of what my religions were about by the end of the conversation. This time I explained first and foremost that the main principle of Unitarian Universalism is respect for the worth and dignity of every person, and that many Unitarian Universalists take part in volunteer work and programs to support social justice as part of their religious life. I talked about how Paganism is a nature-based religion, and that as such it is concerned with the environment and the natural world. Both religions are concerned with promoting the greater good, but one focuses more on people and one focuses more on nature, and the two dovetail nicely in their perspectives. After clarifying what I felt to be the most important aspects of my religions, I then felt safe to move into the realms of theology.

Do Unitarian Universalists believe in God? Some do, and some don't, and some aren't really sure. Unitarian Universalists tend to be a rational bunch, so varying levels of agnosticism usually prevail, but the range of beliefs is immense.

What about Pagans? Do they believe in God? Many Pagans believe in a duality-based system of a God and a Goddess. Some believe in a single androgynous deity that may or may not be anthropomorphic, and some believe in whole pantheons of deities, ranging from Greco-Roman and Norse deities to elementals to nature spirits. Some believe in all of the above. And again, all of this varies according to the individual.

By the end of the conversation, all the people in the room had a fairly good idea of what my religions were about. They knew that my beliefs consisted more of philosophy than theology, they knew that concern for social and environmental issues was important, and they understood a little bit of the variety of theologies that exist within my two religions.

The main point, then, when explaining your religion(s), is to decide what the most important aspects are and to explain those. All religions have innumerable twists and turns in their belief structures, and it's easy to get caught up in explaining the minutiae. But interesting though it may be for people already familiar with the religion to discuss said twists and turns, that level of minutiae is impractical to discuss with people who do not already have some familiarity with the religion at hand. It is better, when beginning with a blank canvas, to start out with the most important aspects of the big picture, the broadest possible outline, so that the image is discernible. Then, like an artist with a fine-tipped brush, you can fill in the details on your theological painting until the image becomes clear.

KOSHER SCANDINAVIAN GOULASH
JESSICA BADINER

In the four years I spent at Brandeis, a lot happened. I changed my major from biology to English, and I gave up singing to make time for ballroom dance. From a religious perspective, I entered as a Reform Jew with a strong sense of family and personal spirituality. I emerged with the same affiliation and values, but with a greater understanding of Judaism and an evolved sense of how I fit into it.

When I began life at college, I knew I would have a lot of amazing and challenging experiences ahead of me. Beyond that, I really didn't know what to expect. I still remember the day I moved into my freshman dorm in the all-girls building. (An unrelated piece of advice for the girls out there in Readerland: I chose an all-girls building thinking it would keep things simple—no boy neighbor to have to constantly contend with. If I had thought it through, I would have realized that the all-girls' dorm is exactly where all the guys go.) Adynna, my new roommate, was friendly and respectful. As our freshman months passed, I admired her calm approach to hectic college life and was awed by her work ethic. In my opinion, those qualities were strongly influenced by her commitment to Orthodox Judaism.

By sharing the room and frequent meals with Adynna, I had my introduction to an observant Jewish lifestyle. For example, like many people I would come to call friends, Adynna keeps kosher.

The basics of a kosher diet include separating meat and dairy. This not only means no meat and milk in the same meal, such as cheeseburgers, but also concludes waiting a period of time to eat ice cream after a chicken dinner. Also, kosher meat is prepared in a specific way and is tastier, as it happens. This is, of course, my limited summary of how keeping kosher works, and it is by no means official. The point is that this was all very new to me, and it was one of many aspects of Jewish life that would find its way into my life. I did not adopt these elements as my own, as you might imagine, but they impacted my life as I learned to share space and time with these friends.

Keeping kosher has varying levels of observance because people commit to the elements that have value for them. Likewise, Shabbat (a period from Friday night to Saturday night) is observed in different ways by different people. In my family, Shabbat means a Friday night family dinner where we light the two Shabbat candles, enjoy conversation, and occasionally attend evening services at my family's synagogue. Adynna, on the other hand, devoted the whole evening and following day to relaxation and Torah study. She refrained from using electronics and doing homework. I still find giving up a full day of study time incredible. But Adynna worked really hard throughout the week and approached Shabbat as a time of rest and refreshment. On several occasions, however, she mentioned to me that she wished she could work on an assignment. And I doubt a Saturday went by when I didn't look across the room and wish I had finished a lab report sooner so I could have time for myself, too. This was a passing and friendly envy that left me with a higher sense of respect for her. Perhaps Adynna felt that way as well.

In addition to impacting my approach to each day, observant people in my life, Jewish and otherwise, stood as a benign reminder that discipline is the responsibility of the spiritual person. My comfort and confidence in my family background allowed me to find my own mode of discipline. My personal practices ranged from a simple deep breath to long walks to sitting in a peaceful spot when I needed comfort. But solitude does not afford the only spiritual moments in my life. On the many occasions I found myself over-whelmed by love and joy or basic silly excitement, I noticed that I was busy with literature, dancing, or, more important, my friends. **It is my personal contention that the greatest blessings in life are the people we share it with.** But I digress.

I find my spirituality in peaceful moments, inspiring environ-ments, and the company of loved ones. I found all three of these in the student-led Jewish services that my second roommate and long-time friend, Shoshana, invited me to join. I attended the Egalitarian Conservative services in our beautiful Berlin Chapel for the first time at the beginning of sophomore year. Conservatism is roughly the level between Orthodoxy and Reform, though it's not quite that simple. Egalitarian means that there are no gender distinctions in who performs the different parts of the service. What this means to this story is that Shoshana and Mike (a fun guy to have around) shared responsibilities in coordinating and leading services. In fact, I went that night to support Shoshana and Mike in this respected responsibility and privilege. It had been a while since I had attended services, and I only chimed in here and there with what I recognized. Part of the issue was that elements of the service were new, the other part was that I frequently became lost in my own thoughts during services back home, and so I hadn't paid much attention. Shoshana, noting that I was quite lost in the service (my Hebrew is minimal), transliterated all the prayers in the evening and morning Shabbat service into the English alphabet so that lan-guage would no longer be a barrier. I did not feel that language or tradition was a barrier, different though both may be. Rather than choose to participate in the group service, I found direction in lis-tening to the voices of others raised together. But to this day, I am grateful for Shoshana's thoughtfulness and dedication in making different options available to me and to many others, as well.

Being in the presence of the singers, readers, and listeners was inspirational to me. I returned to many more services with Shoshana and a handful of other people who were close to me (in addition to those I was just getting to know). I got into the habit of

God's spirit moves through us and the world at a pace that can never be constricted by any one religious paradigm. I love that.

—BONO

standing alone behind the rows of seats. It was a tradition among this group that people—especially seniors—stand in the back to pause from the services for some light and hushed socializing. In my experience at Reform services, no one got up from his or her seat except for special circumstances, such as to hold a crying baby. Come to think of it, the fact that I did not approach these services that way is a surprise to me. Instead, I managed to stand off to one side in order to think about the things that troubled or confused me, the things that had brought me there that night. After all, what better place to be left in peace to pray than at services? Or so I thought. I couldn't help chuckling slightly at what so often happened next.

People I was friendly with would come to the back to visit with me. Conversations about how lovely the service was that day would become conversations about weekend plans. Once I was even interrupted by someone pointing out some lint on my shirt. The idea of asking someone to hold his or her conversation until after a religious service so that I could pray seemed so bizarre to me that I could never bring myself to do it. I made a comment to a few people after services—which felt like a more appropriate time—and they eventually got the idea. Of course, they had only the friendliest of intentions, not the least of which was to make me comfortable in a somewhat new environment, so you can see the culture clash here. Different kinds of piety, one room.

This experience perhaps stands out strongest in my mind among these examples because it was such an eye-opener. I learned about the spiritual life of other people, and I also learned a lot about my own. Attending these services began as an exchange of friendly gestures of support: my attendance and Shoshana's transliteration packet, to pick two. It developed into a place for me to come when I needed to think or sit quietly and clear my head. By adapting an observant practice to my personal needs, I found the element of discipline I was searching for on a level that made me comfortable. After three years of attending sporadically, and occasionally contributing by performing the prayer over the candles that I had learned at home, I became familiar with the details of the service. In the end, my time in services was split between my spot in the back and a seat among my friends. I think this was an important experience because I learned about what my friends do and my friends learned about what I do.

It is very common to say that there are as many belief systems as there are believers. Everyone has a unique perspective and personal contribution to the group. I discovered that my own spiritual growth demanded that I get involved with people I could trust and who would challenge me and that I be that kind of person in return. There were times when an open mind and patience were not enough. There are times to agree to disagree, to recognize that fundamentally different vantage points are what make diversity, even within the same group. Attempts of two people to justify their choices to each other and compromising beliefs are not what spiritual coexistence is about. When you live with people, your spiritual time is still your own. However, this private life often extends into your relationships with others. These opportunities, such as my year with Adynna, challenge what we think and result in deeper knowledge of these thoughts. They are also the opportunities to find harmonies among differences, such as those I made at Egalitarian services.

Junior year, Shoshana and I had a campus apartment and shared a kitchen. She kept kosher and could not have some of the meals in my family's recipe book, and I refused to prepare a meal my friend and roommate couldn't share in. But we found some common ground. I proclaimed, "We all eat goulash, or no one eats goulash!" So we bought and browned some kosher ground beef, baked it with noodles and corn and tomato soup, and ate kosher Scandinavian goulash (350°F for about an hour).

THE POWER OF A POTLUCK

Leaving home and establishing yourself in a new environment can be good fun, and the diversity of the people around you can be very exciting. But at some point the excitement may wear off, and you may start to miss the traditions and comforts of your life at home. Instead of feeling isolated by your differences, share them with the people around you. For instance, if there's a holiday or festival you really love that you haven't been able to celebrate since you've been at school, invite your friends over to celebrate it with you, even if they've never heard of your holiday or festival.

- Treat a traditional meal as a potluck. Give everyone a recipe to make for the meal. This is fun when your friends don't even know what the end product is supposed to look like. You may need to explain uncommon ingredients and tell your friends where to buy them. Ask your friends if they have any dietary restrictions and inform everyone who will be attending the meal about guidelines followed by anyone else in the group.

- Invite your friends to join in the service. If you are reading something out loud, offer your friends a chance to read. If it's appropriate, encourage your friends to interpret part of the service, perhaps adding contemporary commentary or reflecting on how it connects with their faith tradition.

- Be open to their questions. Even if something is obvious to you, it may not be to them. Your friends may disagree with you. They may not like the food.

- Don't push it. These are your friends. Don't try to recruit them. It's great to share your background with your friends and to teach them something new, but it could get uncomfortable if they feel pressured. This applies even if the people around you are of the same religion. School may just leave you missing the way your family cele-

brated. Let everyone in your new community bring some
aspect of their tradition to your new celebration.

Whatever it is you love about your religion, share it with your
friends and community at school. They are bound to be just as
excited about your diversity as you are about theirs.

—CAROLYN GRAHAM, STUDENT, UNIVERSITY OF GUELPH

HINDU AT HOLY CROSS
TEJAL PATEL

Being a minority is hard enough without having other people
remind you time and again. To put a twist on the story, add being
not only a cultural minority but also a religious minority. Again, to
spice it up, add being a Hindu student at a Jesuit institution where
the majority of the students are Irish Catholic.

I am an Indian Hindu student at the College of the Holy Cross.
As one of the few "non-Christians" on campus, I've gotten a lot of
attention from people who want to learn about Indian culture and
Hinduism. I've been asked to do it all, from having lunch with
people who were interested in my background to sharing my faith
in my religious studies class to speaking on panels. One of these
panels I spoke for was an experience I will never forget because of
the challenge I faced.

The topic was "Faith, Struggle, and College." When one of my
mentors asked me to participate, I agreed but was nervous: What
was I going to talk about? Finally, the night of the program arrived.
After going through several drafts (and doing several mock talks for
my roommate), I finally came up with an outline I could live with.
I got to the basement, which is where the panel was to take place,
and took a seat at the front of the room with the other panelists. I
was one of five people who had been asked to speak. As I looked at
the other four members of the panel, I realized that I was the only
"non-Christian" up there. My nervousness increased slightly, but I

I'm happy to work with people to spread a message. And it's a beautiful message we all share:

Chill out.

Peace.

Shalom.

—PERRY FARRELL

thought to myself, "This isn't going to be so bad. Maybe everyone will be interested in what I have to say about my faith because it's so different." The first three panelists spoke about their own spirituality and faith, going through what beliefs they held and what tests of faith they'd encountered.

Finally, the fourth speaker began to talk. Although a very good speaker, he sent my nerves into overdrive by sharing his faith and belief that no one could be saved unless he or she went through life the way his religion said a person should. To boil it down, he said that anyone who was not Christian was not capable of achieving salvation.

I was speechless. I could not even think of how to begin telling the audience about my faith, seeing as I was not even remotely close to being Christian. So I abandoned my outline and began by introducing myself and telling the group that I am a Hindu. I shared my experience of spirituality honestly with the group. As I concluded, members of the audience started raising their hands, anxiously waiting to ask questions and make comments. The response and support the audience gave me was amazingly overwhelming. They really wanted to hear what I had to say, and they wanted to learn about what I believe. I was relieved and excited that the audience cared about my faith.

A week or so after the program, a girl I didn't know too well asked me to lunch. I was curious as to why she had invited me to eat with her, because we'd never exchanged more than a few words at a time. I accepted and found myself sitting at a table in a tiny restaurant with her. We ordered and made small talk for a few minutes, then finally she told me that she was fascinated by Hinduism and wanted to learn more. We sat in that restaurant for more than an hour, discussing our faiths. I gave her detailed accounts of my experience with faith and answered her questions, and she did the same for me, telling me about her life as a Christian. We talked about how different our religions were and how it was so cool to have so many different ways of life. Finally, we had finished our meal and really couldn't sit there anymore, so we paid and went our separate ways.

I walked away that day with a new friend, some extra confidence I hadn't had before, and a lot to consider. I had learned about a new religion and a new way of life. I had heard a new voice, and I had a better understanding of this girl's experience growing up. I learned about the trials of faith she had encountered. **In the end, I realized that our situations were quite similar; although I grew up as a religious minority in a society dominated by Christianity, and she grew up as a Christian, both of us had to work to be accepted.** After that deep conversation with her, I wondered how I could have overlooked the difficulties that members of majority religions have. We were so different, yet so alike. I never noticed all this before, but now that I have, I have a better, richer sense of the experiences that people of differing traditions have with their faith.

GET OUT THERE AND LEARN

Finding faith—that is, identifying with an existing ideology or support structure that you connect with on a profoundly meaningful level—is no casual task, no intramural sport. For many people it is a lifelong endeavor. Luckily, college is a great time for such soul searching. Perhaps no other time in your life will afford you the opportunity to maneuver as fluidly through such a diverse range of people and beliefs. Here are a few suggestions for navigating your educational environment:

- Keep your eyes and mind open. There are always people holding events, sponsoring discussions, and forming new groups. Be sure to scope any activities fairs where campus groups publicly present themselves. Ask questions and see whether anything interests you. And keep an eagle eye on the ever-changing flyers on campus walls. You never know what you may find.

• Join multiple organizations, especially ones that contradict each other. This way, you'll get a broad range of discourse and an understanding of where you might gravitate and why. And if you do begin to specialize and secure your beliefs, it will be beneficial to understand respectfully the fundamentals of other viewpoints. It will ultimately help you communicate with a broader range of people.

• Keep a journal. Write what your faith means to you on a regular basis. It's important to stay active in your definition of yourself. This is also a valuable form of self-empowerment. During discussions with people who are firmly entrenched in the dogma of their belief systems, it may be easy for an open mind to lose its perspective. Keeping a journal will help regularly ground you and keep your head from spinning too fast.

• Be honest with yourself and others. Understand the difference between solidarity and fraternity, spirituality and community, and make sure your needs are met with little sacrifice to your evolving beliefs. Never join a faith out of anything other than faith.

• Don't allow the secular academic environment to dismiss your faith and spirituality-based beliefs or motivations. Every single theory, calculation, war, novel, painting, and machine came to be because someone believed in something. There are faiths of all kinds that lay the foundation for all of human life. These faiths will often be glossed over in classrooms because they initiate intense discussion and debate. If it is important to you, simply do a little extra research, or bring up academic issues in a faith-based setting and see how the discussion changes.

- Don't allow your religious or spiritual faith to dismiss the value of the academic environment. Although you may not realize it, there is a lot to learn about faith from a nonreligious education. The absence of religion from the discussion in classes such as history, economics, and physics speaks volumes about the contemporary view of faith. For a self-empowered faith finder, academia is a fascinating collision of worldviews; where is the line drawn between secular (textbook-friendly) and religious (avoided)?

—ADAM GROSSI, STUDENT, CARNEGIE MELLON UNIVERSITY

TRADING TRADITIONS
SHARON SERVILIO

I grew up in a small, rural, and very homogenous town. It was absolutely teeming with white Christians, and rarely, if ever, did I have the opportunity to meet believers of other faiths. So at age seven, having just made my First Communion, I thought nothing of asking my Jewish cousin when she would make hers. "I won't have one," she replied. Shocked, I asked, "Then what will you have?" "A Bat Mitzvah." These strange words, along with the many other practices of non-Christian religions, were shrouded in mystery for my young mind. Little did I know that, eleven years later, I would enter the world of Brandeis University, a predominately Jewish institution, where I would not only encounter other faiths but also be surrounded by them on a daily basis.

For me, going to Brandeis was like a sugar-deprived child entering a candy store for the first time. It seemed that every day I learned something new about Judaism and other ways of looking at the world, and it was as if doors and windows kept appearing and

161

opening around me. Sometimes I would have religious discussions with my new friends, who came from a variety of backgrounds. I was invited to attend Jewish services, where the prayers and songs, though mostly in Hebrew, were strikingly similar to those of my own tradition. Often it was simply a day-to-day situation that enlightened me about some new concept. Eating in the dining hall, I learned about the kosher rules that many Brandeis students keep strictly. Sometimes a hallmate would pointedly hint that she *really wished* her light were off so she could sleep, and thus I learned that some Jews may not operate anything electrical on the Sabbath, and it was against the rules to ask even a non-Jew for help. And so I have quickly acquired a budding interest in interfaith relations, which over the past two years has grown through the nourishment of countless experiences.

At times, the discoveries I made about other faiths were delightfully unexpected. I am privileged to count a Buddhist among my closest friends, and one day she was teaching me how to meditate. After this instruction, she began to explain, "Sometimes, to help us focus during meditation, we repeat a chant. Some people hold a string of beads and say one chant for each bead." Astounded, I responded, "Catholics do that, too!" Ours is called a rosary, and we say a prayer on each bead, but the purpose is the same: to help us focus on the spiritual. Looking beneath the surface differences of our religions, we found a fascinating connection.

Not only have I gained much knowledge of other faiths at Brandeis, but I have also been able to share my Catholicism with those who have not encountered it before. On Ash Wednesday, the first day of Lent (forty solemn days leading up to Easter), Catholics receive ashes on our foreheads to remind us we are entering a time of repentance and death to selfish desires. In my hometown, this practice is well known and never questioned. But I found that at Brandeis, walking around campus with a black mark on my head made me a visible target for questions about Catholic practices. Complete strangers would approach me with inquiries about Lent and the meaning of the ashes. I discovered that wearing a simple sign of my faith could open up countless discussions. It could also be a source of amusement, as it was when a girl discreetly pulled me aside, whispering, "You have some dirt on your face," and nearly did me the favor of wiping it off!

One of the most rewarding experiences is when another faith enriches my understanding of my own. Every week, Catholics receive Communion, taking bread and wine in memory of Jesus, as he requested at the Last Supper. What escaped me as an uninformed seven-year-old at my First Communion is that the Last Supper was actually a Passover Seder, the Jewish celebration of freedom from slavery in Egypt. At Brandeis, I had the opportunity to attend a Seder, and as a result I feel more connected to my religious roots.

Although interfaith communication is very rewarding, it would be misleading to leave the difficulties unmentioned. What challenges me most is the knowledge that I am the face of Christianity for many of my peers. I must do justice in representing my faith, and this responsibility can sometimes be downright scary. It is on my shoulders to dispel the stereotype that all Christians are judgmental proselytizers who believe everyone else is condemned to eternal damnation. This stereotype is not unfounded and stems mainly from two things: centuries of persecution of non-Christians by the Catholic Church and personal experiences with Christians who, though well-meaning, patronize others for their beliefs and view them simply as potential converts. I feel that I need to make an extra effort to show people that I respect their beliefs, and my priority as a Christian is to love others, not to judge and convert them.

A more specific difficulty arose when the priest sex-abuse scandal swept Boston, where my university is located. Suddenly, the faith I treasure was engulfed in shame. Many students asked tough questions, ranging from, "What do you think of the scandal?" to "Do you agree with the Church's doctrine on celibacy?" to "How did the bishops get away with

Who is wise? He who learns from all.

—SIMEON BEN ZOMA

such a cover-up?" I had to reflect and rethink a lot of my ideas. I had to come to terms with the fact that corruption in church leadership is not just a thing of the past. I had to form thoughtful answers to the questions my peers posed, and sometimes I had to admit that I didn't have all the answers.

If interfaith endeavors can be so difficult and frustrating, why bother with them? One event reminds me why. Two weeks into my freshman year, when my biggest worries were fitting in with my classmates and keeping up with the higher-caliber workload, 9/11 happened. Deeply troubled by the loss of life and fearful of what violence or war would follow, I felt that the world I knew was swept out from under me. That afternoon, the Brandeis population gathered on the library lawn for an interfaith prayer service. As Jews, Muslims, and Christians all offered up prayers, tears welled up in my eyes and I felt strangely comforted. Perhaps it was consoling to know that, although such a great act of hate had been committed that morning, on my campus there remained understanding and peace. Although thousands of lives had been lost in the name of religion, here different religions were coming together to share the burden of this tragedy. **Religious conflict is one of the leading causes of bigotry and violence in the world, and I think that somehow, when I have discussions and open up understanding with those of other faiths, I achieve a small but triumphant victory over hatred.**

UNCOMFORTABLE AND AWARE
NATHAN BLACK

Somebody once told me that he thought he would enjoy going to the funeral of a person he didn't know. I thought that was odd. More odd, though, is that I'm pretty sure I beat him to it.

This past summer I volunteered for a movement called Different Religions Week. During this week in mid-July, people were encouraged to attend a religious service of a faith different from their own. I saw the week as a valuable opportunity to make a statement of tolerance. Because I was not a complete stranger to different religious experiences, I had certain notions of how I might be affected by my time at an Islamic prayer service. I am a

Only in growth, reform, and change, paradoxically enough, is true security to be found.

—ANNE MORROW LINDBERGH

Congregationalist (liberal Protestant), but I had previously gone to Baptist services, Catholic masses, and more.

What had always struck me at such services was not a yawning gap of disparity between my creed and "the other," but instead the multitude of similarities that existed between the various denominations of Christianity. An Islamic service, I figured, would show many of the same parallels—they weren't within the bounds of Christianity that were so familiar to me, but, after all, we were worshiping the same God.

I was wrong, and I began to realize it when I decided to take my mother along with me to the mosque. She had to cover her hair and enter through a separate door. Then, when I spoke to the imam, the prayer leader, he explained that someone had died the day before and that a funeral service was now to be performed.

Nothing in his tone seemed to indicate that my mother and I should take our leave, and we had planned to go at this particular time for at least a week, so I timidly asked, "Do you mind if we participate?"

"Of course not!" assured the imam.

So in I went to a small, still room with taped lines across the carpet floor. My mother, not allowed on the ground level, went upstairs to a balcony shielded by darkly tinted glass. The women there also assured her we were perfectly welcome at the funeral service.

Then the truly disorienting part—the service itself—began. For some reason, I had never given much thought to the possibility that the prayers would be in Arabic, but most of them indeed were. As the unfamiliar words whisked through my brain, I thought to myself: What am I ever going to get out of this?

But I soon noticed what was happening. We weren't simply required to listen to the recitation of the prayers; there were also repetitive physical motions to go through as the service progressed. First we knelt, then we prostrated ourselves, then we were back on our knees, then we were standing. (The lines of tape on the floor told us where to align our toes while we did all this.)

It was without doubt a sad occasion; there was a coffin, and no one was smiling. But as I repeated the physical rituals two, three, four times, and more, I felt a sense of comfort—of routine, normalcy, and simplicity. Although there was neither the time nor the appropriate mood to talk to anyone about what I was observing, those feelings, I imagined, were similar to what the participants were "getting out" of the service in their time of grief.

After twenty minutes of prayer and motions, the coffin was driven away to a cemetery, and my mother and I drove home. The similarities between Islam and my religion, while perhaps there theologically, had not stood out to me. I had instead observed a segregation of the sexes, the use of a different language, and an unfamiliar construction of a religious service. Yet I had also seen a value in Islam that I had not appreciated before—the value of ritual simplicity and comfort.

I had certainly felt awkward, but afterward I thought: What better place to see a religion in action than at a funeral? A funeral is the service where the line between life and death is blurred, where people are sad, angry, and afraid, and where faith and spiritual solace are needed the most.

The power of a religion cannot be fully appreciated by reading a book or taking a class. Like most things in life, it has to be experienced, and for that reason I am glad an Islamic funeral service is now a part of my worldview.

Different Religions Week is held the second week in July. Please consider attending a service that will make you both uncomfortable and aware.

CHAPTER 8

SIGNIFICANT OTHERS:
FAMILY, FRIENDS, AND MENTORS

You walk out of your advisor's office and realize that you haven't felt this energized in months. You made the appointment to see whether you could add a class after the add/drop deadline. But then your advisor asked how things were going. You began talking about how invigorated you have been since you led two discussion groups at last weekend's retreat.

Your advisor asks a few more questions that help you clarify why the experience was so inspiring. She remembers that you have already taken two religious studies courses, and she suggests that you take a minor in that area. The idea of exploring religion through additional coursework had never occurred to you because you had been on a focused track to complete your business degree. She also tells you about a two-week summer study abroad opportunity that would relate to your religious studies interest. Near the end of the conversation, she mentions that you could do an honors thesis on business ethics and tie together your major and minor.

Finally, someone supports your interest in religion and even identifies it as an academic pursuit. You are thrilled, and you promise to return for another meeting soon.

Your family, of course, is already part of your life. But, you will get to make conscious choices about friends. A mentor is someone you will have to seek out. All of these people are likely to impact and influence your spiritual development and commitments.

Family

You may find that your spirituality will continue to help you stay connected with your family as your college experience inherently brings about separation. Not only might you be separated by geography, but, if you are the first in your family to go to college, your parents may also not be able to relate to your university experience. Or you may become either more liberal or more conservative than your parents as you begin to strengthen your identity. Your faith may become even more important as one of the primary means of connecting and finding common ground with your parents, siblings, and other family members.

If you and your family share a strong spiritual connection, then leaving home for college will present some tough emotional challenges. Can you find a spiritual community on campus that will give you the same source of strength as the foundation given to you by your parents? Will you choose to practice with your new community, or will you return home whenever possible?

If you are struggling to find a spiritual community on campus, then identify the elements that make your spiritual community at home so special. Perhaps you need to try a wider range of groups on campus to find one that more closely matches your beliefs and commitments. Or maybe you will be more comfortable connecting with a faith community off campus (see chapter 9). It could be that your reluctance to commit to a community on campus is really about missing your family. If that is the issue, then you would be wise to talk with a counselor on campus and explore this further. A counselor can help you retain the

No person is your friend who demands your silence, or denies your right to grow.

—ALICE WALKER

strong connection that you have with your family while also helping you feel better about being on your own.

What happens when you encounter people and ideas that challenge the beliefs you learned at home? Will you seek out or avoid people who come from traditions other than your own? How about people from your tradition who practice differently than you do? Will you choose to integrate new ideas

Promises are the uniquely human way of ordering the future, making it predictable and reliable to the extent that this is humanly possible.

—HANNAH ARENDT

into your existing framework, or will you hold fast to the principles on which you were raised? What happens if you feel yourself pulled toward new ideas? If your tradition teaches that you should embark on your own spiritual journey, then these new ideas may feel exciting. Conversely, if your tradition doesn't encourage exploration, you may feel as though you will disappoint your family if you pursue your own spiritual identity. This is a tension that many students face. Sometimes parents anticipate that their children will grow and change in unknown ways in college, and they are more accepting than we expect them to be. However, if your parents have been clear that they expect you to follow their beliefs closely, then you will have to work harder to explore, understand, and feel secure in your newfound spiritual identity.

Going home may never be more difficult than walking in that door, knowing that sometime over the break you will be telling your parents that you have converted to another faith tradition or dramatically changed the way you practice the faith tradition that they passed on to you. Other life experiences, such as coming out as gay, lesbian, bisexual, or transgendered; dating outside your faith; or getting involved with a tradition different from the one you were raised with, may also create challenges depending on your parents' religious and political views.

Trouble at Home

Going home to parents who may not support the ways you have evolved can provide a tremendous challenge. If your parents are firmly entrenched in their views, nothing will cause them to accept immediately whatever you are going to tell them; however, you can plan ahead to give yourself a safety net as you enter this difficult conversation.

Clarify your sense of self. You will speak from a stronger position if you can clearly articulate your new beliefs and identity. Some parents, upon realizing that you are making thoughtful choices, will be more accepting than if they think you are taking your faith lightly and experimenting impulsively.

Talk with others who have dealt with similar experiences. Find friends who have faced difficulty in talking with their parents and other family members. Your friends may be able to give you advice, and connecting with someone else who has gone through the same thing can be powerful and centering.

Have a friend ready to help. Know where a few of your friends will be over break and how you can reach them. You will find comfort in talking with someone accepting who knows the new you while things at home are difficult.

Check out resources in your home community. Before you leave campus, see whether your hometown or city has a faith group similar to the one you have connected with at school.

Pack a good book. Whether it's a book of spiritual readings or a biography of someone who had profound spiritual courage, a good book can provide an important refuge from tension and loneliness at home.

Deal with questions of blame. If your parents are unhappy with the ways you have grown spiritually, they may blame themselves. They may believe that they "should have raised you differently," as if taking you to church more often would have prevented you from discovering that you feel more at home in an Eastern religion. Be ready to tell your parents how you discovered this new faith tradition and why you connect with it.

Give them time. Remember that you have probably been dealing with your evolving identity for months or years, but you may be catching your family by surprise. They may say things in the heat of the moment that they will regret later. You deserve respect and shouldn't passively take in their anger. Keep in mind, however, that they will also need time to adjust.

If it all falls apart. If your parents won't accept you for who you have become, then you may choose to create your own spiritual community and support system. If your growth is in a definitive spiritual direction (if you have converted to another faith tradition, for example), then you are probably already connected with a spiritual group. Get to know the people in that group, find friends who can be a good peer group, and look for a mentor. If your growth is in a direction that alienates you from your parents and faith tradition (if you are dating outside your faith or coming out, for example), then look for more liberal communities within your tradition. Most faith traditions, even the most conservative ones, have smaller communities that deal with and accept these issues. The Internet may be your best resource to connect with these communities.

In addition, evaluate your broader support system; if it isn't strong enough, then seek to strengthen it. Are you reaching out? Talk with a supportive spiritual leader, a trusted friend, your resident assistant, an advisor, or a professional counselor. The transition you are going through takes strength, courage, and support.

Finally, if no one in your family supports the changes you are making, and particularly if your new faith group encourages you to separate from your family, then consider the new group more carefully. This group may be taking you in an unhealthy direction (see "What You Need to Know about Cultic Behaviors" in chapter 3).

Friends

So what happens when you grow in a spiritual direction that doesn't resonate for your friends? Perhaps you have moved on in a positive direction and your current friends aren't connecting with it. You may be able to regain some link by talking with them about your newfound faith. Or you may need to seek new friends who will better understand where you are headed. You should also consider your friends' feedback. If they say that you have gone too far in your new commitment, you would be wise to at least contemplate their observation. They are your friends for a reason—you connected at some point, and if you believe they got to know the real you initially, then perhaps their concerns have merit. Or you may decide that they simply don't understand and that you are confident in your choices. Keep in mind, though, that your friends' concerns may be an important red flag that you are letting yourself be controlled by others and aren't making independent, conscious choices about your faith commitments.

Also be on the lookout for "fast" friends. There are people on campus who appear to become your instant best friends, when in fact they are trying to recruit you into their tradition or organization. Real friends will not ask you to separate from other friends or family. They will respect your ideas and not demand all of your time. "Friends" who seem to take over your life in terms of time, thought, or energy may very well have their own agenda for you. Be careful.

Mentors

One of the smartest things you can do while in college is to find a mentor. Finding a mentor takes initiative and patience. Get to know your spiritual leaders, professors, advisors, coaches, deans, and other adults on campus. You can and will definitely learn from other students, but a true mentor needs to have more life experience than you have.

A good mentor will help you come to understand yourself, your values, and your goals. A good mentor will teach and inspire you by exhibiting an obvious integrity as she or he makes decisions and takes action. She or he will also exude a more subtle integrity, a consistency over time. When the chemistry is right, you will know it, because when you leave the company of your mentor, you will be energized and eager to take the next step. A mentor may also serve as part of your support system, providing a safe haven to discuss fears and concerns, and may even be someone to seek out during a crisis.

FAMILY TIES
TEJAL PATEL

It was the summer before my senior year of high school, and I hadn't looked at any colleges, because I knew that I wanted to attend the College of the Holy Cross. Long before school started, I had filled out my application, sent a release request to the College Board for my SAT scores, and had my interview at Holy Cross. After some debate and argument with my parents, I visited and applied to four other institutions on the East Coast.

The year flew by, and before I knew it, I was receiving response letters from the colleges I had applied to. I got four letters; the only one missing was the one I was waiting for. Finally, I received an envelope from Holy Cross, and as I opened it, I prayed for acceptance into the school. That's when I noticed the word *Congratulations* in bold print at the top of the letter. I had gotten in, and I was going to Holy Cross! Little did I know, I was about to enter a spiritual rollercoaster.

My parents were excited for me because they knew how fond I was of Holy Cross. However, when my grandmother heard that I was going to attend a Jesuit institution, she was disappointed in my decision. She was convinced that I would forget my religion and my faith if I was surrounded by so many people of another faith. After I explained my position to her, she put aside her fear and let me follow through with my decision to attend the College of the Holy Cross.

As a Hindu and a religious minority on the predominately Catholic campus of Holy Cross, I, like all students, was never pressured to participate in religious services. But many students, including me, find themselves in the campus chapel or at masses to seek serenity in a sacred space. I found myself going because my visits were never required and students of all faiths were welcome to attend.

Although my grandmother's insecurity about my attending a Jesuit institution was not necessary, I can certainly understand her fear. Recently, one of my closest friends and I discussed how children follow the practices and rituals of their parents' religions. As each child grows, however, it is up to her to decide whether she believes in the faith she grew up with. Until I got to college, I blindly followed the concepts that Hinduism taught. I knew the myths, and I understood the rituals that I performed as a Hindu, but there was so much I didn't know about Hinduism.

During my second semester, I got an opportunity to broaden my knowledge of my faith. In a course that was designed to study religious worlds and their interactions, I was forced to step out of my religion and take a look at it from a new perspective. I read the assigned books and listened to the lectures. I finally appreciated my faith. I grew spiritually after I spent a year away from home.

I also learned something that surprised me. While reading, if I came across something unfamiliar that I didn't understand, I automatically called my parents. Both my parents are Hindus who were born and raised in India, which is predominately Hindu, so I figured if anyone would have the answers, it would be them. To my surprise, my parents didn't have all the answers. They were following the teachings of Hinduism with just slightly more knowledge than I had!

I left school knowing that I understood so much more about Hinduism than I ever had. My parents decided that they wanted to learn about Hinduism, too, so they began reading through my books. **This new desire to learn about Hinduism has definitely brought my family together, as we attempt to open our eyes to all the information we never knew about our religion.**

Although my choice to attend Holy Cross was initially met with disapproval, I found that I have grown as a person. I've had my share of difficulties as a religious minority on campus, and I've experienced different reactions from the Hindu community regarding my decision. However, I've learned and grown spiritually and can honestly say that I am no longer blindly following; I know the myths, I know the rituals, and I know the teachings.

ROOMING WITH MOM AT CHURCH CAMP
MARIANNE SCHILER

The summer after my semester of study abroad was a hard one. Reverse culture shock is enough to deal with on its own, but I had the added bonus of moving back into my parents' house. After six months of total independence it would be an understatement to say that reentry into the role of "child" was difficult. I had grown in so many ways, and my parents had no awareness of it.

My time in Edinburgh, Scotland, had changed me. I was never the adventurous type—I always wanted to stay home and watch TV. But being dropped in another country without anyone familiar to guide me cured me of that. I turned to God for comfort, and for the first time in my life, I took the initiative to step outside my own door. I found a church and friends. I made connections that led to involvement with a swing dance club. Suddenly I was going out every weekend, if not every night, more than I ever had in the combined nineteen years of my life. By the time Easter break rolled around I was desperate to begin backpacking solo across Europe. My mother just about had a heart attack. That month of lonely travel proved to have the greatest impact of all.

And so I returned home at the end of June, having finished classes in Scotland and what felt like a lifetime of living. I had thought that I was ready to go home . . . until I got there. The people I spent time with, went dancing with, were all back in Scotland. And my mother, always a nervous woman by nature, was not about to let me go out with anyone she didn't know personally. Suddenly, having my time planned for me, after being the one in control for six months, did not go over well.

I began really looking forward to church camp, which would roll around in August. It seemed like a great idea. My parents would pay for me to visit all my friends in the Midwest, where I could essentially show off everything that I had learned and bought while I was away. True, my mom would be coming with me, but she had her own friends to occupy her. And besides, they separate the children from their parents. We would at the most run into each other at meals or adult forums.

What I had not counted on was that I was now old enough that I no longer qualified as one of the "children" (a great irony, because my mother so clearly thought I did), and someone, in a fit of perversity, assigned me to the same room as my mother, on a floor with older women who were either single or attending without their husbands. This was not what I had in mind. True, we had managed not to kill each other on the plane from California to Ohio, and truer still that the drive from Ohio to Indiana had actually yielded pleasant conversation between the two of us. That did not mean I wanted to be stuck in the same room with Mom for an entire week.

However, if there was one thing I had learned in Scotland, it was how to make the best of things. So I did, and it seemed that the best of this situation was better than what I had hoped for in my original plans. To my surprise, my mom and I actually had things in common. More than that, we had in common the most important thing in our lives: our faith—I was raised Apostolic Christian (most closely related to Mennonites). Our room became my favorite place to be, and not just for the air-conditioning. We giggled, we talked, we kept each other awake until the wee hours of the morning, discussing life and love and God. I looked forward to when we would come together and share what we learned in our classes or compare notes on a forum speaker. For a week we were equals. And we were best friends.

Then toward the end of the week, one of the camp leaders asked whether some of the younger adults would be willing to share, during the evening service, how God has worked in their lives. It meant getting up and speaking in front of the entire camp of more than three hundred people, but I volunteered anyway. I, at least, had something to share. After all, I had just been in Scotland, right? Maybe.

I spent an entire afternoon of free time writing what I would say in advance, and yet somehow I still cried when I got up on stage and started talking. I told them all about my time abroad, how I had felt that it was God that led me to my friends there. I spoke of the difficulties of returning home, and I spoke of my annoyance at discovering I would share a room with my mom at camp. And then I shared what a blessing it turned out to be. I told them how all my life my mother had shared her faith with me, and this week had been my chance to share my faith with her.

It was not surprising that my mother wept. She likes to be emotional. It was surprising that almost every parent and almost every high school- and college-aged child had tears in his or her eyes, too. I don't think my mom has ever been so proud of me as she was then. For what was left of camp she bragged to anyone who didn't know that I was her daughter. And sometimes to people who did know.

We fought again as soon as we got home, but it really didn't matter. That week changed our relationship. I'm still her baby. I'll always be her youngest of three. But now, at least, her youngest is all grown up and growing still.

MY SISTER SOPHIE
SAKIB QURESHI

I've known Sophie for a long time. I'm her brother, so it wasn't a choice. But I've really *known* her since we became good friends in high school. And in the time that she went through high school, and then made her way through college, I have been more than proud of her. She literally has reversed the tables on me, and although I am two years her elder, I now ask *her* for advice. I ask *her* for help. And I look to *her* as a role model. I never thought it would happen. Perhaps if someone had asked me whether a situation could exist where that would happen, I would acknowledge,

"Yes, it's possible, Sophie's a nice person," but I have to admit, I'm surprised. Pleasantly.

In high school, I just thought of Sophie as a good girl with a great sense of humor. At any given moment, she would explode in laughter like a *desi* hyena (*desi* is slang for Indian subcontinent "countrymen"). She especially loved any impressions of our father or mother, who, Sophie will admit, are the root of all that she thinks is funny and absurd in the world. Our dad was born and raised in Lahore, Pakistan, and is admittedly "a simple man." Our mother was born and raised in Srinagar, Kashmir. I would say she is more complex but also, in our eyes, innocent in the context of fast-paced *amrikan* culture.

"Oh yeah, Sophie *rani* (princess), she's the best one! She's always go! go! go! I like it!" My dad will say now with energetic eyes, thinking of his daughter.

Ironically, in high school, his belief in her abilities was almost perfectly stereotypical of a *desi* father. When it came time to write essays for her college applications, he handed her photocopies of all the essays I had written two years earlier.

"Sophie, reeeeeally, look at your brother's essays. He's such a good writer. Just, you know, use his ideas. He is such a good writer. Okay, *rani?*"

And he didn't see his advice as condescending or disrespectful to her abilities. He really just thought that *she* was a terrible writer and I was a much better one. Innocently. And I suppose, looking back, Sophie had to deal with a lot of innocently negative forces. Just silent cultural biases that did not seem as apparent in our household because, well, compared to many others in the *desi* community, our parents were actually quite open-minded.

But the narrowness of his thoughts about my sister definitely rose to the surface when it came to choosing a college and a career. There was a giant push for her to be a doctor, the only respectable thing for any *desi* child to do. It didn't matter that Sophie (a) hated science and (b) sucked at science.

Looking back, I realize Sophie felt that *desi* culture was oppressive to women in a lot of ways—in domestic life, professional life, and basic attitudes. Combined with the fact that we are a Muslim household, she had built a case in her head against the South Asian culture and Islam. What kind of liberation did the culture and religion offer her? My brother and I visibly received more attention, more freedom, and more support in our pursuits than she did. Spiritually, she shied away from talking about God and life and death and was repelled by thoughts of going to the mosque for prayers—a place for men, often admittedly so. The religion didn't speak to her and, in fact, she felt it neglected her. And in the Pakistani community, it seemed these assumptions were echoed by the examples of its women. Many mothers were somewhat submissive to their husbands, and often, if they had anything to say, it would fall under three main categories: their children, their gold/*shalwar kameez* (traditional dresses), and what new gossip they had on other families. Of course, that was certainly not the rule, but there were enough examples to make her case. My mother surely shared some of Sophie's sentiments as well.

Still, I don't remember Sophie ever being disrespectful or so naïve as to completely cast culture and religion aside; she kept an attitude that easily showed those around her that they were irrelevant to her. She just kept it *on the side.* She was not ready.

She fought for her right to go to college and study as she wished, and through some pain and struggle she made it to the University of Georgia and got the opportunity to prove herself. Okay, the phrase "prove herself" is probably where I'm wrong, and probably where I should focus. I don't really think she's ever really been driven by the "I'll show them!" attitude. She somehow escapes that somewhat typical motivation and instead has an attitude that resembles a philosophy based on the simple tenets of truth, love, and action. Oh, and a damn low threshold for laughter.

If I look at the way she has treated college, it is with this philosophy in mind. It is amazing to see her progress, because she literally *grows*. What is it to grow as a human being? For Sophie, she has made her life a work in progress. She lives and acts with what *she* knows. What *she* believes is right. In all honesty, the other members in our family often whispered behind her back that Sophie was "selfish." I don't really think we understood what was going on at all.

Sophie's methodology of growing was indeed a methodology based on her sense of self and what was directly known to her based on her experiences. If we tried to give her wisdom, she often would not accept it, because it was not something she could understand or at least see as a direct extension of her actions. Instead, as she moved along in life and discovered something true, she would work as hard as she could to incorporate it into her life. The easiest way to see her method of living is through her personal health and fitness. She runs. Every day. Wakes up at 6 or 7 a.m. and is off. She comes back and eats an apple. Or oatmeal. She started realizing, "Hey, meats and oils don't make me feel as good as 'healthier' foods," and she literally made no fuss and just changed her lifestyle. Immediately. No difficulties, no complaints; she simply changed, just like that.

This seems like it has nothing to do with spirituality. But it does. It completely does. With her health, she started realizing that being active and eating nutritious foods feels better, feels right, makes her life better. And so it was that she *realized* it. She made such actions her reality. And she did it with love. (A friend of hers once said that she had never wanted an apple as badly as when she saw Sophie bite into one—the utter delight in her eyes.) And this girl will rarely compromise. To revert to a different lifestyle simply does not make sense to her. "*Why would you?*" It would be illogical not to act on such truths as basic as the fact that eating right and being active make you feel better and give you more energy.

With college, living on her own, and having days replete with new experiences, new perspectives, and opportunities to learn, Sophie's growth accelerated to a point of no return. I must concede that most students have an acceleration of growth and also have such overwhelming learning experiences in school. I did, definitely. *But,* I must also admit, incorporating, applying, and living the truths that we find is such a struggle that most of us get lost along the way. Next to her, my diet, my health, the way I compromise who I will spend time with, what activities I pursue . . . I can see it is often *so far away* from what I know to be true of life and, more important, true of myself. And when I look at how simply Sophie lives her truths, I cannot help but feel silly in how complicated I make the route from *me* to *being me.*

Sophie began holding truth and love as paramount and illusion and hurt as things to avoid as simply as possible. We all wonder how she began her studies in international relations. It would be easy to connect the dots between her international background and her growing passion for resolving the differences in Kashmir, Pakistan, and India, nations she naturally feels connected to. And indeed, I think that was how she became interested. She believes people should be true to one another, be loving and selfless with one another, and uplift one another through humor and goodwill. I cannot but speculate that she subconsciously chose the most challenging field, where illogical actions and relationships cause pain and suffering throughout the world.

I think what most amazes me about Sophie is how she effortlessly realized her connection with God, with piety, and with Islam. I suppose it makes sense, in that she was on a path toward having a one-on-one connection with herself and subsequently found that she felt seamlessly connected with others. She believes in the simplicity of action upheld by the oneness of heart and mind, as well as in the sanctity of life. It was only natural that she began to see that the great spiritualities of the world uphold the very same devotions. Sophie loves the great Sufis who imbibe truth and live as truthfully as they possibly can. I've seen Sophie be in such awe of the beauty of these people that she is brought to tears. I've seen Sophie be in such awe of my mother and father— their struggles and sacrifices—that she sheds tears and increases her resolve to be all that she can be. And then she'll have a damn good laugh at how funny it

> *A person who says "I'm enlightened" probably isn't.*
> —RAM DASS

is that she is madly in love with such cliches. A Sufi teacher will often say, in fact, that a sense of humor is a prerequisite to spirituality. You *must* be able to LET GO in order to submit to truth.

Yes, I'll take a minute to say that I realize how far I've claimed Sophie has traveled in a few short strides in college—from eating an apple to finding God. Sounds ridiculous. And I swear, I can see that it does in fact sound ridiculous. But it actually is so logical. Acquire truth. Live truth. And soon, you are truth. **The search for truth is what people say is indeed the hardest, most challenging aspect of life. But, from knowing my sister, I say:** *Just live the truth that you know, and once you've done that, more truths will follow.* I could certainly find a million and one quotations that say the same thing. I could find a million and one great human beings who may have done the same things. But there's no need to be redundant. Or repetitive. Or to dwell on "the name of action" in the face of truth. That's so silly.

PRAYING FOR AN EXTENSION:
THE BORDER BETWEEN FAITH AND NECESSITY
JOSHUA GRUENSPECHT

I've heard the one—you probably have, too—about the student who goes off to college to find the truth. He's a starry-eyed child of the Lord carrying the Holy Word in his breast pocket. Or she's a hard-nosed atheist who's seen it all and wants to know the reasons. So he realizes that his roommates speak holy words he never knew, and she finds out that science never promised all the answers. Classic stuff, that.

Unfortunately, this isn't that story. I went to college confused and came out just as confused, but with better hair. There was no great awakening, no spiritual crisis, and no fantastic late-night conversation that opened the skies and rained down enlightenment. O my brothers and sisters in youthful confusion, I've come to share that lack of enlightenment with you here tonight! I want to bring you closer to my absence of comprehension! I want to lead you into indecision! Can someone give an Amen? Or not, that's fine, too.

A few snapshots of understanding made me happier than a lavishly produced feature film of the truth. Although I also had friends who experienced revelation and who buttressed their faith in ways they wouldn't have imagined. I've stuck to Judaism mostly because otherwise I might have to use terms like "Eucharist," which I still don't exactly grasp, but most of my friends in college weren't Jewish, and there are plenty of good stories there, too. Especially the one about the inflatable Buddha.

With fair warning, then, here are the Commandments of Collegiate Faith (keeping in mind always the First Commandment of Collegiate Composition: never turn in Ten Commandments when Seven will do).

1. **Hang out with all sorts of people from all sorts of faiths. All sorts of revelations will follow.** Depending on your school, your hair can say at least as much as your religion does about how you want to be perceived. For most of college, I wore shoulder-length hair that was chopped rarely, if at all. Even when it was cut, it listed slightly to one side. For a short time, I also sported a beard like a scrawny patch of seaweed. I wanted to be perceived as fashion-impaired and faintly piratical.

   At one point, I dropped in on a friend of mine, an evangelical Christian. He wasn't exactly in a state of perfect sobriety. As he rolled over to the door to greet me, he looked up in momentary wonder and remarked on my resemblance to Jesus.

   Why not, I pointed out to him. Named Joshua, scion of a Jewish family, coming of age at the dawn of the new millennium. Coincidence? Or a hint of predestination?

   "If you're my messiah," he said, "I quit."

   He was right, though I would never have noticed. It was the Jesus 'do, except that even cutting his hair with carpenter's tools Jesus could have done a better job.

2. **Just because it's a place for your people doesn't mean it's a place for you**. If you don't know who your friends are by halfway through sophomore year, you may want to consider a transfer.

Three semesters have gone by; you've had your second chance at a new beginning. You have a fairly good idea about who will keep you going and who you wouldn't trust to get wet in the rain. There are places you want to hang out and places that aren't your style.

Halfway through sophomore year, I was stuck in a place that was emphatically not for me with a bunch of people who I was pretty sure were not going to be my friends. The campus Jewish center was having a Seder, and, because I wasn't joining my family until the following night, I tagged along with some acquaintances to get into the spirit of the season.

"Are you a freshman?" asked one of my tablemates almost immediately. "I don't think we've seen you here before." I owned up to sophomore status and mentioned I'd been down for lunch a few times. "But have you come to services?" she pressed. I hadn't. "Oh, well!" she said, "We'll have to make sure you have a good time tonight!" And the hunt was on.

For the rest of the evening, as we sang unfamiliar tunes with familiar words, I sat uncomfortably deciphering the placemats and monopolizing the wine. It was that party at the house of a friend of a friend of a friend, where all of a sudden everyone is discussing currency devaluation and you're desperately looking for an exit. Every time I pushed a topic out onto the table, it became fodder for an ongoing discussion of personal responsibility to God. These were people who took their religion very seriously, and I didn't have the background to take part. Occasionally, there would be a throwaway line about something discussed in Torah study last week or in the sukkah some time back. The implicit sales pitch—be all that you can be! Join up! Go Torah!—may have been well-meaning, but by late in the dinner, the atmosphere was dense and airless. Thoroughly claustrophobic, I made my excuses and escaped to a spiritually unaffiliated dining hall.

3. **Then again, your people might be pretty cool. Hey, you're one of them.** I quietly made a promise not to return to the center for

another holiday gathering. As it turned out, I broke it more than once. I was invited the next year, on Purim, to drop by a concert by the Klezmer Band. Klezmer, a traditional form of eastern European Jewish music influenced by jazz in its most recent incarnations, had never made an impression on me, but I knew a couple of the band members and needed to catch a concert once before leaving.

I was standing against a wall in the back when it began. High-spirited, reckless music, bursting with brass, caught me off guard. It was music for dancing and celebrating, and not far into the first song, a few of the spectators in the front threw down their shoes and swung onto the parquet floor in front of the band. I had planned to slip in and slip out without partaking in the dance, but the freewheeling tune swept all of us up. After a few songs, almost nobody was still seated. Inexperience and inelegance were irrelevant. We would leave the floor flushed, only to rejoin the circle a few minutes later.

That night I left with a buzz that lasted for hours, or would have had I not come home and found that someone had thrown up in our shower. Don't drink and dance.

4. **Define and redefine your commitments to your religion on your own terms; if you don't, angry people with purpose will be more than happy to define them for you.** Over four years, there were at least ten extracurricular activities that claimed sizable chunks of my time. I edited a newspaper, wrote book reviews, juggled, and performed music, but only one group sent me e-mail from the week I arrived to the week I left. And I never attended a single meeting or responded to a single message.

A high school associate who had preceded me by a year was a big shot in the Yale Friends of Israel, a group whose raison d'être was authoring angry letters to the editor whenever the Arab-Israeli conflict came up in campus conversation. Entering the freshman bazaar as fresh meat, I tried desperately to pretend I hadn't seen her, but campus gadflies learn quickly not to take no for an answer. She slipped out from behind her table and placed her ninety-some-pound frame in my path.

"Hey!" she said, with the bright and brittle telemarketing voice used universally to reel in freshmen, "sign up for YFI!" It couldn't possibly have been mistaken for a question.

"Er, what's it all about?" I asked, discreetly searching the crowd for an exit.

She slurred her lengthy pitch into near incomprehensibility and proffered a clipboard: "Don't worry, Israeli rights, you'll get the e-mail, hear all about it, Mondays and Thursdays, sign here."

"The Israelis bear at least a little responsibility for some of the problem, too, though, I mean, uh . . . " I trailed off into a mumble as her eyes blazed up. Not the right response. She sped up to a hummingbird whine of irate didacticism, "How could you say the Western Wall and settlements bombing over 90 percent of small children with Yasir Arafat and guns over the Gaza Strip and American support democratic solidarity . . . " The real Jews, I was given to understand, were the ones who stood up and were counted. Blinking and retreating, I scrawled a name and left in a hurry.

I let them count me on the membership rolls for four years. I had been manipulated into signing up. And I would have resented it, except, well, the internal sniping on the mailing list was pretty amusing. You can never have too much comedy in your inbox.

5. **Maintain a careful balance between upsetting your family and neglecting your school.** The Metro-North railroad ran to Grand Central, always a thrill at holiday time. From there, the unwary rider had to fight his way down the escalator, hop the shuttle to Times Square, take the A train to 175th street, get out and walk to the George Washington Bridge bus terminal and catch a cab across the bridge to Fort Lee.

My first year in college, I went to my grandparents' for Rosh Hashanah using that route. When I started college, they had been thrilled that I had chosen a school so convenient to New York, and I assumed that I would be down for all the holidays. But that weekend, I was in the middle of my first set of midterms, negotiating a new girlfriend, writing two newspaper articles at once, and I hadn't slept the previous night. I fell asleep between dinner and dessert, then made my way back to New Haven the same night to keep working.

Initially, I felt like I was letting the family down by showing up tired, unshaven, and incoherent. Soon I realized that if coherence were their ideal, they'd have adopted a new grandkid a while back. What I needed to think about was keeping sane. I started looking for ways to save time on the trip, negotiating a terminal pickup, or a ride to Grand Central. And, occasionally, I didn't make it down. But I'd always show up for the next holiday, just to make sure no one missed the familial bonding involved in seeing me fall asleep in the soup.

6. **If you feel like you've been excluded, you're always within your rights to complain really loudly.** The agonizingly appropriately named Yale Glee Club holds an annual Christmas concert in which they exhume several turn-of-the-century Christmas carols collected by the New Haven Choral Society. And truth be known, they're some of the best arguments for Christianity I know. These are songs that malls could never play, because people would stop to listen instead of purposefully striding around buying portable massagers and cheese platters, and soon Christmas would be in ruins.

Nevertheless, a member of the choir asked why the club sang only Christmas songs. **We were a multicultural university, filled with preppy liberal angst, weren't we? Where was the love for the good fifth of the choir that was Jewish? Where were the Chanukah songs?**

The director hemmed and hawed and brought out the traditional argument in full regalia. Of course, the real answer is that there are no Chanukah songs. Chanukah, for generations, was a holiday in the same way that Columbus Day is a holiday. I'd offer the Christian equivalent, but I wouldn't know it. Proximity to Christmas boosted it into at least welterweight contention, but even most Jews would be stuck singing:

Oh, dreidel, dreidel, dreidel
I made it out of clay

And something something something
And then I get to play.

(Uncomfortable Silence.)

OH . . . dreidel, dreidel, dreidel . . .

But this particular member was not to be dissuaded and suggested a number of possible celebratory songs appropriate to the season. And in the following year's concert, a traditional Jewish number was somehow found and added to the repertoire. Maybe it was a token gesture, but watching those kids try in vain to spit their way through a mouthful of Hebrew consonants, well, it just made me feel all warm and fuzzy inside.

7. **You can't win an argument with a street preacher.** If you have enough time to start down this road, you aren't studying enough.

Remember that college is just one step along the way. Prepare to question yourself there, but don't think you'll have all the answers four years later. If you do, though, send me a postcard. I'd like to read them.

ON FRIENDSHIP AND FINDING GOD
SARAH KELLER

The night before I went to college, I wrote myself a long letter in my brand-new journal. The journal was a graduation gift, leather and bound with gold binding, and my name was even engraved on the side. I knew that the journal would be something that I would always keep, and I wanted to remember what I was thinking when I took that step forward from adolescence to independence. That's really what I thought college was—a step away from every ignorance and insecurity that coupled itself with "coming of age" toward a limitless existence of understanding and knowing.

"Dearest of all dear sweet little Sarah Jane Cecilia," I wrote fondly, "this is what you know, here, on August 30th." I wrote for pages about the lessons I had taken from high school, advice, well wishes, and challenges. Among them, "Never settle; write more songs," and maybe the most important, "Work harder to find a strong spirituality." There is one little sentence that has since become foreboding, a single line where I reminded myself, *"And watch out for Lacey."*

Lacey was my best friend. Have you ever had a best friend—I mean, a true best friend, not just an acquaintance or a very funny partner in crime, but a person with whom you feel an inexplicable equality, a connection that can't be fully explained but only envied? Lacey was the real deal, a friend I'd follow to the ends of the Earth in a rickety raft. She was a girl I admired, a girl who always seemed to have the right thing to say even in the most terrible situations, the one who always had a date for every dance. I was one of the first friends she made in high school, and I was in awe of her. She encouraged me to speak up in my classes, to talk to that surfer with the green backpack that I had a crush on, to start writing poems. By the time we were sixteen, she knew by the way I was walking whether my day was going all right, and I knew by the pitch of her loud laughter whether or not it was genuine. It isn't enough to say just that we always watched out for each other, because what we did was so much more than that. At that tender teenage time when it was so hard to be proud or sure of ourselves, we were proud and sure of each other. We shared every success and every failure, taking the highs and the hits as they came and went. It was empowering to be around her, because it honestly felt like together we could take on the world . . . and win.

When I wrote that letter to myself the night before college started, I wasn't as afraid as most other kids would have been, because Lacey had decided to go to the same school. I'd be starting off college with my faithful sidekick, and I felt optimistic about how wonderful the next few years would be. In retrospect, it is almost humorous how ready I thought I was for this freedom, how easy I thought this new challenge would be. Finally I was in college! I would become the master of my fate! I had some lofty questions that deserved loftier answers than I could offer in my youth, but college meant that I was an adult now. I was going to start taking these questions, and taking myself, very seriously. Yes, I thought that I would look the hard questions straight in the eye until I solved them. I honestly thought that every problem or query *could* be solved, logically, like a math equation. I was determined, with an unrestrained idealism, that my first act as an adult would be to find "God." Oh, I'd find him all right . . . and figure him out as best I could. I resolved to be a religious studies major, almost thinking that my professors would hand out helpings of faith along with their syllabi. When I finished my letter that night, I turned off the lights and slept like a baby. School would be the realization of all my dreams; nothing could go wrong. And after all, Lacey would be there, as she'd always been there, if I needed any help.

So school started. Lacey and I settled in to our different dorm rooms and different schedules. For a while, everything went well. I was making what I thought was considerable headway on my quest to pinpoint faith, and she was off on quests of her own. We both were making friends. But then the seasons started to change, and Lacey got "sick." It wasn't the flu, or chicken pox, or cancer. It was a fight she'd always been fighting, valiantly, since I'd known her . . . a quiet battle against some genetic chemical imbalance in her brain that made her world seem sad. Almost no

> *Opinion has caused more trouble on this earth than all the plagues and earthquakes.*
>
> —VOLTAIRE

one in our high school had known the full extent of her struggles with depression, but she'd told me in the kind of confidence that had characterized our closeness. *"And watch out for Lacey."*

Sure, she'd had attacks of depression before, but they seemed to be getting stronger and stronger, and more and more serious. She would call sobbing at 2 a.m. She would break down in the middle of classes. I stopped sleeping, tried to spend all my time with her, and prayed incessantly that wherever God was, He would appear and ease whatever pains were making her cry all the time, were making her so critical of herself. I couldn't understand what was upsetting her, and she couldn't explain. Day after day, nothing I said or did seemed to help her. I noted, with a sense of profound despair, that my invitations for God to show himself were being either not received well or simply ignored. And even though Lacey tried time and time again to assure me that I shouldn't be so hard on myself because of the whole thing, that it wasn't my fault, I couldn't help feeling responsible for her condition. She was my best friend. Have you ever had a best friend? You feel like it's your job to take care of her, even though sometimes you can't. I thought that I could solve her grief somehow, that if I looked at the problem for long enough its answer would come to me . . . like a math equation. *"And watch out for Lacey."*

For such a long time I'd been looking forward to college's independence, but every night I'd wish I were six again, being tucked safely to sleep by my mom after she'd read me my favorite bedtime story. The first big thing my adulthood had made clear was not God's precise location but that Lacey's sadness was too real for me to bear. I felt colossally alone, too far from my parents, devoid of the understanding that had marked my relationship with Lacey, and deserted by God. I stopped looking for him because I stopped believing I could find him. I questioned his existence, and for the first time in my life, not even a full year into my "adulthood," I was at a real loss for something I'd taken for granted when the days seemed sunnier and life was easier: faith.

You know, everyone comes to a first time when she realizes,

When the student is ready, the master appears.

—ZEN BUDDHIST PROVERB

rather embarrassingly, that she has been defeated, that something is bigger than her hands can rework. It is an essential part of growing up, coming to accept that you cannot always "fix" everything, right everything, and do everything on your own. I was defeated when I suggested that Lacey leave school, head home, and get some serious help. I hated that I couldn't be that serious help she so needed. I was defeated when she packed her dorm room back into the cardboard boxes it had come from, and defeated at all of her good-bye parties as she smiled for flash photographs and promised to keep in touch with the girls from her hall. I was a miserable person, an idealist who'd lost her idealism, a little girl who'd somehow grown out of her chance to be uninvolved, a young woman who was losing her best friend. The five months of Lacey's sickness had convinced me that God could not exist, because He was cruel if He did. I was angry at Him, more so than I knew how to handle. I thought that saying good-bye to Lacey the day she left would do nothing but reassure me of how right I was not to have faith.

Just the opposite. When I was hugging her in my room right before she left for the airport, I remembered all the other times I'd hugged her, or she'd hugged me. She had always been there to hug me right when I needed it most—when I was a mess when my heart was broken by that surfer with the green backpack, when I got an A on the big English paper, when I lost the student council election. When I hugged her that night and she was saying good-bye, I almost wished that I never had to let go of her, that I could hold her long enough until she had all the strength I had inside of me, until she was okay again, until she was happy. But instead, I just found myself telling her that I'd miss her. "You're going to get better," I said, "you're going to be just fine."

That's when it happened; I realized that I'd been wrong in saying I was faithless. I believed what I was telling her, I believed it with my whole heart. I had faith that she would recover, and that Something would be watching her footsteps in my absence—that Something already was watching, because I could really feel for the first time that it was the right decision to send her home, even though it was the hardest. Through my sniffles, I was peaceful for the first time in months, thinking about what a journey she had ahead of her, thinking of how her laugh would sound when she rediscovered her happiness. *"And watch out for Lacey."*

You know, human beings live their lives entirely based on small helpings of faith. When we go to sleep every night, we do so with the faith that we'll be met in the morning by a new sunset and a different day. When we find ourselves crippled by tragedy, we persevere with whatever courage we can because we have faith that our pain will lessen in its due time. It's easy now to look back on the night I wrote myself the letter and know what I *should* have said. I should have sat there and told myself and the journal with the crisp new pages not to expect only knowledge and concreteness from college but also bursts of uncontrollable laughter and nights of unprecedented tears. "Sweet little Sarah Jane Cecilia," I should have written, "know that you will sometimes meet with difficulty, because being an adult is not about easiness, and wisdom was never won simply. You cannot always answer questions in the definite terms that comfort you in their definitiveness . . . and you might not find 'God' as easily as you expect to. **Following your faith may lead you many places, though possibly never to a single solitary point like the one you think you'd be most satisfied with, but having faith in your fight for faith is the best you can hope for. Don't give up so easily . . . that is a sign of faith. Love in spite of adversity . . . that is a sign of faith.**" If only my letter had said that, if only I'd known to say that. "Watch out for Lacey, and trust that there will be a sunrise," I should have ended it, with a drawn heart and my name signed underneath.

THE BUDDHIST GODFATHER
LODRÖ RINZLER

I grew up with two Buddhist parents and never considered my religious beliefs to be anything other than an offshoot of theirs. I attended talks and sat there quietly, pretending to meditate at times, and generally looking forward to any social atmosphere afterward where I could hang out and act semisophisticated. Because I expressed such an interest in the teachings my parents attended, they decided when I was eleven years old that I was ripe to attend my own weekend retreat. I'm not quite sure what they were thinking, dropping a shy eleven-year-old off at a Buddhist retreat center in the middle of downtown Manhattan, but they made sure I had someone to take me out to lunch and gave me a hug good-bye. I found myself confronted with an intense retreat. Needless to say, I was left blown away and feeling incredibly groundless (which some people might consider the best time to meditate and receive teachings).

At that moment, Eric Spiegel walked into my life. I had known him as a family friend and met him on several occasions, but in this case Eric had taken on leading the weekend retreat, and he became my first Buddhist teacher. The retreat was incredible. I remember long portions of the talks he gave on my inherent basic goodness, his incredible warmth and sincerity, and how he manifested the teachings he presented. **I left the retreat feeling just as groundless as I had before but more confident in my own meditation practice; most important, I had found that Buddhism was my own path, not just my parents'.** My parents encouraged me to attend further retreats of a similar nature, but none was as good as Eric's presentation of the teachings.

I saw Eric infrequently after that, but he became a strong presence in my life again when I was eighteen, shortly after I had gotten into a near-fatal car accident that left me emotionally shaken and, once again, groundless. I had fled to a Buddhist retreat center in Vermont and was working on staff there when a visiting teacher came to lead a program I was interested in. I took a few days off work and registered for the weekend retreat, and sure enough, Eric was the visiting teacher. I had little time with Eric that weekend, as he was often in staff meetings, but I finally caught him at the end of the retreat as he was humbly doing the dishes from the reception we had just had. I related to him the awful occurrence that had gone down just a few weeks before, how shaken I was, how glad I was to be living at Karme Choling, the Buddhist center, and how much better I was feeling because of it. "Hmm . . . " he lamented as he dried a glass, "that does sound yucky. Are you okay?" I nodded. "Well . . . good." And that was that. It was at this moment I realized that Eric would never overly indulge me and that I had found a true spiritual friend. Eric knew when I needed a shoulder to cry on, and in this case, I was fine and just showing off my experiences, and he would have none of it.

The following summer, I had tentatively planned to sit a two-month meditation and study retreat in Colorado. I was terrified to go, and so I called up Eric, hoping that he would talk me out of it. "Eric, I'm having some doubts about this retreat," I offered. "What doubts?" He sounded unimpressed. "Well, what if I don't really connect with the teacher there?" The retreat I was about to attend bound me to the teacher in a guru/student relationship, and I wasn't sure whether I was ready for such a commitment! "I think you should go." I tried several tactics to work my way out of it, but Eric knew that in my heart I was dedicated to going, and he wouldn't let me evade that feeling. Eric ended up teaching a class during the two-month retreat, and the highest compliment I received during that time was from another teacher who introduced me as the "student who will follow Eric Spiegel until he becomes just as amazing a teacher." Eric was an amazing teacher; his words connected with my heart each time he presented the teachings. He always made time for me during this retreat as well, feeling that I was struggling during the retreat and offering his shoulder this time. I got to know him as a person and understand the teachings I had studied so hard through his very presence.

Sometime around then Eric became my Buddhist godfather, an

interesting term because Buddhism does not include a god. It was my parents' idea, and an indication that Eric was a very kind mentor to me, someone who I learned from just by watching his interactions with people. I admire his warmth and generosity, while acknowledging his basic humanity. I have seen him frustrated, upset, angry, and yet still hold his heart open for all to see. My biggest privilege in my relationship with Eric was when I was able to host him at my school last year. I had organized an introductory meditation retreat on my college campus, the same one I had sat when I was eleven, and had asked Eric to lead it. His words were still pure, his meaning true, and the fourteen participants fell for Eric just as I had nine years before.

AN ALPHABET OF ADVICE: YOU AND YOUR MENTOR

Mentors are people who can help you move toward a goal. They can help you consider alternative routes you might follow and help you select a good one. Because they have traveled along similar paths, you can benefit from their experiences and insights into challenges you will meet as you move forward. Mentors can help you recognize landmarks along the way, ensuring that you continue in the right direction to reach your destination.

The mentoring relationship can be defined in many ways and in many contexts. My view is that, in all cases, it is about dialogue, meaningmaking, and personal growth. The term *dialogue,* as used by philosophers Hans-Georg Gadamer, Karl Jaspers, and Martin Buber, involves the participants being actively engaged in a mutual effort to seek meaning and truth/s.

Your mentor will engage you in meaningful dialogue to assist, stimulate, and support your efforts. Exploring questions with your mentor will help you reflect more deeply and probe ideas, beliefs, and goals. You will find that during your struggle for clearer, deeper, and broader knowledge, awareness, and better-defined convictions, you will clarify your beliefs and values and you will come to understand yourself better. If this work is accomplished during the mentoring partnership, it will be reflected in decisions and choices that genuinely express your personal intellectual and spiritual commitments. However, a mentor can only point out the path; it is up to you to travel it. Here are a few tips for developing a productive mentoring partnership:

- **Action:** After careful thought about your choice, take the initiative and discuss with a prospective mentor that you would like to establish and maintain a mentoring relationship.

- **Brain:** Bring yours to all meetings! Responsive, active listening shows you are giving your complete attention to the interaction.

- **Communication:** Lots of it—before, during, after—nurtures the mentoring relationship and keeps it productive. Ask questions, expand on ideas offered, and let the mentor know you are considering carefully what is said.

- **Development:** Ideally, the mentoring relationship evolves gradually from teacher-student to colleague-colleague and, perhaps, to lasting friendship.

- **Education:** Help your mentor learn about your skills, capabilities, ideas, and goals; this understanding is crucial for effective mentoring.

- **Follow-up:** Keep your mentor informed about pertinent activities, progress, achievements, and areas in which you need assistance.

- **Gratitude:** No need to overdo it, but we all like to hear occasionally that our efforts have been useful, valuable, and appreciated.

- **Humor:** This is the oil that lubricates any relationship; it alleviates the intensity, seriousness, and purposefulness that are hallmarks of a mentoring relationship.

- **Information sharing:** Exchanging information about interests, expertise, and experience enriches the relationship and centers it on what each partner can best contribute.

• **Judgment:** Use it! Selecting appropriate objectives and means of achieving them is central to using the mentoring process well.

• **Kindness:** This value from both partners characterizes a good relationship; disagreement and criticism can be expressed honestly and helpfully, without rancor.

• **Limits:** The mentoring relationship should be focused effectively; good mentors are busy people who appreciate efficient use of their time.

• **Mutuality:** Your mentor is giving a lot to you; what can you give in return?

• **Negativity:** This is a no-no; a positive attitude in approaching problems will elicit respect, as well as assistance, from your mentor.

• **Outcomes:** Keep your mentor fully aware of results originating from the work you have done together; mentors welcome evidence of progress.

• **Preparation and promptness:** Set the tone for productive dialogue at meetings.

• **Quality work:** In other words, don't waste your mentor's time with half-hearted efforts.

• **Responsibility:** Accept it!

• **Study:** Be conscientious, research ideas, and bring new learning to each meeting.

• **Tact:** Courtesy facilitates discussion, builds a positive relationship, and generates good references.

• **Unity:** You and your mentor are working together; disloyalty, harsh criticism, backbiting, or mockery kill cooperation.

• **Victories:** Your successes are immensely meaningful to your mentor, so share the joy and, maybe, some of the credit.

- **Willingness to work:** Show it! This is the foremost quality a mentor looks for when deciding to take on the role.

- **Xenophobia:** This is totally unacceptable because precisely what your mentor is trying to do is broaden your horizons.

- **Yield:** For a mentor, the primary reward that makes the mentoring effort worthwhile is your progress.

- **Zest:** This is the enthusiastic dynamic that makes a good mentoring partnership fulfilling and fun.

—ROBERTA BELDING O'CONNOR, INSTRUCTOR,
ECKERD COLLEGE

CHAPTER **9**

TAKING IT OFF CAMPUS

You walk into the community food pantry for the first time. You've been assigned to help stock shelves, and so you begin.

There is that moment when you stop to think about what you are really doing. It's easy to get lost in the rhythm of unpacking and shelving bottles of shampoo. It's boring, and yet there is a cadence to it, and your mind wanders back to school. But when you really stop and think about it, you are amazed that someone who comes to this food pantry next week will be grateful to get a bottle of shampoo. Previously, when you thought of soup kitchens and food pantries, you thought about people in line to get a hot meal, and that was troubling enough. But your work at the pantry has made you realize all those other things you take for granted—soap, toothbrush and toothpaste, toilet paper, and so on. Imagine not being able to get clean.

When you are captured by these thoughts, you begin to feel sad. These problems—hunger and homelessness and poverty—are so big; is stocking this shelf with shampoo really going to make a difference? But then you remember the wisdom passed down through the words of the elders of your faith tradition: that it isn't up to you to solve all of the world's problems, but it is up to you to do your part. Although you remain disturbed by the reality in front of you, you also take comfort in knowing that you are making a difference. It may be a small difference, but fact is, someone will have shampoo next week, and you helped make it happen.

You stop to marvel at how your spiritual commitments led you to the pantry. You felt a tug at your heart each week when your community's prayers mentioned helping to feed the hungry. And so you finally decided to take action, and you volunteered two hours a week on Saturdays. And now, as the reality of those dealing with poverty hits you even harder, you draw on your faith to keep going.

Community service is one endeavor that gets you off campus as you put your spiritual commitments into practice. There are many other reasons you may venture away from campus, some that have spiritual issues at their core, such as finding a community with whom to pray or meditate. Or your motivation for going off campus may not be primarily spiritual—you may be looking for a job or decide to sing in a choir or choose to advise a youth group. Regardless of why you are stepping out into the larger local or global community, you will encounter exciting opportunities to get to know yourself better and further connect with your faith.

Searching for a Faith Community

Whether the campus faith groups fail to meet your needs or you are looking to add to your spiritual involvements, off-campus faith communities can give you a wider range of possibilities. Certainly, if your campus does not feature a group from your faith tradition, your only option may be to look off campus. Some students find a spiritual home on campus, yet still seek to connect with an off-campus group. Praying and meditating with a community faith group puts you in the company of a more diverse collection of people. Rather than being surrounded by people who are stressed at the same time you are about midterms or finals, you are surrounded by people celebrating births, weddings, and other life-cycle moments. This can be a refreshing change of pace from the intense world of academic work.

Finding a faith community off campus may also give you the opportunity to enhance your study or practice through adult education classes, retreats, and the like. Or you can spend time with kids and perhaps make some extra cash by teaching religious school or advising a youth group. Talented musicians also find an outlet through singing or playing in their spiritual community. Getting involved as a musician or a teacher off campus may seem a bit daunting, but almost any faith group will be glad to have you. Pick up a phone book and start calling around. Introduce yourself and offer your skills and experience, then offer to drop off a resume that substantiates your teaching or performing experience, and before you know it, you'll have a new home away from home.

WALK DOWN TO THE COFFEE SHOP AND TAKE A LEFT: FINDING A FAITH COMMUNITY OFF CAMPUS

Okay, so you get to college and decide that—unlike some folks you know—you don't want your faith to go into a coma for four years. There are some good things happening on campus, but you're thinking of maybe exploring some worship and involvement opportunities *off* campus. The options are there; what are the advantages? For starters:

- **You get to meet older adults who don't know your parents or your history.** They don't remember when you burned the drapes at the Chanukah feast. You have a clean slate. You can be whatever you want to be, and they'll probably love you anyway.

- **You're not just another student in an off-campus, multigenerational, microcosm-of-the-world faith fellowship.** You bring a diversity, a depth, and a difference that will enrich a lot of other people, as you are enriched by them.

- **You make financially helpful contacts.** I'm not talking filthy lucre or anything here, just opportunities to earn some money babysitting or pet-watching or get a home-cooked meal just for being a nice person.

- **You get a new perspective.** They don't call the campus a "bubble" for nothing. There are more voices, new songs, and different keys in community-wide fellowship. For even more perspectives, try visiting several groups—some of your own tradition, some of another, if you want to be challenged above and beyond.

- **You get to be the big kid.** Those middle schoolers really need someone to affirm them. There's no extra time commitment; just remember their names the next time you see them. They'll look up to you. And you'll feel good about it.

Now that you've decided to try an off-campus faith community, how do you find one? How about:

- **Ye Olde Yellow Pages.** It could be simple: only one Reform synagogue in the county. It could be hard: fifty-two Baptist churches in the city. It could be harder: NO mosques in the whole area! But it's a place to start.

- **Your student affairs or campus ministries office.** Let's face it— these guys get paid to know the answers to your questions. See whether they're earning their money.

- **E-mails to faculty, staff, and other students.** You could even end up with a ride! And make some new friends. Or other perks— what if the director of financial aid goes to meditation group each week and is delighted that you want to join her? Now, how could she show her gratitude . . .

- **Your home spiritual leader.** Many denominations have national college groups that track students and offer ways to keep them involved. One of those is to help you find local faith communities that welcome and encourage college students.

College is the time for challenges, for changes. Try out some new things in the form of off-campus faith communities. See how they work. You don't have to wear them forever. But you do have to keep your soul forever, so give it some attention.

—MONA BAGASAO, CHAPLAIN AND DIRECTOR
OF CAMPUS MINISTRIES, ECKERD COLLEGE

Community Service

Most colleges offer a wide range of opportunities to get involved in community service. Finding a community service experience that is a good fit for you is vital in terms of making a meaningful commitment that you can fulfill. You may want to start by clarifying which issue calls to you. Think about spiritual readings you have done, sermons and teachings you have heard, discussions with others— which issue has most touched you? Next, look within. What skills do you have to offer and are you most comfortable using? Do you see yourself working behind the scenes or with people? Do you want work related to your planned profession or something totally different? Do you want work that is physically, emotionally, or intellectually demanding? If you want to work with people, what demographic appeals to you? How much time do you have and how often? Are you someone who would best fulfill a commitment to be somewhere for two hours once a week throughout the academic year? Or would you be better off, given your other commitments, to wait and volunteer over a break period?

How do you want your service commitment to connect with your spirituality? Is this connection a private thing for you—you just want to do the service and know that you are guided by your spiritual commitments? Or, at the other end of the spectrum, do you want to serve with other people of your faith and pray or meditate as part of your volunteer experience?

Answering these questions will help you make a smart choice about your

All labor that uplifts humanity has dignity and should be undertaken with painstaking excellence.

—MARTIN LUTHER KING JR.

service commitment. There are people on campus who can then help you find a service opportunity to match the commitment you are looking to make. Ask someone from the campus faith center or a student organization to advise you, particularly if you want your service to happen in a faith-specific context. Most colleges also have a volunteer office or community service coordinator, someone in the residence life or student activities area who can help you connect with service opportunities. Your city or town may also have a volunteer center.

Finally, if you have been too busy to serve and find yourself "stuck," as in not growing spiritually, try to carve out some time to serve. It will bump your thinking in ways that are likely to present you with new questions and a change in perspective that will rekindle your spiritual self.

Study Abroad

Although heading off campus to find a faith group or perform community service both have a spiritual mission at their core, study abroad is, for most students, a different sort of endeavor. Study abroad may be motivated by a spiritual quest, but more often it is driven by a wish to add a specific element to your academic studies or attain immersion in a new and different culture. Nonetheless, study abroad presents its own set of issues relating to spiritual development and practice.

If you are already strongly rooted in your spiritual tradition and have chosen a study abroad destination, chances are you have thought about the implications of your choice. But if you haven't considered finding a faith community abroad, then you may want to do some homework ahead of time. Ask members of your campus faith community, particularly staff, whether they have recommendations for finding a community. You can also contact officials at the campus where you will be doing your foreign study. And of course, the Internet is a good resource as well.

If you have chosen a destination that will not include a faith community from your tradition, then plan ahead as to how you will maintain your practice while abroad. Faith leaders on your home campus can help you develop a strategy and recommend readings, rituals, and sacred objects that you can take with you. Perhaps you can even find another student or staff member who will be willing to correspond with you via the Internet (if you will have access) or snail mail to maintain a spiritual dialogue while you are away.

The same strategy may be even more important if you are just beginning to explore your spirituality. Ask one or two trusted advisors to recommend a few books for you to take along, books that are a good fit given where you are on your spiritual journey and that are rich enough to challenge and support you during your time away (and that will fit in your suitcase!). Ask these same trusted advisors to guide you on how to look for a faith community abroad and how to find sources of support for your spiritual exploration.

Regardless of where you are spiritually, your time away will present new opportunities for challenge and growth. Reentry to your home campus will also be a challenge on many fronts, including your spiritual identity and practice. In fact, many students later say that returning home is a more difficult transition than adjusting abroad. While away, prepare for your reentry. Consider how you have evolved spiritually and what this may mean to your routine, commitments, and connections upon your return. Once you arrive back on campus and get your bags unpacked, seek out a study abroad advisor. They are skilled at helping you plan your trip abroad and settle back in after your time away. In addition, your campus faith leader will also be a valuable support as you begin to integrate yourself back into your old campus community.

MY OTHER COLLEGE CLASSROOMS
BETH KANDER

In all honesty, I didn't attend services much my freshman year. I didn't go to Hillel events, either. Wasn't really my thing. I didn't feel that the Brandeis University Jewish community was *my* Jewish community. I had a negative experience my first week at school, and I mostly steered clear for first semester that year. Pretty much only holidays—Rosh Hashanah, Yom Kippur, and the first night of Chanukah—drew me to services. One February Friday, though, I decided to go to regular Shabbat evening services. I can't recall the impetus, but for whatever reason, I went.

Toward the end of services each week, community announcements were made—volunteer opportunities, upcoming events, and so on. At the end of the community announcements, a junior named Sarah chimed in, "Oh! If anyone is going to be around over February break and is interested in subbing for a great group of fourth graders, see me after services!"

I thought about it as we sang the concluding song. I was going to be stuck on campus that February break and would definitely have some free time. In high school, I had served as a junior youth group advisor and worked as a teacher's aide in third- and seventh-grade classrooms. I had really enjoyed working at the religious school and realized that I missed being around kids. I felt guilty about not having much of a role in Jewish life since starting college. Not to mention that being a poor college student working a $6-an-hour administrative assistant work-study scholarship job, I could always use some extra money. Maybe this was worth a shot . . .

I arranged with Sarah to sub for her fourth-grade Hebrew school classes on Tuesday and Thursday of the February break. Sarah left me lesson plans and a few general notes about her class. I went into the classroom that first Tuesday with relatively low expectations. I knew I could survive for two hours in the classroom, and that was the primary goal. Hey, this was just a one-shot subbing deal, right?

Well, life's funny sometimes.

I didn't just survive in the classroom. I thrived. I loved it. I loved the kids, I loved their questions, I loved challenging them to think and challenging myself to make the lesson engaging and exciting. I approached Sarah after the break and told her I'd be happy to sub for her anytime. As it happened, Sarah had a week-long vacation coming up and I subbed for her once again. This time, I left my resume with the Hebrew school office and told them how interested I was in working as a full classroom teacher.

Over the summer, I received a call from the religious school director. After a phone interview and a few days of waiting, an e-mail confirming my appointment as teacher of both a second-grade and a sixth-grade classroom filled me with excitement. Thrilled excitement, but also nervous excitement: *second graders, fine. Sixth graders, too? I'm only going to be a college sophomore! I'm little—they're going to be taller than me! Can I really write two curricula over the summer? Can I handle this?*

If I am not for myself, who will be for me? And if I am only for myself, what am I? And if not now, when?

—RABBI HILLEL

Home in Michigan, I worked hard over the summer to develop lesson plans. I spoke with my former religious school director and conferred with my parents, both of whom had taught various classes. Fall rolled around, and I returned to Massachusetts with a twofold role: university student and religious school teacher.

That first year was at least as much a learning experience for me as it was for my students. My second graders were high-energy and enthusiastic, and I had to learn to deal with seven-year-old attention spans, sensitivities, and learning needs. My sixth graders were insightful but sometimes liked to push the envelope—they were more of a challenge, but also more of a reward. They, too, were sensitive. They were sometimes hormonal, sometimes unbelievably cerebral and seeking knowledge, and sometimes still just eleven-year-olds who wanted to do arts and crafts.

They were also all looking around to find Jewish role models, and there, plunked down in front of these seeking eyes, stood I. More so than I had ever imagined possible, I felt the full responsibility of being a good role model. I also felt the importance of community. As I deepened my involvement with this off-campus Jewish community in my role as teacher, I also began to increase my involvement with the campus Jewish community. How could I teach my students the importance of maintaining a Jewish identity, taking pride in their heritage, and being involved with the larger Jewish community if I wasn't living these ideals myself?

I'm not a big charts-and-graphs girl, but I can confidently say that were I to track my service attendance on a graph, there would be a huge spike highlighting the dramatic increase in my involvement after I began teaching religious school.

By my junior year, I was co-services coordinator for BaRuCH (the Brandeis Reform Chavurah). I was also teaching religious school five days a week: second grade, sixth grade, and seventh grade, as well as music at a different school. People also started asking me to tutor students for their Bar and Bat Mitzvahs, and to sing at services. I was recruited as a curriculum pilot-teacher by the Jewish Women's Archive. Without ever planning it, I had jumped into a career in the world of Jewish education.

Even with the curriculum development and service projects, I still felt the classroom moments were at the heart of my Jewish—and Jewish education—experiences. I loved my education director, Pat, and her guidance and support. Most of all, I loved my students. Junior year, I had the most incredible group of sixth graders I had ever encountered. They were so bright, so motivated, and so trusting—whatever current events issue or archaic Hebrew teaching I brought in, they wanted to probe and explore it.

They were also hilarious. One week we were studying immigration, and after a more serious study and debate about issues of immigrants and community support, I decided to lighten the mood. I told my students that they had to act out a skit to demonstrate how American Jews tried to aid incoming immigrants, but the support was far from enough, and to find some memorable way of presenting it. The students had me close my eyes, and when I opened them, they were all standing on one side of the room, arms outstretched, acting as though they were trying to grasp something just beyond their reach. Following the direction of their fingers, I looked to the opposite side of the room, where they had taped up a giant sign reading "Enough."

Their smiles were huge when I started laughing. Even though they knew I understood, they all began chiming in. "Get it, Beth? Get it? We're FAR from ENOUGH!!"

My own life and education were enriched by my constant quest to keep up with this class and provide them some new teaching each week. I became close with their families, as well, and found myself wishing I could drag my feet and slow down the clock as the end of that school year approached. We had an "awards ceremony" at the end of the year, presenting "The Justice Award," "The Compassion Award," and so on to the various figures in Jewish history we had studied. Our awards ceremony was followed by a sparkling-cider-and-cheese reception for the students and their families. As I gave the year-end wrap-up speech to segue from our program to the reception, I spoke about how incredible this class had been and how much I had learned from them.

One of the parents stepped forward, eyes shining. "Beth, you have meant so much to our kids. They have learned so much this year, and they just love you. Thank you for all you've done for them, and for our community. You've really become a part of this community, and we're really going to miss you when you leave." They presented me with a card and gift, and my eyes filled with tears.

That's when I realized how much I was going to miss *them* when I left.

I always find myself at a loss for words when I attempt to articulate the impact that teaching religious school has had on my life. Going off campus led me back to campus, and farther from campus than I ever could have imagined. Teaching religious school has clearly influenced my life choices—at college, and now. I spent the remainder of my undergrad years being an active member of the Jewish community on campus and off. I'm currently working in the deep South as a traveling educator, doing education, culture, and coexistence programming, while also training and working with teachers in small religious schools throughout the region. Would these doors have opened for me had I not accepted that substitute job my freshman year of college? Maybe. Would I have known to walk through those doors? Maybe not.

Teaching religious school certainly doesn't lead everyone to life as a Jewish professional. I carpooled to work junior and senior year with "my boys," four Brandeis undergrad guys who also taught at my school. Of the four, one plans to be a Jewish educator; the others are interested in medicine, accounting, and business. Three of the four were not involved in campus Jewish life even minimally—but for them, teaching at a religious school provided a connection to the Jewish world.

Teaching was my connection, too. **Religious school was my "in"—by teaching about the importance of heritage and identity, I learned how important my community is to me.** I took some incredible classes at Brandeis and had several memorable and inspiring professors. I also wound up learning a lot by praying each week in the round, classroom-by-week, sanctuary-by-Shabbat room that BaRuCH used for our services. But I learned at least as much in my other college classrooms—the ones located miles off campus, filled with brightly colored Hebrew letters, student artwork, and a piece of paper with the word "ENOUGH" hastily scribbled across it, taped to the far side of one wall.

FAITH AND LEADERSHIP IN ACTION: THE HABITAT EXPERIENCE
BRETT IAFIGLIOLA

Construction is hard work. Would anyone ever want to *volunteer* to work in this field? But what if it was a way to serve others, not only through construction but also by building communities, all while disproving stereotypes, such as those stemming from racism, poverty, and homelessness? What if building homes in partnership with God's people in need is something that appeals to you? Well, then, do I have the opportunity for you, and it's known as Habitat for Humanity.

Habitat is dedicated to the mission of making decent shelter a matter of conscience and eliminating poverty housing. Unwilling to accept the fact that millions of people live without adequate shelter,

Habitat for Humanity challenges individuals, congregations, corporations, foundations, and other organizations to change the conditions in which they live. Habitat for Humanity International is a worldwide ecumenical, grassroots Christian-based housing ministry with more than 1,600 affiliates in the United States and representation in more than eighty countries. The houses are definitely not free; they are paid over the life of a standard mortgage by the homeowners, but with an interest-free loan. The homeowners are required to work a set number of hours on their own home, "sweat equity," as well as on those of other Habitat owners, and this serves as their down payment.

By volunteering in a faith-based organization such as Habitat for Humanity, I have found a way to stay connected to my faith not only through words but also with action. Several stories immediately come to mind about leadership qualities and the collaboration required to plan and execute a Collegiate Challenge building trip. Collegiate Challenge (CC) is a program run through Habitat International that enables high school and college students to participate in a weeklong building trip, usually during spring break and usually to other affiliates across the country. Although I have been to Florida and West Virginia during my early college years, it was my recent trip to Valdosta, Georgia, that has been the most successful overall.

Before beginning to plan the trip, a select few people volunteered to manage various aspects of it (such as transportation, paperwork, financial issues, and affiliate coordination) and report back to the group as necessary. This delegation's first step was to alleviate the workload being dumped all on one person, and it also clearly defined each person's role—both of these points proved to be critical. The people who accepted these roles displayed three skills of a top-quality team player: a *self-initiator* recognizes what else needs to be accomplished, a *hard worker* completes the necessary tasks, and a *good communicator* informs the rest of the group of what has been done and what step to take next. Despite some roadblocks on our way, we eventually arranged our transportation, completed all the necessary paperwork, secured our financing, and coordinated times with the affiliate. With the advance planning all set, we were finally ready to head south!

Nearly every aspect of the trip flowed smoothly, and though that may seem like sheer luck for most people (including me most times), we took several steps to ensure the trip's success. First off, the planners and the participants had clear-cut roles. For instance, one person in particular, "Kelsey," went above and beyond her role in kindly assisting anyone who needed it. Everyone respected Kelsey for her work, and she accepted that leadership role. No one had a need to question her because whatever she suggested was both fair and reasonable, two additional keys to success. Successful undertakings require a "champion" to carry the project through to completion, and Kelsey definitely fulfilled that role. Interpersonal problems on the trip were also nonexistent, partly due to the friendly interaction among the group both during the day at the site and at night during evening devotions, and also because of the prevailing attitude that we should and could indeed cooperate with one another. Of all the keys thus far, attitude certainly is the hardest to change, but with proper planning, fairness to everyone, and the proper attitude starting at the top of the leadership pyramid, I am certain it can be done.

Our work for the week consisted of building wall sections in a warehouse. Yeah, it may not sound like that much fun at first, but as we soon found out, it was an experience that will not be forgotten. We were split into teams of five on Monday morning, and we stayed in those teams for most of the week. The teams included some people from my college, but mostly people from the other four schools that were with us that week. I can speak only from my own perspective, but during those short five days, I experienced something incredible.

First, as I worked more and more with the same people, I quietly began to notice what skills the other people had and how comfortable they were in using them. After only the second day, everyone seemed to understand that the group's mantra was "See a need and fill it." For example, if I needed more wood on my wall section, someone had it almost immediately. If a particular wall needed two windows and a door, the need was recognized and quickly filled. Even more impressive was that all this coordination took place without even needing to talk; the job was done even before someone could ask for it! To me, that credo was simply amazing and a testament to our group. "See a need and fill it." Imagine how many problems would simply disappear if needs were just filled, instead of the usual "That's not my problem" or "Do it yourself, I'm too busy!"

Second, but certainly no less amazing, is the theory of successful empowerment in action. Habitat not only builds houses, but it also empowers people who would not otherwise have the chance to build and own their own home—empowering others to become all that God intended them to be. However, empowerment does not apply only to homeowners but to volunteers as well. For example, having construction experience, I often attempted to empower the other people in our group so they could work more safely, efficiently, and skillfully. To see the skills our group developed over the week should have been enough to demonstrate successful leadership. However, on the last day, the construction leaders decided to build an entire house-worth of wall in the shortest time possible, using all available people to build it. Because several other people had been working on other aspects of wall construction (such as windows and doors, but not specifically the final wall product), they had to learn how to build the walls correctly.

My group, which had been learning new skills all week, took a lead role for this final project. To my great exhilaration, my group was everywhere, teaching the new people how to build the wall safely, efficiently, and skillfully! One person in particular took a strong leadership role on this final project. Although she never had a shortage of leadership skills anyway, she demonstrated what I call the two mantras of a good leader. First, she became an even better leader than the one who came before her, and second, the people following her lead did not necessarily know that she was in charge.

215

The second part means that instead of bossing people around and demanding answers, she handled the problems and kept the work moving, and the followers simply followed along without needing to question her. It may sound dangerous that the leader is not immediately known, but notice that the next time a project seems to flow smoothly, one person is behind the scenes making it work.

The trip ended with great success, notably that we all returned to Indiana with no mortal flesh wounds and no traumatic experiences, only a great time had by all. We had more than enough food for the trip, our finances covered all our expenses, and I still cherish the friends and memories. Certainly many aspects came together at the right time to make the trip such a success, but remember the essential items for future planning. First, delegation of the total workload saves one person from being overloaded and includes other people in the project and gives them a sense of importance in the planning. Second, a clear definition of roles is critical to eliminate leadership-grabbing later, which can be highly detrimental to any cause. In addition, choose people with great team-player qualities, such as self-initiation, hard work, and good communication. Furthermore, strive to find a "champion" for the project, someone who has all the necessary qualities of a team player and a leader. Fairness in the decision-making process, combined with the right attitude from the leaders on down, is also key.

So maybe you do not want to be a construction worker, let alone volunteer with Habitat's mission to eliminate substandard housing around the world. There are, however, innumerable worthy causes for which you may find God calling you to serve. I challenge you not to "make a difference" but to "be the difference." So many of my ideas and projects fail simply because I am lacking the one person to make it happen. Perhaps I have been looking for you, or perhaps you are called somewhere else. I look forward to working with you in the world of leadership, and even if I do not ever get to meet you, know that we are still working for the same goal. If you happen to work for Habitat, remember—the world can always use another good carpenter.

MOMENT AFTER MOMENT: A ZEN RETREAT
MICHAEL POPPER

Thus far, my decaying 1986 Oldsmobile has safely navigated the Catskills of upstate New York. I approach Dai Bosatsu Zendo, a Zen Buddhist monastery and my home for the next week. A rickety wooden bridge emits a thunderous clap as I slowly roll across. I fear my car might plunge straight into the stream below. There is one parking spot left in the rutted grass lot. The lake is surrounded on all sides by a mountainous green forest. At the water's edge, my lungs fill with cool air; my heart thumps to the rhythm of the waves. I cannot imagine a better place for a meditation retreat.

Upon entering the monastery, I am greeted by a young monk named Shin Din. My first instinct is to follow the advice of my father, "Look everyone you meet right in the eye and shake hands firmly." But as I approach, Shin Din brings his hands together and bows. He informs me that the retreat will be conducted in silence and that I am not to make direct eye contact with the monks or the other participants. Perhaps silence is necessary to sustain the concentrative atmosphere of the retreat. I see meditation practice as a way to become more at ease in the company of others. In any case, the instruction leaves me feeling confused.

There are thirty other lay practitioners attending the retreat. We are taken through the daily itinerary for the week, given robes, and lined up outside the zendo. All the formal meditation takes place in this large, open room. We file noiselessly into the zendo. The monks stand, and after all the practitioners enter, a small gong is struck. Immediately, everyone bows to the Buddha statue four times, bows to the person across from him or her, and sits down.

Despite coming from a religious heritage that forbids idol worship, I gladly follow along. Each year, during Passover Seder at my house, the non-Jewish guests recite the Hebrew blessings because they respect my family and our traditions. In the same spirit, I bow to the Buddha statue because I respect this community of monks and the tradition we will be practicing together for the next week.

A beautiful, high-pitched bell is rung to signify the beginning of meditation. We are not to move or make any sound during the forty-minute session. I cross my legs and close my eyes, straighten my back and relax my shoulders. Breathe in and breathe out.

I have to walk around all the grounds before I leave here.

Breathe out.

"I just meditated for seven days," I'll say when I get back.

Breathe out.

Already I'm like a kid counting down to the last day of school.

The bell sounds. Work period.

We walk out of the zendo, return to our rooms, and change into work clothes. Ten of us follow Shin Din down the road to the garage. There are empty garbage cans squeezed into every open space. A massive pile of mulch sits outside. Armed with pitchforks and shovels, we repeatedly attack the mulch, unleashing the steaming stench of its hot underbelly.

The transition from noisy quads of busy students to silent halls of meditating monks is a difficult one. I do not see how an hour of manual labor in the sweltering heat will help me complete that transition. I thought my previous study and practice of Zen Buddhism would provide me with a sense of belonging, but it hasn't—perhaps because no one has asked me what I know about Zen. When I arrived, the monks didn't say, "This is what we believe, this is what we don't believe, this is Zen." Instead, we were brought into their daily routine and forced to discover things on our own.

An hour later, the cans are back in their original spots in the garage and filled with mulch. I survey the area where we worked. How did this job get done? It seems like the cans were empty, the mulch piled high, and the shovels unsoiled just moments ago.

I change position and posture throughout the remaining meditation sessions, but my knees still ache. I hobble back to my room and apply BenGay to relieve the pain. The first day has finally come to an end.

At 4:30 a.m. I stumble out of my room. The wake-up gong still reverberates through my body. Shin Din shuffles by, notices the sleepy-eyed, bewildered look on my face, and ushers me into line. We all enter an elaborately decorated room and sit in rows. Shin Din and a giant elderly monk box me into the back corner of the room; my view is completely obstructed. All at once the chanting starts. I feel like a loud, unprepared bass in a women's choir.

Love cannot remain by itself—it has no meaning. Love has to be put into action and that action is service.

—MOTHER TERESA

Shin Din is chanting in rhythm with everyone else. Despite my attempts to seem calm and unworried, a sudden wave of panic surges through me. Luckily, Shin Din detects my distress. He adroitly snatches a little book from under his cushion, turns to the third page, and begins following along. It is clear the chant is imprinted in his memory, but he coolly feigns ignorance. I reach under my cushion and join in the chanting.

The bell sounds for breakfast. We file into the eating room, sit at long, rectangular tables, and bow in unison. Chanting begins as I disassemble an intricately folded napkin containing three stacked bowls, a wipe rag, a chanting card, and chopsticks. I make sure the points of my chopsticks do not face toward another person, and place the napkin, rag, and chanting card on my lap. Since I came from a relaxed dinner table with the television blaring in the background, the formal, synchronized structure of the meal troubles me.

A steaming pot of rice starts moving down the table. I glance at Shin Din, who sits across from me. The instant the people to our right are finished, we grab the mat under the pot and pull over the hot food. When we are done serving ourselves, the pair sitting to our left grab the mat and the pot continues down the table. It takes intense concentration to keep the food moving quickly. If one person makes a mistake, all forty people are held up.

Once meal chants are over, sounds of slurping, chomping, and inhaling fill the air. Rice explodes out of the bowls, chopsticks fly, and everyone quickly finishes the food. Huge kettles of hot water are passed down the table. We each take as little water as possible to clean our bowls and chopsticks. The entire meal lasts thirty minutes.

After another work period, I am back in my room. I sit down and let my mind pour out onto the pages of my journal. This is how I plan to keep my sanity in the face of our intense daily meditation schedule. I have decided to keep the personal judgments and reflections to a minimum in my writing. When this entire experience is behind me, I'll have some perspective, but for now I'm keeping to the straight facts. I take a quick nap and apply more pain ointment before our next session.

In the zendo, I bow four times, bow again, sit, straighten my back, and close my eyes.

What is the point of this schedule? Ten hours of meditation a day! How am I going to last?

Breathe out.

I don't care if we're not allowed to move, the entire lower half of my body is asleep, I'm changing position.

Breathe out.

This is more painful than before!

While surreptitiously adjusting my cushion, I become aware of the woman sitting across from me. Her irregular breathing and grimacing face evince intense pain. Tears run down her cheek. She seems about ready to stretch and collect herself. Suddenly, her neighbor places a tissue on the ground, but she refuses to take it. It is as if the thought of moving to take that tissue drives her to overcome the pain. After a few deep breaths, she stops crying, recovers her composure, and resumes meditating. For someone who restlessly shifts throughout every meditation, this is an empowering and inspirational scene.

Before the last sit of the night, we have *teisho*, a talk given by the abbot of the monastery, Eido T. Shimano Roshi. Rain begins to fall as Eido Roshi expounds the importance of practicing with intensity.

"It is not up to the teachers; it is up to you. You get what you give. The more you give, the harder you practice, the more energy you will have. You can't save your energy; then it will be gone." At that, a deafening clap of thunder booms.

He smiles, "Thunder."

The bell is rung. We stand up, form lines, and enter the zendo. I begin the meditation without any concern for posture or pain. Despite many desperate urges to move, I remain completely still for the entire session. Walking back to my room, it dawns on me. Perhaps it is time to sit through the pain rather than just get around it.

THINGS TO DO IN AUSTRALIA #7: GETTING BEYOND "SORTA CHRISTIAN"

IAN DALE

During my junior year in college, I had the privilege of participating in a semester of study abroad in Australia. I chose Australia for academic reasons: The school had a good art program for my major; practical reasons: I already spoke the language; and personal reasons: I had a childhood obsession for Australian wildlife. All of these were important reasons to go—and I do enjoy my souvenir stuffed wombat—but as it turned out, the greatest benefit by far was one that had weighed little on my choice to go abroad. My unintentionally well-timed excursion "Down Under" was most precious not for the sightseeing or cultural exchange but for the incredible opportunity it provided for spiritual growth.

I had grown up in a Christian family, attending church all through my childhood. But from about age nine onward, I rejected the faith I was raised with, thinking it irrelevant, burdensome, and untrue. For the next nine years of my life, I lived secretly as an atheist. A very shy, private, and unsociable teen, I never actually shared my beliefs with my parents or my few friends. This privacy enabled my atheism to go unquestioned for many years, until I went off to college. New coursework, new friends, and new freedom led me to think more about my beliefs, raising important issues and implications that I hadn't previously considered. At first this strengthened my "faith" in atheism, but during my second year of college I began to see a futility to my thinking, as new struggles exposed the weaknesses in myself as well as in my belief system. I needed hope, and I began looking for it in other options. The summer before my junior year, after several months of searching and reading, I found that hope in the Christian faith.

I was amazed at how my faith began immediately to improve my outlook and my life, but I was still hesitant about it, with many issues unresolved. I was also still quite private and shy about personal matters. So while I began to pray and visit churches and read more about living a good life, I revealed none of this to family or friends, nor did I seek out a church or campus group of Christians. I also felt that I should undergo baptism, a public confession of belief and a Christian's first step of obedience, but I just kept putting it off. Although I knew there was an inconsistency between my appreciation for my new faith and my secrecy about it, I just couldn't bring myself to share it with anyone.

Little did I know, there was a solution brewing from the start. I had already been planning a semester abroad before my conversion, and I continued with the arrangements afterward. A few weeks before my departure, I finally started to read the Bible and was further convicted of my need to mature spiritually. It occurred to me that Australia would be an excellent opportunity for this, allowing me to pursue Christianity in a more organized fashion, while still having the benefit of secrecy from my friends and family back home, just in case it didn't work out. I resolved, rather halfheartedly, to add "check out some Christian groups" to my lengthy "Things to Do in Australia" list.

Fortunately, fate prioritized my schedule better than I had, and when I arrived in Australia, the first batch of students I encountered were part of a local congregation. On my third day in the country, I visited their Saturday night youth group, and then went along to their church, a lengthy bus ride from campus. This first church seemed okay to me, but I planned to visit a few others before getting involved in any one group. The following week, I visited one of the student churches on campus, and I found its approach more appealing. There were even a few people there whom I recognized from my dorm, but I was still reluctant to meet them. I guess I needed a bit more time on this whole "church" thing.

I took a couple of weeks off from the church search before I again crossed paths with a girl from that first youth group. Knowing that I was, in my own words, "sorta Christian," she invited me to attend a study group her church offered. When I was reluctant to commit, she confronted me, questioning where my priorities and beliefs really were. We barely knew each other, yet the things she said somehow characterized me perfectly, and I knew I had to make a choice. I had been waffling for too long, allowing my introversion to hold me back from the path I knew to be right. Looking back upon all that I had learned and experienced already, I concluded that Jesus Christ was the truth, and, intimidating as it may be, my only hope was to follow him. I went to the study, and then back to the church, where I made a formal, public commitment to Christ, and I was baptized the following Sunday.

In a way, it felt like a cheat, that I made my "public" confession in the presence of total strangers from another country. But I knew it was an important start, and now that I was really moving, I would have to at least tell my parents. At the end of our weekly international phone conversation, I awkwardly told them what I had done. The last thing they knew concerning my spirituality was my refusal to go to church when I was seventeen, and now, at twenty-one, I was a Christian. It was quite a surprise, I'm sure. But it opened the door to a much closer relationship between my mother and me as we began to discuss issues of faith over the following weeks.

The next few weeks were exciting but difficult as I began to attend the church regularly, making acquaintances and taking classes. I received some solid teaching, but still had many gnawing questions that went unanswered. I began to associate with other Christians,

You must be the change you wish to see in the world.

—MAHATMA GANDHI

223

but because I would see them only on Sundays, I found it hard to relate to them in any other context. And while I grew more accustomed to church life, I soon discovered some beliefs of this particular church that didn't seem right. Without the ability to justify my reaction theologically, though, I had to give them a chance. I continued to attend church and classes several times a week, but it was often motivated by a sense of obligation rather than desire.

Even with all the new people I was meeting, I felt very lonely. I couldn't yet trust or find comfort with the church and its people, but I didn't think my nonreligious Australian friends could help with these matters either. Looking back, the solitude was an important period of testing, because I was forced to trust primarily in God to get me through my problems with the church. I read the Bible and other books on my own time, seeking answers to my countless questions. In the States, it had been a rare occasion when I could find time for independent reading. But overseas, I was able to start fresh, designing a lifestyle built around my new priorities, relatively free of the usual distractions. With time for both reading and writing, I was able to work through my concerns at a steady pace. Also of great help were my weekly phone calls home, as my mother proved to be a trustworthy "outside" source of guidance and encouragement.

Mid-semester I received a much-needed break from the pressures of church life, as I traveled the country for two weeks and continued to read. After my return, things began to brighten up. Some dormmates invited me to a "barbie" (barbecue); they all belonged to the campus church I had visited earlier in the semester, and they had seen me there. Afterward, I tagged along to the church with them, and this time, something was different. I had fun! I really felt comfortable with these people, and we had a great time. I started going to their Bible study in our dorm and their church on Sunday evenings, and I found a theology that made more sense to me. Because these Christians lived so close, I was able to spend "normal" time with them as well, at meals or just hanging out after class; and that made a big difference in how I could relate to them.

I was finally beginning to feel comfortable around other Christians, which, in turn, helped me to accept my own identity as one and not see it as something that I needed to hide or be ashamed of. Most important, **they showed me how wonderful it could be to seek after God in the company of other people, after I had been trying it alone for so long.**

Eventually, of course, the semester had to end, and it was hard to let these friends go, especially because we had just begun to grow close. It wasn't just one or two friends I was leaving behind, but a community, a family, so in a way it hurt even more because I knew they would continue to live and worship together without me. I regretted that I hadn't found this group earlier in my stay, but I eventually came to accept that it was all part of God's plan, even the difficult parts. Whether I had had the full four months with them or only two, it would still be sad to leave. I had, however, made friends I would truly miss, and for that I was extremely grateful.

I spent several more weeks traveling Australia solo, which was nice, and it gave me a great opportunity for reading and prayer (and zoos). But I found that I really wanted to be one of two places: back with my new Australian friends or returning to the States, so I could begin the next phase of this new life. Really I wanted to stay in Australia, but I knew the only option was moving on. I was a little worried about going back, now that I was a "full-on" Christian. I dreaded the possibility of forgetting all I had been through when suddenly thrust back into my old life. My friends at school were still in the dark on all of this, so it would certainly be a challenge breaking the news to so many people right away. And after all my struggles to find the right church in Australia, I was anxious at the thought of starting all over again back at my own college.

Fortunately, I faced all these uncertainties coming home with a much stronger faith and foundation than I had when I left the States. Once again, I had to trust that God would get me through, and once again, he did. It was a struggle sometimes to integrate my new life with my old, to explain my experiences to my skeptical friends, and to find a church that could replace the one I left behind. But with time, it has worked out, and I've begun to realize that this life at home offers everything I left behind, while somehow being more "me." I see now that my Australian journey was only a taste of things to come, a glimpse of the treasures I know God has in store, thanks to the best souvenir I could possibly bring back: faith.

A CAP, A GOWN, AND A COMMITMENT TO FAITH

Sunday is commencement. But today feels like the more important day. This afternoon, your campus faith group had its senior picnic. For you, this marked four years of spiritual growth, growth that happened in the company of these friends. You remember staying up late to debate topics of spiritual importance. You remember the community service trips, where you put your commitments into action. You remember the ethical dilemma you had earlier this year as the group's student coordinator. And you also remember marking important celebrations with these friends. And that's just it—more than the students in your academic department, more than various roommates, these students have been your closest friends.

Although you feel ready to be finished with your undergraduate studies, you are sad to be leaving your friends. How will you find a group of people with whom you can share this degree of spiritual comfort, challenge, and support? In retrospect, it seems as if this was almost built in, as you were all part of the campus community. There was a structure, a way to find each other. How will this happen when you relocate to a different city? Will you ever find a community as amazing as this one?

Career goals, the job search—these are the topics that get a ton of airtime during the senior year. But if you are like many students, you are just as concerned with the broader topic of starting over in a new place, whether it is graduate school, the location of your new job, abroad for a service or military commitment, or even a return home. How will you find a spiritual community? How will leaving your campus community impact your spiritual growth and commitments? Along with this, you are probably concerned about your career. If you have already landed a job, then you may feel mixed with excitement and a touch of nervousness about the transition. If you don't have a job yet—well, there's pressure to get one.

Exploring Careers

As you think about your career goals, you may consider a career of service or some other form of leadership within your spiritual community. To explore these options further, identify which skills you most enjoy and most effectively use. Also consider your values and other interests. Your career counselor can help you explore these. There are a number of ways to work within your spiritual community, some more obvious than others. You may be feeling strongly about serving your spiritual community, and the most obvious option may be to train for the clergy, or maybe you know deep down inside that serving other people directly is not something you are suited for or would enjoy. Look at your other skills. Maybe you have strong management skills and could work as an organizational leader within your tradition. There are other ways to serve as well—many spiritual communities need lay leaders to run organizations, teach in schools, provide human services, administer philanthropies, write and edit publications . . . the list of opportunities is long.

Or, like most students, you may decide that while you are profoundly committed to your spiritual life and

Every man has a vocation to be someone: but he must understand clearly that in order to fulfill this vocation he can only be one person: himself.

—THOMAS MERTON

community, you prefer to pursue a career outside this realm. In one way or another, your values, and thus your spirituality, will impact how you approach your work—if not the work itself, then certainly your integrity on the job.

Finding Community

Whether you have thought about it or not, you are already experienced at starting over. You made that first transition from high school to college, and here you are four or so years later. In some ways, that earlier transition happened with more support. You walked onto a campus that had a built-in community, and opportunities for prayer, meditation, study, service, and leadership were readily available. If your postgraduate plans are taking you to a community that is new to you, then you will probably have to take more initiative to get connected this time around.

There are many approaches to seeking a new spiritual community. You can ask members of your current community to help you—they may know someone you can connect with in your new community. Also, if you are moving to a major city, your college or university may have an alumni club. Attend one of their gatherings and meet other alumni—this is a terrific way to network for all kinds of connections. In addition, you can also start simply by looking online or in the phone book to identify spiritual organizations that may interest you.

Starting Again

More than looking to continue your present spiritual path, you may be seeking a change. Perhaps you have been wanting to alter your spiritual practice or commitment but have found it hard, given how immersed you are in your campus community. This time, starting over in a new community affords you the opportunity. For example, perhaps you have been strongly connected to a group in college and now you want something more progressive. You may have had trouble breaking away while still remaining close with your friends in the group. Or possibly you wanted to make a steady service commitment but just couldn't find the time. Now that you are starting over, you can build it into your routine. A fresh start gives you new freedom.

NOTHING IS ROUTINE
SUMI LOUNDON

One of the thrills of being a young adult is that everything is a first-time experience. My first semester of college—making new friends, picking my own classes, decorating my dorm room—was exhilarating. My first short haircut and manicure felt amazing. My first true love, first kiss, first skinny-dipping in a mountain lake on a summer's night—every experience was new and fresh.

By my last semester of college, some things had ceased to be so new. I once found eating in the dining halls a culinary adventure because of the wide selection of foods. Four years later, deciding on yet another pizza or pasta night with orange juice from concentrate seemed like such a burden that I would simply forgo trekking to the dining hall altogether. When I considered that, in the future, food would pretty much taste the same, I despaired at the bleakness of it.

I was getting bored by routine matters. Another class. Another discussion group. Another paper to write. Another load of laundry. I even began to tire of dance parties. I could feel myself going numb, becoming jaded, losing that freshness I felt during the first few months of being away from home.

Then it hit me. Four years of college was nothing; I would be doing these things for the *rest of my life*. Even if I had servants to do things I did not like, I would still have other matters, such as brushing my teeth and peeing. Nobody could do that for me. I faced the fact that at least 70 percent of my time would be dedicated to things that had

To be successful, the first thing to do is fall in love with your work.

—SISTER MARY LAURETTA

absolutely no long-range purpose or greater meaning but were simply done for survival. Bummer!

Then I began to think about it. What if one day I found out that it was my very last day to take a shower, put on my socks, and brush my teeth? Wouldn't those things suddenly seem like an incredibly precious act? The feel of warm water and soap, the texture of my socks as I pulled them up against my ankles, the taste of toothpaste and that zingy feeling in the mouth after rinsing. To really experience these things intimately felt profound, joyful, and relaxing. Rather than getting high off obvious first-time experiences, I considered how to awaken to each seemingly insignificant moment.

From there, I began examining supposed routines with full attention to my actual experience. I discovered that there are worlds of variation in what seems to be mere repetition. When I brought my mind into the present moment of what I was doing, I found there was as much freshness and newness to the experience as my first kiss. There were marvelous worlds of beauty, motion, sound, creation, existence, and passing away in the smallest of sensations. Having been raised in the Buddhist tradition, I was finally beginning to understand why the Vietnamese Buddhist master Thich Nhat Hanh says that meditation, rather than a practice of simply sitting on a cushion with closed eyes, is being mindful to daily life.

Interestingly, by the last few weeks of my senior year, those last papers, last dances, and last dining hall meals felt anything but ordinary. **Each moment took on a precious quality. I found, in bringing myself fully into the present, observing with fascination and attention everything about my experience, that nothing is routine.**

COUNTING SHEEP AND COUNTING MY BLESSINGS
LEAH RACHEL BERKOWITZ

"Tell me *exactly* what happened this morning!" my friend Liz said as she handed out drinks. I couldn't believe this moment had finally come. We were about to toast my acceptance into rabbinical school.

Everyone in the room looked a little disappointed by my first answer: that I opened my campus mailbox and found an acceptance letter. So I smiled and told them that when I opened my box in the campus mailroom, there was a huge burning bush inside and a booming voice from the heavens.

"Leah!" The voice thundered from the mailbox. "This is G-d. I want you to become a rabbi." People laughed and took a sip of their drinks.

But it really wasn't like that at all. All there was in my mailbox was a plain white envelope.

Still, holding that letter in my hand, something that had been a dream for almost ten years had suddenly become a reality. I had started thinking about becoming a rabbi when I was twelve years old, and by the time I was sixteen there wasn't a doubt in my mind that this was what I was meant to do with my life. There were doubts, however, about whether or not the admissions committee would agree with me.

The month of waiting between my interview and my acceptance was the most excruciating. I kept telling myself that it was out of my hands. My interview had proved that.

I went down on the train from Boston to New York one Thursday afternoon in February to complete a psychological interview on Friday morning. I spent the weekend dragging a suitcase around New York City in the snow while wearing a "power suit" and high heels, shuttling between my grandmother's house in the suburbs and my Aunt Hadassah's apartment in the city. I even had the rare New York experience of having a pedestrian stop and ask me whether I needed directions. I looked that lost.

The crown jewel of the experience was facing a panel of nine people on that Monday morning.

You often find your destiny on the path you take to avoid it.

—CHINESE PROVERB

The preparation for the interview had been intense: sending in two essays and six recommendations, taking entrance exams, talking to past applicants, choosing the perfect suit, carefully

232

selecting accessories and makeup, and trying to figure out what they were going to ask me and what I might say. I even gave up my daily fix of Diet Coke to keep myself calm.

We have to sleep with open eyes, we must dream with our hands.

—OCTAVIO PAZ

By Sunday night, all I needed to do was get a good night's sleep.

My mother had come to meet me in the city on Sunday afternoon. We excused ourselves from dinner with my aunt early so I could get to bed by nine. I had to wake up at six a.m.

My mother had insisted that staying with family would be better than staying in a hotel. We unfolded the sofa bed that we were to share for the evening and the thin mattress curled up on both sides. After an hour or so of tossing and turning and switching sides, the two of us fell into a light sleep.

At one a.m., a car alarm went off. For three hours. My mother called the police three times, reminding me each time that, if the alarm went off, I could still get X hours of sleep. A few times the noise would stop, and just as one of us would breathe a sigh of relief, the rhythmic screaming of the disturbed car would start up again.

I was close to crying. For years I had prepared for the moment that was only a few hours away, and it was all going to be ruined by a stupid car alarm.

Instead, I turned to my mom, who was stroking my hair and trying to keep me calm, and said, "Remember that time on Sesame Street when Ernie is counting sheep to fall asleep, but there's only one sheep, so every time it jumps over the bed it has to run back to the other side and start over?"

It was dark, but I could hear my mother smiling.

I turned toward her. "Baaaaa . . . clomp, clomp, clomp . . . baaaa." The two of us started giggling and "baaa"-ing quietly in my aunt's living room. And I knew that it was going to be all right.

"I'm glad that you can see the humor in the situation." My mom was still giggling. "Now at least you'll have a funny story to tell."

Man has a purpose in the universe. That particular mission which he must fulfill is uniquely his and cannot be accomplished by even billions of other humans.

—RABBI ABRAHAM TWERSKI

"This will only be funny if I get in." I scowl.

"You'll get in." She murmured. Somewhere around four a.m. we fell asleep.

In the morning, we reminded each other that two hours of sleep would be plenty and I just had to get through the next few hours before going back to sleep on the train ride home. We didn't mention that within those hours I had to prove to a panel of nine that I would make a good spiritual leader and had to take a written test in a language other than my own.

An hour before my interview I met with one member of the panel for some final preparation. After I explained my lack of sleep, the woman offered me a cup of coffee.

"No!" I almost shouted. "I'm sorry, I mean, I had to give up caffeine."

The woman smiled. "Well, you get to ask yourself the first question. What do you want us to ask you?"

I had spent months thinking about what they might ask and what I hoped they wouldn't ask. I hadn't really thought about what I wanted them to ask. Should I ask myself about my experience in the Jewish community so that I can tell them how experienced I am? Should I ask myself some sort of factual question so that I can impress them with the breadth of my knowledge?

Instead, I took a deep breath and said, "Ask me, 'What's the most important thing you brought with you today?'" She wrote my question down on a legal pad.

I reached into my shoulder bag and rooted through it. There were a few "lucky" pieces and a book that had belonged to my late grandfather. There was a folder full of Hebrew verb conjugations and a package of mechanical pencils.

Finally, I touched a small blue compact mirror shaped like a flower.

The compact was part of a care package that my roommates from college had given me the night before I left for New York. The bag had been full of crossword puzzles, books and magazines to read on the train, emergency cosmetics, and cards with inspirational messages on them.

At the bottom of the bag was the little compact mirror, on which they had written in tiny letters, "What a *shayna maydele!*" ("pretty girl" in Yiddish).

"You can do this." They had hugged me and told me not to be nervous. "No one is more ready for this than you are."

An hour later, I sat in front of the panel and listened to my question being asked. I told them about the mirror and the bag of goodies. I told them how wonderful and supportive my friends had been during this process, how they believed in me.

And even though I didn't say anything about the other people in my life, I thought of all the people who had "put something in my bag" to take with me that day, all the people who were more certain about my abilities than I was. And I thought about my mom and the sofa bed, and of the two of us making each other laugh when we should have been crying.

When I thought I had finished answering the question, I suddenly added, "And having friends like that is really what makes me believe in G-d." The words flew out of my mouth before I could think about them, but I realized as I heard them that they were true.

The people on the panel nodded and smiled. Someone at the table asked the next question. I took a deep breath and began to speak.

I can do this.

My faith had been in my bag all this time, but not only my faith in G-d. Tucked between the books and crossword puzzles and extra lipsticks, I carried with me faith in the people in my life and, ultimately, faith in myself.

RELIGION ON THE RESUME

Wanted: research assistant. Must have working knowledge of qualitative research methods, pay attention to detail, work well on deadline, and have strong writing skills. Monotheists need not apply.

Fortunately, employers cannot make belief in a higher power or religious affiliation part of a job description. So should you include such information on your resume? Clearly you aren't going to simply list your religion, yet you may wish to include your involvement or leadership in a faith-based organization that, in turn, indicates your affiliation.

The easiest scenario is if you are applying for a position in a religiously affiliated organization or an organization that has overt spiritual or religious content (e.g., a record company that specializes in spiritual music). Then your prior leadership and involvement helps make the case that you are a strong candidate, and thus you should feature these items on your resume.

For positions outside the religious sector, however, the situation is more complicated. Fact is, you rarely know who will be reading your resume (unless Uncle Steve is the CEO and you are applying to him for a summer internship!). One potential employer may see that you are president of a student religious group and make the assumption that you are an ethical and trustworthy candidate. Taking this even further, if you happen to be of the same religion as this potential employer, he or she may consciously or subconsciously feel a connection that will act in your favor. On the flip side, this potential employer may knowingly, or unknowingly, make negative assumptions about you based on your religious affiliation. Positive or negative, religious involvement on the resume tends to stand out in way that is different from leadership in many other kinds of organizations (though it is similar to the impact of listing political activities), so you must decide whether it's a risk you wish to take.

If you are clear that you would only work for an employer who is totally cool with your involvement in religious organizations, then it's best to include your involvements, because you want to screen out a situation that isn't a good fit. If, however, you tend to keep your outward practice (as opposed to your ethics and other inward manifestations of your faith) separate from your workday, then you may want to focus your resume on only work-related skills and experience. This keeps you in control, because you can aim to get the interview and visit the employer, and then assess whether the environment feels right for you.

READY FOR VOCATION
JEREMY D. POSADAS

"So, what are you gonna do when you finish? With your life? With that major?"

Are you tired of these questions yet? Don't you sometimes wish you could just answer something like, "Gee, I guess I was thinking about being a professional hippie," or "As a child of postmodernism, I don't think in terms of 'doing' something with my life"? Of course, it's even better when you start to feel that the person asking the question—regardless of the appearance of sincerity—already has the answer and is just waiting for you to guess: "Oh, well why don't you think about (fill in some hallowed profession)" or "There's always (random, allegedly prestigious job)." As though you haven't really thought about the question and just needed some encouragement to decide what you would do with the forty years of labor ahead of you.

Then again, maybe you *haven't* thought about these questions, or wish you didn't have to.

Whether or not you are tired of the questions, whether or not you've thought about them, whether or not you're terrified of them, it's time for a reality check:

1. These are not the most important questions;

2. There are others that *really* matter; and

3. Everything's gonna be okay.

(Feel free to use these as a mantra whenever you're tempted to tell someone that you've decided to be a licensed procrastinator.)

So if "What are you gonna do when you grow up?" *isn't* the most important question, what is? Here are some possibilities:

- What would you do if you knew you couldn't fail?

- What would it be like if you really believed that God—however you understand God's being—had some idea in mind for your life?

- What do you do that makes you feel most alive, most human, and most in touch with other humans?

- Which kinds of work do you admire the most?

Put another way, **the important questions are not really about doing, so much as they are about being: not what will you do, but who are you and who do you want to be?** *Vocation,* though it seems like a heavy Christian term, does not have to be particularly Christian if that is not your tradition. It means nothing more than asking who you want to be while God is overhearing. And it means being ready for the possibility that God might actually speak back to you in response, if you ask honestly.

Maybe speaking isn't the way you relate to the Divine—and maybe you have a particular name for the Divine, besides simply "God"—so fill in whatever expression or metaphor best captures how you understand that relationship. The point is, always remember that something vastly greater than you is the source of the answers to the most important questions. To care about your vocation, then, you have to see yourself and your life in relation to God and, through God, to the humans with whom you share the planet.

CONCLUSION

A few more questions . . .

So who do you want to be?

What gets in your way?

How might you deal with those obstacles?

And how does it feel when you are that person, the person you want to be?

This spiritual quest is a lifelong journey. We enjoy times when we are in a good spiritual groove, and we work through times when we can't find our spiritual rhythm. Learn from it all and continue to grow.

Keep asking spiritual questions. Look for patterns. Which questions challenge and excite you? Which questions frustrate you? Which questions do you avoid at all cost? Notice what all this tells you about where you feel secure and where you feel vulnerable. Discover the kinds of challenges that energize you versus the ones that drain you.

Find a good spiritual mentor. And be one.

Give yourself spiritual checkpoints—times of the day, week,

month, year—when you stop to reflect and examine whether your behaviors and commitments reflect the person you are trying to be. Your spiritual tradition may provide these checkpoints. If it doesn't, then create your own.

Like the writers in this book, take risks. Don't take risks that put you in danger, but occasionally seek experiences that make you uncomfortable and will ultimately help you grow. Have tough conversations that explore difficult spiritual questions. Attend a service of a tradition different from your own. Seek out someone from another tradition and search for common ground.

Stop and take note of the bad stuff. Whether it's someone saying something offensive in conversation or the larger problems on our planet, identify at least one thing that you wish were different. Take a stand. Take action.

Look for opportunities to share your story. If you have questions about this book, or wish to be considered as a writer for a future edition, contact me at edgewise14@hotmail.com or by mail in care of the editors at SkyLight Paths Publishing in Woodstock, Vermont.

Peace.

FURTHER RESOURCES

NATIONAL TRADITION-SPECIFIC ORGANIZATIONS

Buddhist:
Buddhist Peace Fellowship
www.bpf.org

Protestant:
InterVarsity Christian Fellowship
www.intervarsity.org
Episcopal Student Fellowship
*(and other similar on-campus groups
representing other denominations)*

Hindu:
The Hindu Universe
www.hindunet.org

Jewish:
Hillel
www.hillel.org

Muslim:
Muslim Students Association of
the United States and
Canada
www.msa-national.org

Roman Catholic:
Catholic Campus Ministry
Association
www.ccmanet.org

Unitarian Universalist:
Unitarian Universalist Association
www.uua.org

NATIONAL RESOURCES FOR DEALING WITH HATE AND INTOLERANCE

Anti-Defamation League
www.adl.org

Civil Rights Coalition for
the 21st Century
www.civilrights.org

National Conference for
Community and Justice
www.nccj.org

Stop the Hate
www.stophate.org

StopViolence.com
www.stopviolence.com

GENERAL INTERNET SPIRITUALITY

www.beliefnet.com

www.spiritualityhealth.com

www.killingthebuddha.com

COMMUNITY SERVICE

Campus Outreach Opportunity
  League
www.cool2serve.org

Corporation for National and
  Community Service
www.nationalservice.org

Idealist and Action Without
  Borders
www.idealist.org

RECOMMENDED READING

Boldt, Laurence G. *Zen and the Art of Making a Living: A Practical Guide to Creative Career Design*. New York: Penguin, 1991.

Fowler, James W. *Stages of Faith: The Psychology of Human Development and the Quest for Meaning*. San Francisco: Harper & Row, 1981.

Hammarskjöld, Dag. *Markings*. Translated from the Swedish by Lief Sjöberg and W. H. Auden. New York: Ballantine, 1964.

Al Huang, Chungliang, and Jerry Lynch. *Thinking Body, Dancing Mind: Taosports for Extraordinary Performance in Athletics, Business, and Life*. New York: Bantam, 1992.

Loundon, Sumi D., and Jack Kornfield. *Blue Jean Buddha: Voices of Young Buddhists*. Boston: Wisdom Publications, 2001.

Matlins, Stuart M., ed. *The Jewish Lights Spirituality Handbook: A Guide to Understanding, Exploring, and Living a Spiritual Life*. Woodstock, Vt.: SkyLight Paths Publishing, 2001.

Matlins, Stuart M., and Arthur J. Magida, eds. *How to Be a Perfect Stranger: The Essential Religious Etiquette Handbook, Third Edition*. Woodstock, Vt.: SkyLight Paths Publishing, 2003.

Merton, Thomas. *No Man Is an Island*. New York: Octagon Books, 1983.

Nasr, Seyyed Hossein. *The Heart of Islam: Enduring Values for Humanity*. San Francisco: HarperSanFrancisco, 2002.

Palmer, Parker J. *Let Your Life Speak: Listening for the Voice of Vocation*. San Francisco: Jossey-Bass, 2000.

Quinn, Daniel. *Ishmael: An Adventure of the Mind and Spirit*. New York: Bantam/Turner, 1992.

Sinetar, Marsha. *The Mentor's Spirit: Life Lessons on Leadership and the Art of Encouragement*. New York: St. Martin's Press, 1998.

Sweeney, Jon M., ed. *God Within: Our Spiritual Future—As Told by Today's New Adults*. Woodstock, Vt.: SkyLight Paths Publishing, 2001.

Taylor, Charles. *The Ethics of Authenticity*. Cambridge: Harvard University Press, 1991.

Twerski, Abraham J. *I'd Like to Call for Help, but I Don't Know the Number: The Search for Spirituality in Everyday Life*. New York: Pharos Books, 1991.

Who Is My God? An Innovative Guide to Finding Your Spiritual Identity, Second Edition. Woodstock, Vt.: SkyLight Paths Publishing, 2004.

ACKNOWLEDGMENTS

My profound respect and appreciation goes out to the student writers and educators who contributed to this book. You have challenged and inspired me, and you have been wonderful collaborators in this project. Much appreciation to all the professionals who helped me connect with student writers.

Maura Shaw, my good friend, development editor, and drumming buddy, coached me through the book writing/editing process. Three important readers—Carolyn Graham, Paul Fowler, and Patti Tihey—provided invaluable perspective on the chapter introductions. Thanks also to the terrific folks at SkyLight Paths Publishing—Jon Sweeney, Emily Wichland, Shelly Angers, Karen Levy, Amanda Dupuis, and the design team.

Several students and colleagues contributed to the early conceptualization of this book: Amanda Chassot, Adam Grossi, Neil Guzy, Jessica Liberatore, Joanna Lovering, Shanna Tellerman, Michael Murphy, Tim Foster, Denny Golden, and Susan Ambrose.

Indira Nair and Barbara Lazarus were actively supportive, encouraging, and insightful as I took on this project and considered my role as editor. In what was a tremendous loss to the Carnegie Mellon community, Barbara passed away last summer.

In addition, I lost a profoundly influential mentor while

working on this book. Bill Fuller was a gentle spirit, quietly confident with tremendous integrity. Bill was consistent and generous with his compassion, wisdom, and love.

An enthusiastic nod to my colleagues in the Carnegie Mellon Career Center, whose intelligence, energy, and humor make every day in the Center an adventure.

Finally, big thanks to my friends and family who have supported me throughout this process. Cathy Anderson, Gigs, Anne Candreva, Donna Smith, Bob Kail, Amy Cush, Judi Mancuso, and my bandmates Serban Maris-Sida, Jeff Dine, and Mike DePace have been wonderfully encouraging, as have many other friends. And thanks to my friend Jim Donovan, whose album *Revelation #9* often helped me find a good writing groove.

My grandmothers, to whom this book is dedicated, have shown me two different, yet substantial approaches to living a spiritual life. My grandmother Mildred encouraged me almost daily as I worked on this book, despite her declining health. She passed away the week after I submitted the manuscript. A steady and loving companion, she remains a daily inspiration.

Mom and Dad, you have taught me how to live the life I choose instead of one others would choose for me. Howard and Joan, thanks for your encouragement. And finally, thanks to Molly for cheering me on, Chris for making me smile, and Carolyn for being my go-to under-twenty-five advisor. And to Brenda, for keeping things going so I could write, walking Jake the wonder beagle, and being by my side.

CONTRIBUTORS

Jessica Badiner is a recent graduate of Brandeis University in Waltham, Massachusetts. An English major and philosophy minor, she was also very active in several dance groups on campus. Jessica presently works for a consulting firm in Boston. To readers, she highly recommends patience with others and with yourself—and laughter.

Merritt Baer is a student at Harvard College in Cambridge, Massachusetts. She expects to graduate with a concentration in social studies and hopes to attend law school. She loves soccer and dance and is the leadership development chair of her sorority, Kappa Alpha Theta. She is a member of the Harvard Fallen Angels, an a cappella group, and of MINHUET, a community service group that performs music in nursing homes and hospitals.

Mona Bagasao earned her B.A. in music from Webster University in St. Louis. She went on to earn her master's of divinity degree from the Pacific School of Religion and is pursuing her Ph.D. in Hebrew Bible from Vanderbilt University. She currently serves as chaplain/director of campus ministries at Eckerd College in St. Petersburg, Florida, and is ordained in the Christian Church (Disciples of Christ).

Hannah Beerbower majored in science education at Indiana State University in Terre Haute, Indiana. Upon graduation, she accepted a position teaching high school mathematics in the Terre Haute public school system.

Leah Rachel Berkowitz received a B.A. in Near Eastern and Judaic studies and journalism from Brandeis University. She served for three years on the board of Brandeis Reform Chavurah and was a staff writer for the *Justice*. Leah is currently pursuing a Master of Arts in Hebrew Letters and rabbinic ordination from Hebrew Union College–Jewish Institute of Religion.

Nathan Black majors in history and policy studies at Rice University. He has written professionally since he was in high school, and he is the founder of Different Religions Week.

Chris Cameron graduated from the University of Virginia in 1991 with a B.A. in international relations and foreign affairs. He earned an M.Ed. degree in student personnel services from the University of South Carolina in 1993. He has worked for the past ten years at Loyola University New Orleans as assistant and associate director for student activities advising the programming board, commuter services, Greek life, and student government, and serves as director of the student union and student activities office.

Laura Carroll attends Smith College in Northampton, Massachusetts, where she studies literature, medieval culture, music, and a number of other similarly fascinating subjects in pursuit of her major of "undecided." She is captain of the sabre squad of the fencing club, and she participates in Unitarian Universalist, Pagan, and interfaith events at Smith.

Conor Cashman is a student at the College of the Holy Cross. He is an English major with a concentration in teaching. After graduation, Conor plans to teach high school English. He is also considering the possibility of law school. Currently, Conor is studying abroad for his junior year in Cork City, Ireland.

Alice Chen received a B.A. in English literature from the Johns

Hopkins University, where she was a member of Hopkins Christian Fellowship as well as the illustrious 3223 St. Paul house. She now is a case manager at Miriam's Kitchen in Washington, D.C., as a part of the Public Allies program.

Ian Dale is a recent graduate of the University of Southern California. A fine arts major, Ian focused his study in painting and drawing, together with an independent pursuit of digital art and animation. Ian currently does animation and painting work on a freelance basis, while also pursuing an internship with Christian Challenge, assisting with campus ministry at USC.

Dave Ebenhoh is the director of campus ministry at Fontbonne University in St. Louis and loves working with young adults as they seek the will of God in their lives. Dave lives for God in his marriage, in his ministry as campus minister and spiritual director, and in his own struggle to live a life of holiness and passion.

Lynne Gearty attends the College of the Holy Cross in Worcester, Massachusetts. She is a history major with an art history minor. Lynne participates in a number of activities including the Big Brother, Big Sister program.

Carolyn Graham is a fourth-year student at the University of Guelph, Ontario, pursuing an independent studies major in visual representation studies. Passover was one of her favorite holidays to celebrate, but there was only one other Jew in her circle of friends. One year they decided they had to share it with everyone else—what could go wrong with a holiday promoting comfort, food, and wine? She encourages everyone to share the things they love.

Adam Grossi recently received a B.F.A. from Carnegie Mellon University. He is currently working as a freelance visual artist and navigating the survival/expression dichotomy. He hopes that he will soon be able to write a bio that does not include any institutional affiliations.

Joshua Gruenspecht would probably not read his own advice if he were you. He graduated from Yale University with a B.S. in English and Computer Science.

Shadi Hamid, a master's degree candidate in Arab studies at Georgetown University, is chair of the Political Action Task Force for the Muslim Students Association of the United States and Canada. As a freelance writer, his articles have been published in variety of print and online publications, wire services, anthologies, and journals both here and abroad. He is also a regular columnist for *PopMatters.Com*, writing monthly on music, politics, and pop culture.

Ben Hochman is studying aeronautical and mechanical engineering at the University of California at Davis. In addition to designing aircraft, Ben spends his time wakeboarding, flying, snow skiing, motorcycling, and attending gatherings with family and friends. Although his plans are not fully decided, Ben intends to develop a career in the aerospace industry and to remain in close contact and support of the community.

Natalie Hunte is a recent graduate of Central Connecticut State University in New Britain, Connecticut, with a major in marketing. She completed her basketball playing career after two seasons with the CCSU Blue Devils and is now an administrative assistant for the team, as she continues study toward an M.B.A. in international business.

Brett Iafiglioa attends Valparaiso University, majoring in civil engineering. He has been involved in Habitat for Humanity since he was in high school. His future plans include working in the construction industry and attending graduate school.

Dale Johnson II is pursuing an M.A. in theology at Creighton University. He is a recent graduate of the College of the Holy Cross, with a double major in political science and religious studies.

Beth Kander is a graduate of Brandeis University. She graduated with highest honors in American studies and Near Eastern and Judaic studies. Beth is the recipient of the Elsie Witt Award for Excellence in Judaic Studies and Community Service. A Phi Beta Kappa inductee, Beth is currently working as an Education Fellow for the Institute of Southern Jewish Life, based in Mississippi. Originally from Michigan, she is involved in theater and also enjoys writing, travel, and bad jokes.

Sarah Keller is an English and religious studies double major at the College of the Holy Cross. She is a resident assistant, a member of the Poetry Circle, and a volunteer at Frances Perkins House, a local family shelter.

Bobbie Koplowitz is the academic/life skills coordinator for the men's basketball team at Central Connecticut State University.

Sumi Loundon spent her first eight years in a Zen community in rural New Hampshire. After graduating from Williams College with a fine arts major and religion minor, she recently received a master's degree from Harvard University's Divinity School with training in Buddhist Studies and Sanskrit. She is the editor of the anthology *Blue Jean Buddha: Voices of young Buddhists* (Wisdom) and is working on a companion volume. Sumi is the assistant director at the Barre Center for Buddhist Studies in Barre, Massachusetts.

Joanna Dorr Lovering studies in Carnegie Mellon University's Bachelor of Humanities and Arts Program with concentrations in drama directing and psychology. Her daily routine at Carnegie Mellon includes residential life, theater management, museum out-reach, and campus social and academic clubs. These rewarding experiences motivate her to pursue opportunities in the advance-ment of the arts community.

Michelle Mandelstein is majoring in history and Jewish studies at Tulane University. She hopes to enter Tulane's 4+1 Master's Program in history and is considering applying to law school. She is organ-izing a second women's seder with the National Council of Jewish Women, New Orleans Hillel, and Hadassah. She is also active in TIPAC (Tulane's branch of AIPAC, the American Israel Public Affairs Committee) and New Orleans ADL (Anti-Defamation League), and she tutors in an after-school program for children from the New Orleans public schools.

Varun Mehta is studying at the University of Texas at Austin on the pre-med track, double majoring in biology and psychology. Presently, he is involved with the on-campus Hindu Students Council Chapter as the historian and an active "core member" (elected club officer).

Meghan Mueller graduated from Fontbonne University with a B.A. in English. Throughout college, she was active in campus ministry and, along with other students, helped found Fontbonne in Service and Humility (FISH), which works to provide service wherever there is a need and to build community within Fontbonne and in the greater St. Louis area. Currently, Meghan is the assistant campus minister and plans on attending graduate school in ministry next year.

Indira Nair, educated as a physicist, is a professor of engineering and public policy and currently vice provost for education at Carnegie Mellon University. Her favorite work involves advising students to reflect on their own quests and teaching interdisciplinary courses on topics such as electromagnetic radiation, the environment, and ethics.

John Newton is a senior at the University of Texas at Austin and will graduate with a degree in business administration. He is a member of the Phi Gamma Delta fraternity, an avid golfer, and an involved leader at All Saints Episcopal church. Though his long-term career plans are uncertain, he plans to spend next year working as the program coordinator at the University of Texas Episcopal student center.

Roberta Belding O'Connor served as associate professor of education and chair of the education department at Springfield College in Springfield, Massachusetts. She currently teaches at Eckerd College in St. Petersburg, Florida.

Tejal Patel is a student at the College of the Holy Cross in Worcester, Massachusetts. She is a mathematics major with a pre-med concentration. On campus, she is the vice president of INDIA

(Individuals of All Nations Developing Indian Appreciation) and a mentor for the freshman participating in the first-year program.

Michael Popper studies anthropology, English literature, and religion at Brandeis University, where he leads Buddhism and meditation groups, mentors first-year students, and performs improvisational comedy.

Sam Portaro is the Episcopal chaplain to the University of Chicago. A graduate of the University of North Carolina in Chapel Hill and the Virginia Theological Seminary in Alexandria, he was Episcopal chaplain to the College of William and Mary in Williamsburg, Virginia, from 1976 until 1982, when he was called to his present position at the University of Chicago. He is the author of five books and numerous articles and reviews.

Jeremy D. Posadas graduated from the University of Chicago's Fundamentals: Issues and Texts Program. In Chicago he also worked for Children's Memorial Hospital. He currently attends Union Theological Seminary in New York City, preparing for ordination. His vocation is congregational ministry.

Sakib Qureshi is currently a fourth-year student at Drexel University College of Medicine in Philadelphia. In recent years, Sakib has studied Sufi expressions of Islam, but he confesses a deep love for all paths toward truth. Sakib plans to practice medicine as well as continue to pursue his interests in writing, art, and political activism.

Lodrö Rinzler attends Wesleyan University in Middletown, Connecticut, where he is a religious studies major. He founded and leads the Wesleyan Dharma Study Group, a campus-based Buddhist organization, as well as the nation-wide Student Buddhist Network.

Randolph Romero, Jr., graduated from the University of Pittsburgh with a B.S. in neuroscience and a B.A. in philosophy. He currently serves as youth director at First Baptist Church of Rancho Cucamonga, California, and is working on a master's of divinity at Golden Gate Baptist Theological Seminary.

Marianne Schiler is a creative writing major at the University of Southern California.

Sharon Servilio is a fine arts major at Brandeis University. She is an active leader of the small but vibrant Roman Catholic community on campus. Some of her other loves include peace, beauty, friends, Italy, nature, tea, Argentine tango, good conversation, and not taking herself too seriously.

Alison E. Siegel is a student at the University of Illinois at Urbana-Champaign majoring in religious studies with a minor in women's studies. She has recently finished a year-and-a-half term as co-president of Hillel at the University of Illinois. A campus activist on various issues and a long-time staffer at the Union of American Hebrew Congregations' summer camps, Alison still works with Jewish-Muslim-Arab relations on campus and is looking forward to a career working with Jewish youth while focusing on outreach and inter-group relations.

About SKYLIGHT PATHS Publishing

SkyLight Paths Publishing is creating a place where people of different spiritual traditions come together for challenge and inspiration, a place where we can help each other understand the mystery that lies at the heart of our existence.

Through spirituality, our religious beliefs are increasingly becoming a part of our lives—rather than *apart* from our lives. While many of us may be more interested than ever in spiritual growth, we may be less firmly planted in traditional religion. Yet, we do want to deepen our relationship to the sacred, to learn from our own as well as from other faith traditions, and to practice in new ways.

SkyLight Paths sees both believers and seekers as a community that increasingly transcends traditional boundaries of religion and denomination—people wanting to learn from each other, *walking together, finding the way.*

We at SkyLight Paths take great care to produce beautiful books that present meaningful spiritual content in a form that reflects the art of making high quality books. Therefore, we want to acknowledge those who contributed to the production of this book.

PRODUCTION
Sara Dismukes & Tim Holtz

EDITORIAL
Amanda Dupuis, Maura D. Shaw & Emily Wichland

COVER & TEXT DESIGN
Sara Dismukes

PRINTING & BINDING
Versa Press, East Peoria, Illinois

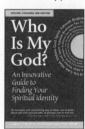 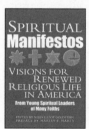  

Spiritual Biography

The Life of Evelyn Underhill
An Intimate Portrait of the Groundbreaking Author of Mysticism
by *Margaret Cropper;* Foreword by *Dana Greene*

Evelyn Underhill was a passionate writer and teacher who wrote elegantly on mysticism, worship, and devotional life. This is the story of how she made her way toward spiritual maturity, from her early days of agnosticism to the years when her influence was felt throughout the world. 6 x 9, 288 pp, 5 b/w photos, Quality PB, ISBN 1-893361-70-5 **$18.95**

Zen Effects: *The Life of Alan Watts*
by *Monica Furlong*

The first and only full-length biography of one of the most charismatic spiritual leaders of the twentieth century—now back in print!

Through his widely popular books and lectures, Alan Watts (1915–1973) did more to introduce Eastern philosophy and religion to Western minds than any figure before or since. Here is the only biography of this charismatic figure, who served as Zen teacher, Anglican priest, lecturer, academic, entertainer, a leader of the San Francisco renaissance, and author of more than 30 books, including *The Way of Zen, Psychotherapy East and West* and *The Spirit of Zen.*
6 x 9, 264 pp, Quality PB, ISBN 1-893361-32-2 **$16.95**

 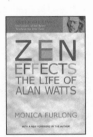  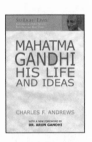

Simone Weil: *A Modern Pilgrimage*
by *Robert Coles*

The extraordinary life of the spiritual philosopher who's been called both saint and madwoman.

The French writer and philosopher Simone Weil (1906–1943) devoted her life to a search for God—while avoiding membership in organized religion. Robert Coles' intriguing study of Weil details her short, eventful life, and is an insightful portrait of the beloved and controversial thinker whose life and writings influenced many (from T. S. Eliot to Adrienne Rich to Albert Camus), and continue to inspire seekers everywhere. 6 x 9, 208 pp, Quality PB, ISBN 1-893361-34-9 **$16.95**

Mahatma Gandhi: *His Life and Ideas*
by *Charles F. Andrews;* Foreword by *Dr. Arun Gandhi*

An intimate biography of one of the greatest social and religious reformers of the modern world.

Examines from a contemporary Christian activist's point of view the religious ideas and political dynamics that influenced the birth of the peaceful resistance movement, the primary tool that Gandhi and the people of his homeland would use to gain India its freedom from British rule. An ideal introduction to the life and life's work of this great spiritual leader.
6 x 9, 336 pp, 5 b/w photos, Quality PB, ISBN 1-893361-89-6 **$18.95**

Spiritual Practice

The Sacred Art of Bowing
Preparing to Practice
by Andi Young

This informative and inspiring introduction to bowing—and related spiritual practices—shows you how to do it, why it's done, and what spiritual benefits it has to offer. Incorporates interviews, personal stories, illustrations of bowing in practice, advice on how you can incorporate bowing into your daily life, and how bowing can deepen spiritual understanding.
5½ x 8½, 128 pp, b/w illus., Quality PB, ISBN 1-893361-82-9 **$14.95**

Praying with Our Hands: *Twenty-One Practices of Embodied Prayer from the World's Spiritual Traditions*
by *Jon M. Sweeney;* Photographs by *Jennifer J. Wilson;*
Foreword by *Mother Tessa Bielecki;* Afterword by *Taitetsu Unno, Ph.D.*

A spiritual guidebook for bringing prayer into our bodies.

This inspiring book of reflections and accompanying photographs shows us twenty-one simple ways of using our hands to speak to God, to enrich our devotion and ritual. All express the various approaches of the world's religious traditions to bringing the body into worship. Spiritual traditions represented include Anglican, Sufi, Zen, Roman Catholic, Yoga, Shaker, Hindu, Jewish, Pentecostal, Eastern Orthodox, and many others.
8 x 8, 96 pp, 22 duotone photographs, Quality PB, ISBN 1-893361-16-0 **$16.95**

   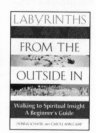

The Sacred Art of Listening
Forty Reflections for Cultivating a Spiritual Practice
by *Kay Lindahl;* Illustrations by *Amy Schnapper*

More than ever before, we need to embrace the skills and practice of listening. You will learn to: Speak clearly from your heart • Communicate with courage and compassion • Heighten your awareness for deep listening • Enhance your ability to listen to people with different belief systems. 8 x 8, 160 pp, Illus., Quality PB, ISBN 1-893361-44-6 **$16.99**

Labyrinths from the Outside In
Walking to Spiritual Insight—a Beginner's Guide
by *Donna Schaper* and *Carole Ann Camp*

The user-friendly, interfaith guide to making and using labyrinths— for meditation, prayer, and celebration.

Labyrinth walking is a spiritual exercise *anyone* can do. This accessible guide unlocks the mysteries of the labyrinth for all of us, providing ideas for using the labyrinth walk for prayer, meditation, and celebrations to mark the most important moments in life. Includes instructions for making a labyrinth of your own and finding one in your area.
6 x 9, 208 pp, b/w illus. and photographs, Quality PB, ISBN 1-893361-18-7 **$16.95**

SkyLight Illuminations Series
Andrew Harvey, series editor

Offers today's spiritual seeker an enjoyable entry into the great classic texts of the world's spiritual traditions. Each classic is presented in an accessible translation, with facing pages of guided commentary from experts, giving you the keys you need to understand the history, context, and meaning of the text. This series enables readers of all backgrounds to experience and understand classic spiritual texts directly, and to make them a part of their lives. Andrew Harvey writes the foreword to each volume, an insightful, personal introduction to each classic.

Bhagavad Gita: *Annotated & Explained*
Translation by *Shri Purohit Swami*; Annotation by *Kendra Crossen Burroughs*

"The very best Gita for first-time readers." —Ken Wilber

Millions of people turn daily to India's most beloved holy book, whose universal appeal has made it popular with non-Hindus and Hindus alike. This edition introduces you to the characters; explains references and philosophical terms; shares the interpretations of famous spiritual leaders and scholars; and more. 5½ x 8½, 192 pp, Quality PB, ISBN 1-893361-28-4 **$16.95**

The Way of a Pilgrim: *Annotated & Explained*
Translation and annotation by *Gleb Pokrovsky*

This classic of Russian spirituality is the delightful account of one man who sets out to learn the prayer of the heart—also known as the "Jesus prayer"—and how the practice transforms his life. 5½ x 8½, 160 pp, Quality PB, ISBN 1-893361-31-4 **$14.95**

The Gospel of Thomas: *Annotated & Explained*
Translation and annotation by *Stevan Davies*

Discovered in 1945, this collection of aphoristic sayings sheds new light on the origins of Christianity and the intriguing figure of Jesus, portraying the Kingdom of God as a present fact about the world, rather than a future promise or future threat. This edition guides you through the text with annotations that focus on the meaning of the sayings. 5½ x 8½, 192 pp, Quality PB, ISBN 1-893361-45-2 **$16.95**

Rumi and Islam: *Selections from His Stories, Poems, and Discourses—Annotated & Explained*
Translation and annotation by *Ibrahim Gamard*

Offers a new way of thinking about Rumi's poetry. Ibrahim Gamard focuses on Rumi's place within the Sufi tradition of Islam, providing you with insight into the mystical side of the religion—one that has love of God at its core and sublime wisdom teachings as its pathways. 5½ x 8½, 240 pp, Quality PB, ISBN 1-59473-002-4 **$15.99**